The Common Worship Psalter
with Chants

Psalms and canticles pointed
for use with Anglican Chant

edited by John Harper

Music for Common Worship V

MUSIC FOR COMMON WORSHIP
GENERAL EDITOR: JOHN HARPER

M
2168.6
.C66
2002

Published by	RSCM Press
	The Royal School of Church Music
	19 The Close
	Salisbury
	Wiltshire SP1 2EB
ISBN	978-0-85402-112-3
Published	2002
Reprinted	2005, 2008, 2011 and 2014
	10 9 8 7 6 5 4 3 2

Copyright — This collection, typography, artwork and layout are copyright © 2001, 2002 The Royal School of Church Music All rights reserved.

The music (unless otherwise noted) and its arrangements are copyright © 2001, 2002 The Royal School of Church Music. All rights reserved.

The Psalter and Canticles from *Common Worship: Services and Prayers for the Church of England* are copyright © The Archbishops' Council, 2000 and are used by permission.

Any reproduction, storage or transmission of material from this publication by any means or in any form, electronic or mechanical, including photocopying, recording, or any information storage and retrieval system, requires written permission from RSCM Press, The Royal School of Church Music, 19 The Close, Salisbury, Wiltshire SP1 2EB.
Telephone: 01722 424848   Fax: 01722 424849
E-mail: copyright@rscm.com   Web: www.rscm.com

Typeset by	Alistair Warwick in Gill Sans
Music set by	Timothy Rogers and Gregor Zednik
Printed by	Halstan & Co Ltd

Contents

Introduction	4
Notes	6
Copyright acknowledgements	6
Psalms	7
Canticles	203
Opening Hymn and Canticles at Morning and Evening Prayer	204
Old and New Testament Canticles at Morning and Evening Prayer	212
Morning Prayer	212
Evening Prayer	218
Gospel Canticles	222
Other Canticles	226
Te Deum laudamus	229
Canticles from *The Book of Common Prayer*	232
Index of canticles	246
Index of chants	247
Division of Psalms by Morning and Evening according to *The Book of Common Prayer*	248

¶ Introduction

The psalms and canticles are the principal scriptural songs of the Church. They have been part of the core of Christian worship since the earliest times. The psalms, taken over from Judaism, are a diverse collection of poems. Some recount Jewish history, others are timeless; some give collective expression, others are intensely personal; some seem obscure, others seem contemporary and direct; some embody joy and praise, others express the most profound human and spiritual feelings. The psalms give expression to the full range of human experience, and encompass the whole of our praying and praising relationship with God.

Despite their individuality and diversity, there has been a tradition of singing the psalms in standard ways – to repeated plainsong melodic patterns, to harmonised chants, to standard metrical patterns in versified translations, to newer melodic formulae with refrains. This provides a basis for sharing the singing of all the psalms in public worship. Although psalms and canticles may be sung in one way, each needs to be treated as an individual expression.

Pointing

In pointing the psalms for Anglican chant we have to balance consistency of method with the individuality of each psalm. The pace of the texts varies from one psalm to another, as do word patterns – partly because of the original Hebrew text, and partly because of the preferences of different translators and text editors. There are some verses where only one pointing solution is possible, others where method dictates choice of pointing, others where it is a matter of personal preference, and some where there is no really satisfactory solution.

All of the pointing observes the convention of the textual and musical caesura at the mid verse which is characteristic of recitation of the psalms. This is indicated by the diamond sign ♦. However, there are times when the musical patterns (and especially the number of chords in the second part of the verse) has required either the caesura to be moved, or for two verses to be combined and treated musically as one verse, or for one verse to be subdivided and treated musically as two verses.

Pointing marks have been kept to a minimum. The upright dash ' corresponds to the bar lines of the chant. Where there are two syllables between the bar lines, one chord is sung to each syllable. Where there are three or four syllables between the bar lines, the second chord is reserved for the last syllable – except where there is a dot • between two syllables. The dot indicates the mid point of the bar, and the chord changes after that dot for the remaining syllables of the bar.

This psalter is being prepared in two editions: one without chants, and one with chants. All psalms are pointed for use with double chants (i.e. chants whose music encompasses two verses of text), even in those psalms where a single chant (i.e. one whose music is repeated every verse) may be preferable. Where there are odd numbers of verses in a psalm, or section of a psalm, the second part of the chant has to be repeated to accommodate this. This is indicated by the sign ‡.

In attending to declamation, the *Common Worship Psalter* provides line breaks where there should be a short break. This always occurs at the caesura (the diamond), but there may be additional line breaks in longer verses. Avoid breaks at commas within lines of text, otherwise the flow of recitation is broken. It may be helpful to mark commas by lengthening the syllable that precedes it.

Section breaks within a psalm are indicated by extra space between verses; these breaks may sometimes call for a change of chant.

Psalms in worship
Psalms and canticles become shared texts when they are sung in public worship. As such they have to be treated as texts to be declaimed through music. They need to be declaimed, with care given to word stress, phrase structure, and meaning. There is a balance to be achieved between singing them as prose, which must follow normal speech patterns, and heightening them as poetry, which requires an element of stylisation. The speed and style of sung recitation will depend on acoustic, and the numbers singing: a small group in a small room has far greater scope for flexibility, momentum, and intimacy in recitation, than a large congregation in a big building.

Ideally the psalms and canticles are songs 'owned' by all God's people. Ownership does not imply that everyone has to sing the whole of every psalm and canticle; there is a place for praying and praising listeners, as well as praying and praising singers.

However, if everyone is to sing the psalm text with confidence they need to be familiar with the text, with the rhythm of the text, and with the chant. That may well define a successive process of familiarisation over several weeks: hearing the psalm read as a spoken text, reciting the psalm together as a spoken text, hearing the psalm sung by a single voice or small group which has prepared it, and finally singing the psalm together.

Developing this confidence in psalm singing is very important: psalms sung tentatively and badly are demoralising for all who are singing and may be painful for anyone listening. Singing a small group of psalms and canticles with confidence and purpose, may be better than trying to use the whole psalter. A combination of psalms and canticles sung, and psalms and canticles read may enable a worshipping congregation to pray and praise with the psalter, and meet the requirements of the Lectionary.

Chants edition of the Psalter
This edition of the Common Worship Psalter with Chants provides chants for all the psalms and canticles, and prints them in the text of the psalter. The chants have been selected so that they can be sung by all present at a service. The vocal range of the chants is limited, with reciting notes that are not too high and vocally taxing; none of the

music is technically difficult. To assist effective recitation, some chants have been simplified or amended to exclude passing and other non-essential notes. An additional small anthology of chants is also available; these chants are particularly suitable for singing without accompaniment.

Acknowledgements

In preparing this pointed psalter for publication, I am particularly grateful for the assistance of David Ogden, Tim Rogers, Tim Ruffer, John Wardle, Alistair Warwick, and Geoff Weaver.

John Harper
24 August 2002
St Bartholomew's Day

¶ Notes

¶ *When singing a psalm, the word 'blessed' is to be pronounced as two syllables: 'bless - ed'. Where spelled 'blest', the word is pronounced as one syllable.*

¶ *For those traditions which omit the word 'Alleluia' during penitential seasons, we have provided an alternative: 'Praise the Lord'.*

¶ *Each psalm, group of psalms, or canticle may end with*

Glory to the Father and ' to the ' Son ♦
and ' to the ' Holy ' Spirit;

as it was in the be'ginning is ' now ♦
and shall be for ' ever. ' A'men.

¶ Copyright acknowledgements

The Royal School of Church Music thanks the owners or controllers of copyright for permission to use the following chants:

H Walford Davies (171): The Trustees of Sir Henry Walford Davies
Edgar Day (103, 231, 268): Mrs E M Webb
Peter Hurford (202, 207): The composer
C Hylton Stewart (2, 16, 67): Mrs M Brazier

Psalms

Psalm 1

William Croft

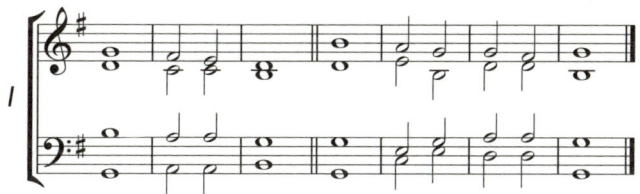

1 Blessed are they who have not walked
    in the ' counsel • of the ' wicked, ♦
  nor lingered in the way of sinners,
    nor sat in the as'sembly ' of the ' scornful.

2 Their delight is in the ' law of the ' Lord ♦
    and they meditate on his ' law ' day and ' night.

3 Like a tree planted by streams of water
    bearing fruit in due season, with leaves that ' do not ' wither, ♦
  whatever they ' do, ' it shall ' prosper.

4 As for the wicked, it is not ' so with ' them; ♦
  they are like chaff which the ' wind ' blows a'way.

5 Therefore the wicked shall not be able
    to ' stand in the ' judgement, ♦
  nor the sinner in the congre'gation ' of the ' righteous.

6 For the Lord knows the ' way of the ' righteous, ♦
  but the ' way of the ' wicked shall ' perish.

Psalm 2

C. Hylton Stewart

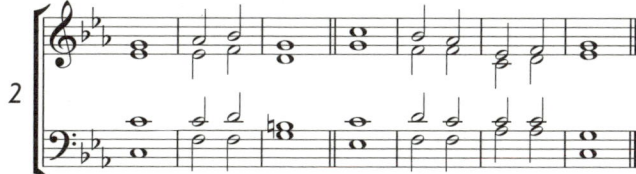

1 Why are the ' nations in ' tumult, ♦
  and why do the peoples de'vise a ' vain ' plot?

2 The kings of the earth rise up,
    and the rulers take ' counsel to'gether, ♦
  against the Lord ' and a'gainst his a'nointed:

3 'Let us break their ' bonds a'sunder ♦
  and ' cast a'way their ' cords from us.'

4 He who dwells in heaven shall ' laugh them to ' scorn; ♦
  the Lord shall ' have them ' in de'rision.

C. Hylton Stewart

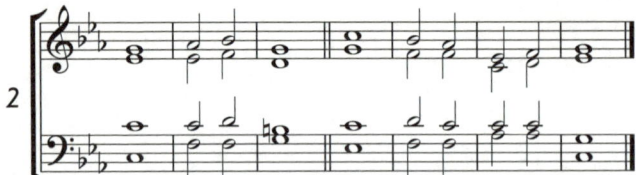

5 Then shall he speak to them ' in his ' wrath ♦
   and ' terrify them ' in his ' fury:

6 'Yet have I ' set my ' king ♦
   upon my ' holy ' hill of ' Zion.'

Jonathan Battishill

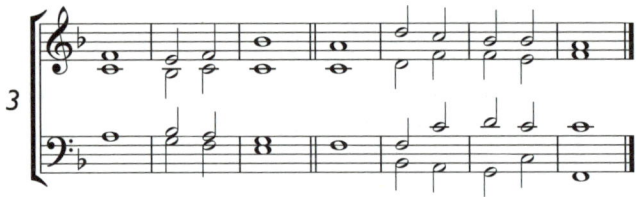

7 I will proclaim the de'cree of the ' Lord; ♦
   he said to me: 'You are my Son; this ' day have ' I be'gotten you.

8 'Ask of me and I will give you the nations for ' your in'heritance ♦
   and the ends of the ' earth for ' your pos'session.

9 'You shall break them with a ' rod of ' iron ♦
   and dash them in pieces ' like a ' potter's ' vessel.'

10 Now therefore be ' wise, O ' kings; ♦
    be prudent, you ' judges ' of the ' earth.

11 Serve the Lord with fear, and with trembling ' kiss his ' feet, ♦
    lest he be angry and you perish from the way,
        for his ' wrath is ' quickly ' kindled.

12 Happy ' are all ' they ♦
    who ' take ' refuge in ' him.

Psalm 3

John Stainer

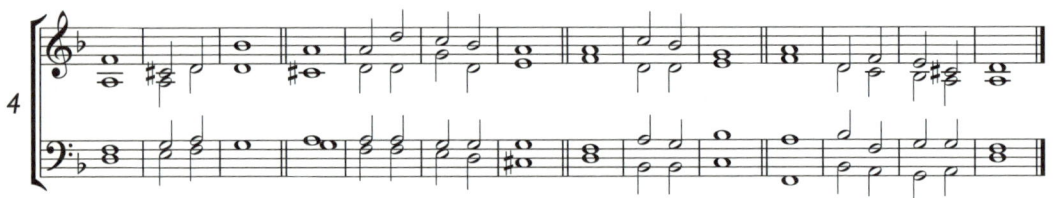

1 Lord, how many ' are my ' adversaries; ♦
  many are ' they who rise ' up a'gainst me.

2 Many are they who ' say to my ' soul, ♦
  'There is no ' help for you ' in your ' God.'

3 But you, Lord, are a ' shield a'bout me; ♦
　you are my glory, and the ' lifter ' up of my ' head.

4 When I cry a'loud • to the ' Lord, ♦
　he will answer me ' from his ' holy ' hill;

5 I lie down and sleep and ' rise a'gain, ♦
　be'cause the ' Lord sus'tains me.

6 I will not be afraid of ' hordes • of the ' peoples ♦
　that have set themselves a'gainst me ' all a'round.

7 Rise up, O Lord, and deliver me, ' O my ' God, ♦
　for you strike all my enemies on the cheek
　　and ' break the ' teeth of the ' wicked.

8 Salvation be'longs to the ' Lord: ♦
　may your blessing ' be up'on your ' people.

Psalm 4

Noel Rawsthorne

1 Answer me when I call, O ' God of my ' righteousness; ♦
　you set me at liberty when I was in trouble;
　　have mercy on ' me and ' hear my ' prayer.

2 How long will you nobles dis'honour my ' glory; ♦
　how long will you love vain ' things and ' seek • after ' falsehood?

3 But know that the Lord has shown me his ' marvellous ' kindness; ♦
　when I call upon the ' Lord, ' he will ' hear me.

4 Stand in ' awe, and ' sin not; ♦
　commune with your own heart upon your ' bed, ' and be ' still.

5 Offer the ' sacrifices of ' righteousness ♦
　and ' put your ' trust • in the ' Lord.

6 There are many that say, 'Who will show us ' any ' good?' ♦
　Lord, lift up the ' light of your ' countenance up'on us.

7 You have put gladness ' in my ' heart, ♦
　more than when their corn and ' wine and ' oil in'crease.

8 In peace I will lie ' down and ' sleep, ♦
　for it is you Lord, only, who ' make me ' dwell in ' safety.

Psalm 5

Joseph Barnby

1 Give ear to my ' words, O ' Lord; ♦
  con'sider my ' lamen'tation.

2 Hearken to the voice of my crying, my ' King and my ' God, ♦
  for to ' you I ' make my ' prayer.

3 In the morning, Lord, you will ' hear my ' voice; ♦
  early in the morning I make my ap'peal to ' you, and look ' up.

4 For you are the God who takes no ' pleasure in ' wickedness; ♦
  no ' evil can ' dwell with ' you.

5 The boastful cannot ' stand in your ' sight; ♦
  you ' hate all ' those that work ' wickedness.

6 You destroy ' those who speak ' lies; ♦
  the bloodthirsty and de'ceitful the ' Lord • will ab'hor.

7 But as for me, through the greatness of your mercy,
    I will come ' into your ' house; ♦
  I will bow down towards your holy ' temple in ' awe of ' you.

8 Lead me, Lord, in your righteousness, be'cause of my ' enemies; ♦
  make your way ' straight be'fore my ' face.

9 For there is no truth in their mouth,
    in their ' heart • is des'truction, ♦
  their throat is an open sepulchre,
    and they ' flatter ' with their ' tongue.

10 Punish ' them, O ' God; ♦
   let them ' fall • through their ' own de'vices.

11 Because of their many transgressions ' cast them ' out, ♦
   for ' they have re'belled a'gainst you.

12 But let all who take refuge in ' you be ' glad; ♦
   let them ' sing out their ' joy for ' ever.

13 You will ' shelter ' them, ♦
   so that those who love your ' name • may ex'ult in ' you.

14 For you, O Lord, will ' bless the ' righteous; ♦
   and with your favour you will de'fend them ' as with a ' shield.

Psalm 6

Norman Warren

1 O Lord, rebuke me ' not in your ' wrath; ♦
  neither chasten me ' in your ' fierce ' anger.

2 Have mercy on me, Lord, for ' I am ' weak; ♦
  Lord, heal me, ' for my ' bones are ' racked.

3 My soul also ' shakes with ' terror; ♦
  how ' long, O ' Lord, how ' long?

4 Turn again, O Lord, and de'liver my ' soul; ♦
  save me for your ' loving ' mercy's ' sake.

5 For in death ' no one re'members you; ♦
  and who can ' give you ' thanks • in the ' grave?

6 I am weary ' with my ' groaning; ♦
  every night I drench my pillow
  and ' flood my ' bed with my ' tears.

7 My eyes are ' wasted with ' grief ♦
  and worn away be'cause of ' all my ' enemies.

8 Depart from me, all ' you that do ' evil, ♦
  for the Lord has ' heard the ' voice of my ' weeping.

9 The Lord has heard my ' suppli'cation; ♦
  the ' Lord • will re'ceive my ' prayer.

10 All my enemies shall be put to ' shame and con'fusion; ♦
   they shall ' suddenly turn ' back • in their ' shame.

Psalm 7

James Turle

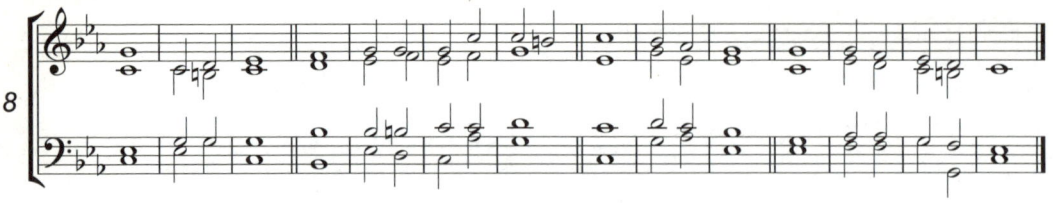

1 O Lord my God, in ' you I take ' refuge; ♦
   save me from all who pur'sue me, ' and de'liver me,

2 Lest they rend me like a lion and ' tear me in ' pieces ♦
   while ' there is ' no one to ' help me.

3 O Lord my God, if I have ' done these ' things: ♦
   if there is any ' wickedness ' in my ' hands,

4 If I have repaid my ' friend with ' evil, ♦
   or plundered my ' enemy with'out a ' cause,

‡ 5 Then let my enemy pursue me and ' over'take me, ♦
   trample my life to the ground,
       and lay my ' honour ' in the ' dust.

6 Rise up, O Lord, in your wrath;
       lift yourself up against the ' fury • of my ' enemies. ♦
   Awaken, my God, the judgement ' that you ' have com'manded.

7 Let the assembly of the peoples ' gather ' round you; ♦
   be seated high above them: O ' Lord, ' judge the ' nations.

8 Give judgement for me
       according to my ' righteousness, O ' Lord, ♦
   and according to the ' innocence ' that is ' in me.

9 Let the malice of the wicked come to an end,
       but es'tablish the ' righteous; ♦
   for you test the mind and ' heart, O ' righteous ' God.

10 God is my ' shield • that is ' over me; ♦
   he ' saves the ' true of ' heart.

11 God is a ' righteous ' judge; ♦
   he is pro'voked ' all day ' long.

12 If they will not repent, God will ' whet his ' sword; ♦
   he has bent his ' bow and ' made it ' ready.

13 He has prepared the ' weapons of ' death; ♦
   he makes his ' arrows ' shafts of ' fire.

14 Behold those who are in ' labour with ' wickedness, ♦
   who conceive evil ' and give ' birth to ' lies.

15 They dig a pit and ' make it ' deep ♦
   and fall into the hole that ' they have ' made for ' others.

16 Their mischief rebounds on their ' own ' head; ♦
    their violence ' falls on their ' own ' scalp.

17 I will give thanks to the Lord ' for his ' righteousness, ♦
    and I will make music to the ' name of the ' Lord Most ' High.

Psalm 8
First version

Joseph Barnby

1 O ' Lord our ' governor, ♦
  how glorious is your ' name in ' all the ' world!

2 Your majesty above the ' heavens is ' praised ♦
  out of the ' mouths of ' babes at the ' breast.

‡ 3 You have founded a stronghold a'gainst your ' foes, ♦
  that you might still the ' enemy ' and • the a'venger.

4 When I consider your heavens, the ' work of your ' fingers, ♦
  the moon and the ' stars that ' you have or'dained,

5 What is man, that you should be ' mindful ' of him; ♦
  the son of man, that ' you should ' seek him ' out?

6 You have made him little ' lower • than the ' angels ♦
  and ' crown him with ' glory and ' honour.

7 You have given him dominion over the ' works of your ' hands ♦
  and put ' all things ' under his ' feet,

8,9 All sheep and oxen,
      even the wild ' beasts of the ' field, ♦
    the birds of the air, the fish of the sea
      and whatsoever ' moves • in the ' paths of the ' sea.

10 O ' Lord our ' governor, ♦
   how glorious is your ' name in ' all the ' world!

Psalm 8
Second version

Joseph Barnby

1 O ' Lord our ' governor, ♦
how glorious is your ' name in ' all the ' world!

2 Your majesty above the ' heavens is ' praised ♦
out of the ' mouths of ' babes at the ' breast.

‡ 3 You have founded a stronghold a'gainst your ' foes, ♦
that you might still the ' enemy ' and • the a'venger.

4 When I consider your heavens, the ' work of your ' fingers, ♦
the moon and the ' stars that ' you have or'dained,

5 What are mortals, that you should be ' mindful ' of them; ♦
mere human beings, that ' you should ' seek them ' out?

6 You have made them little ' lower • than the ' angels ♦
and ' crown them with ' glory and ' honour.

7 You have given them dominion over the ' works of your ' hands ♦
and put ' all things ' under their ' feet,

8,9 All sheep and oxen,
even the wild ' beasts of the ' field, ♦
the birds of the air, the fish of the sea
and whatsoever ' moves • in the ' paths of the ' sea.

10 O ' Lord our ' governor, ♦
how glorious is your ' name in ' all the ' world!

Psalm 9

George M. Garrett

1 I will give thanks to you, Lord, with my ' whole ' heart; ♦
I will tell of ' all your ' marvellous ' works.

2 I will be glad and re'joice in ' you; ♦
I will make music to your ' name, ' O Most ' High.

3 When my enemies are ʼ driven ʼ back, ♦
   they stumble and ʼ perish ʼ at your ʼ presence.

4 For you have maintained my right ʼ and my ʼ cause; ♦
   you sat on your throne ʼ giving ʼ righteous ʼ judgement.

5 You have rebuked the nations and desʼtroyed the ʼ wicked; ♦
   you have blotted out their ʼ name for ʼ ever and ʼ ever.

6 The enemy was ʼ utterly laid ʼ waste. ♦
   You uprooted their cities;
      their ʼ very ʼ memory has ʼ perished.

7 But the Lord shall enʼdure for ʼ ever; ♦
   he has made ʼ fast his ʼ throne for ʼ judgement.

8 For he shall rule the ʼ world with ʼ righteousness ♦
   and ʼ govern the ʼ peoples with ʼ equity.

9 Then will the Lord be a refuge ʼ for the opʼpressed, ♦
   a refuge ʼ in the ʼ time of ʼ trouble.

10 And those who know your name will put their ʼ trust in ʼ you, ♦
   for you, Lord, have ʼ never failed ʼ those who ʼ seek you.

11 Sing praises to the Lord who ʼ dwells in ʼ Zion; ♦
   declare among the ʼ peoples the ʼ things • he has ʼ done.

12 The avenger of blood ʼ has reʼmembered them; ♦
   he did not forget the ʼ cry ʼ of the opʼpressed.

13 Have mercy upon ʼ me, O ʼ Lord; ♦
   consider the trouble I suffer from those who hate me,
      you that lift me ʼ up • from the ʼ gates of ʼ death;

14 That I may tell all your praises in the gates of the ʼ city of ʼ Zion ♦
   and reʼjoice in ʼ your salʼvation.

15 The nations shall sink into the ʼ pit of their ʼ making ♦
   and in the snare which they set will their ʼ own ʼ foot be ʼ taken.

16 The Lord makes himself known by his ʼ acts of ʼ justice; ♦
   the wicked are snared in the ʼ works of their ʼ own ʼ hands.

17 They shall return to the ʼ land of ʼ darkness, ♦
   all the ʼ nations • that forʼget ʼ God.

18 For the needy shall not always ʼ be forʼgotten ♦
   and the hope of the poor ʼ shall not ʼ perish for ʼ ever.

19 Arise, O Lord, and let not mortals have the ʼ upper ʼ hand; ♦
   let the nations be ʼ judged beʼfore your ʼ face.

20 Put them in ʼ fear, O ʼ Lord, ♦
   that the nations may know themʼselves to ʼ be but ʼ mortal.

Psalm 10

Samuel Wesley

1 Why stand so far ' off, O ' Lord? ♦
  Why hide your'self in ' time of ' trouble?

2 The wicked in their pride ' persecute the ' poor; ♦
  let them be caught in the ' schemes they ' have de'vised.

3 The wicked boast of their ' heart's de'sire; ♦
  the covetous ' curse • and re'vile the ' Lord.

4 The wicked in their arrogance say, 'God will ' not a'venge it'; ♦
  in all their ' scheming God ' counts for ' nothing.

5 They are stubborn in all their ways,
      for your judgements are far above ' out of their ' sight; ♦
  they ' scoff at ' all their ' adversaries.

6 They say in their heart, 'I shall ' not be ' shaken; ♦
  no harm shall ' ever ' happen to ' me.'

7 Their mouth is full of cursing, de'ceit and ' fraud; ♦
  under their ' tongue lie ' mischief and ' wrong.

8 They lurk in the outskirts
      and in dark alleys they ' murder the ' innocent; ♦
  their eyes are ever ' watching ' for the ' helpless.

‡ 9 They lie in wait, like a lion in his den;
      they lie in wait to ' seize the ' poor; ♦
  they seize the poor when they ' get them ' into their ' net.

10 The innocent are broken and ' humbled be'fore them; ♦
   the helpless ' fall be'fore their ' power.

11 They say in their heart, ' 'God has for'gotten; ♦
   he hides his face away; ' he will ' never ' see it.'

12 Arise, O Lord God, and lift ' up your ' hand; ♦
   for'get ' not the ' poor.

13 Why should the wicked be ' scornful of ' God? ♦
   Why should they say in their hearts, ' 'You will ' not a'venge it'?

14 Surely, you behold ' trouble and ' misery; ♦
   you see it and take it ' into your ' own ' hand.

15 The helpless commit them'selves to ' you, ♦
   for you are the ' helper ' of the ' orphan.

16 Break the power of the wicked ' and ma'licious; ♦
search out their wickedness un'til you ' find ' none.

17 The Lord shall reign for ' ever and ' ever; ♦
the nations shall ' perish ' from his ' land.

18 Lord, you will hear the de'sire of the ' poor; ♦
you will incline your ear to the ' fullness ' of their ' heart,

19 To give justice to the orphan ' and op'pressed, ♦
so that people are no longer driven in ' terror ' from the ' land.

Psalm 11

Matthew Camidge

1 In the Lord have I ' taken ' refuge; ♦
how then can you say to me,
   'Flee like a ' bird ' to the ' hills,

2 'For see how the wicked bend the bow
   and fit their arrows ' to the ' string, ♦
to shoot from the shadows ' at the ' true of ' heart.

3 'When the foundations ' are des'troyed, ♦
what ' can the ' righteous ' do?'

4 The Lord is in his ' holy ' temple; ♦
the ' Lord's throne ' is in ' heaven.

5 His ' eyes be'hold, ♦
his eyelids try ' every ' mortal ' being.

6 The Lord tries the righteous as ' well as the ' wicked, ♦
but those who delight in ' violence his ' soul ab'hors.

7 Upon the wicked he shall rain coals of fire and ' burning ' sulphur; ♦
scorching wind shall ' be their ' portion to ' drink.

8 For the Lord is righteous;
   he loves ' righteous ' deeds, ♦
and those who are upright ' shall be'hold his ' face.

Psalm 12
Henry Smart

13

1 Help me, Lord, for no one ' godly is ' left; ♦
   the faithful have vanished from the ' whole ' human ' race.

2 They all speak falsely ' with their ' neighbour; ♦
   they flatter with their lips, but ' speak • from a ' double ' heart.

3 O that the Lord would cut off all ' flattering ' lips ♦
   and the ' tongue that ' speaks proud ' boasts!

4 Those who say, 'With our tongue will ' we pre'vail; ♦
   our lips we will use; ' who is ' lord ' over us?'

5 'Because of the oppression of the needy,
      and the ' groaning • of the ' poor, ♦
   I will rise up now,' says the Lord,
      'and set them in the ' safety ' that they ' long for.'

6 The words of the ' Lord are ' pure words, ♦
   like silver refined in the furnace
      and purified ' seven times ' in the ' fire.

7 You, O Lord, ' will watch ' over us ♦
   and guard us from ' this • gene'ration for ' ever.

8 The wicked strut on ' every ' side, ♦
   when what is vile is exalted by the ' whole ' human ' race.

Psalm 13
J. Harrison

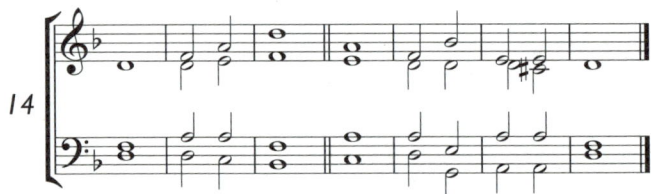

14

1 How long will you forget me, O ' Lord; for ' ever? ♦
   How long will you ' hide your ' face ' from me?

2 How long shall I have anguish in my soul
      and grief in my heart, ' day after ' day? ♦
   How long shall my ' enemy ' triumph ' over me?

3 Look upon me and answer, O ' Lord my ' God; ♦
   lighten my eyes, ' lest I ' sleep in ' death;

4 Lest my enemy say, 'I have pre'vailed a'gainst him,' ♦
   and my foes re'joice that ' I have ' fallen.

J. Harrison

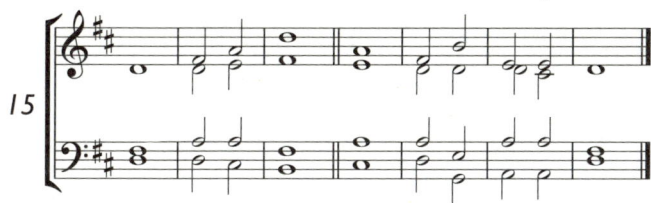

15

5 But I put my trust in your ' steadfast ' love; ♦
my heart will re'joice in ' your sal'vation.

6 I will ' sing to the ' Lord, ♦
for he has ' dealt so ' bounti•fully ' with me.

Psalm 14

C. Hylton Stewart

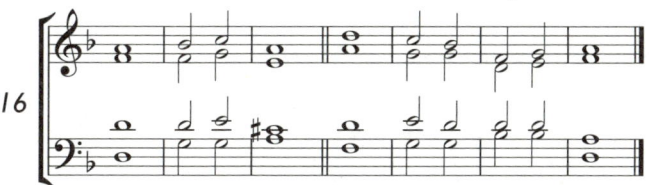

16

1 The fool has said in his heart, 'There ' is no ' God.' ♦
Corrupt are they, and abominable in their wickedness;
there is ' no one ' that does ' good.

2 The Lord has looked down from heaven
upon the ' children of ' earth, ♦
to see if there is anyone who is wise
and ' seeks ' after ' God.

‡ 3 But every one has turned back;
all alike have be'come cor'rupt: ♦
there is none that does ' good; ' no, not ' one.

4 Have they no knowledge, those ' evil'doers, ♦
who eat up my people as if they ate bread
and do not ' call up'on the ' Lord?

5 There shall they be in ' great ' fear; ♦
for God is in the ' company ' of the ' righteous.

6 Though they would confound the ' counsel • of the ' poor, ♦
yet the ' Lord shall ' be their ' refuge.

7 O that Israel's salvation would ' come • out of ' Zion! ♦
When the Lord restores the fortunes of his people,
then will Jacob re'joice and ' Israel be ' glad.

Psalm 15

George A Macfarren

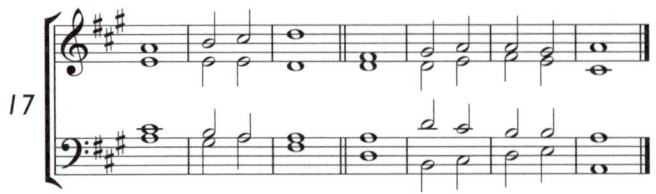

17

1 Lord, who may ' dwell in your ' tabernacle? ♦
Who may rest up'on your ' holy ' hill?

2 Whoever leads an ' uncorrupt ' life ♦
and ' does the ' thing that is ' right;

3 Who speaks the ' truth • from the ' heart ♦
and ' bears no de'ceit • on the ' tongue;

4 Who does no ' evil • to a ' friend ♦
and ' pours no ' scorn • on a ' neighbour;

‡ 5 In whose sight the wicked are ' not es'teemed, ♦
but who honours ' those who ' fear the ' Lord.

6 Whoever has ' sworn • to a ' neighbour ♦
and ' never goes ' back • on that ' word;

7,8 Who does not lend money in hope of gain,
nor takes a bribe a'gainst the ' innocent; ♦
Whoever does these ' things shall ' never ' fall.

Psalm 16

Edwin Monk

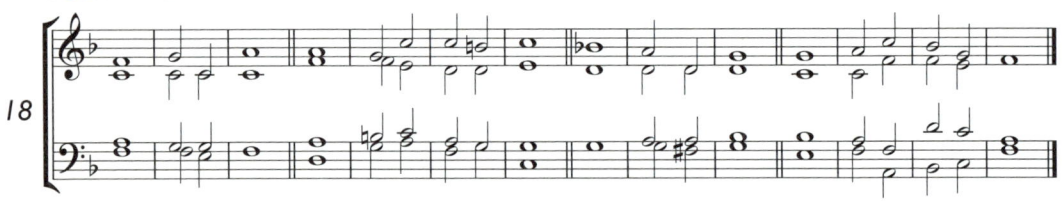

18

1 Preserve me, O God, for in you have I ' taken ' refuge; ♦
I have said to the Lord, 'You are my lord,
all my ' good de'pends on ' you.'

2 All my delight is upon the godly that are ' in the ' land, ♦
upon ' those • who are ' noble in ' heart.

‡ 3 Though the idols are legion that ' many run ' after, ♦
their drink offerings of blood I will not offer,
neither make mention of their ' names up'on my ' lips.

4 The Lord himself is my portion ' and my ' cup; ♦
in your hands a'lone ' is my ' fortune.

5 My share has fallen in a ' fair ' land; ♦
indeed, I ' have a ' goodly ' heritage.

6 I will bless the Lord who has ' given me ' counsel, ♦
   and in the night watches ' he in'structs my ' heart.

7 I have set the Lord ' always be'fore me; ♦
   he is at my right ' hand; I ' shall not ' fall.

8 Wherefore my heart is glad and my ' spirit re'joices; ♦
   my flesh ' also shall ' rest se'cure.

9 For you will not abandon my ' soul to ' Death, ♦
   nor suffer your ' faithful one to ' see the ' Pit.

‡ 10 You will show me the path of life;
      in your presence is the ' fullness of ' joy ♦
      and in your right hand are ' pleasures for ' ever'more.

Psalm 17

Thomas A. Walmisley

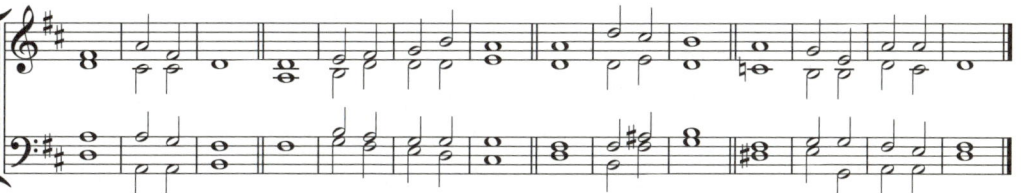

1 Hear my just cause, O Lord; consider ' my com'plaint; ♦
   listen to my prayer, which comes ' not from ' lying ' lips.

2 Let my vindication come ' forth from your ' presence; ♦
   let your eyes be'hold ' what is ' right.

3 Weigh my heart, ex'amine me by ' night, ♦
   refine me, and you will find ' no im'purity ' in me.

4 My mouth does not trespass for ' earthly re'wards; ♦
   I have ' heeded the ' words • of your ' lips.

5 My footsteps hold fast in the ways of ' your com'mandments; ♦
   my feet have not ' stumbled ' in your ' paths.

6 I call upon you, O God, for ' you will ' answer me; ♦
   incline your ear to me, and ' listen ' to my ' words.

7 Show me your marvellous ' loving'kindness, ♦
   O Saviour of those who take refuge at your right hand
      from ' those who ' rise up a'gainst them.

8 Keep me as the ' apple • of your ' eye; ♦
   hide me under the ' shadow ' of your ' wings,

9 From the wicked ' who as'sault me, ♦
   from my enemies who surround me to ' take a'way my ' life.

10 They have closed their ' heart to ' pity ♦
    and their ' mouth speaks ' proud ' things.

Thomas A. Walmisley

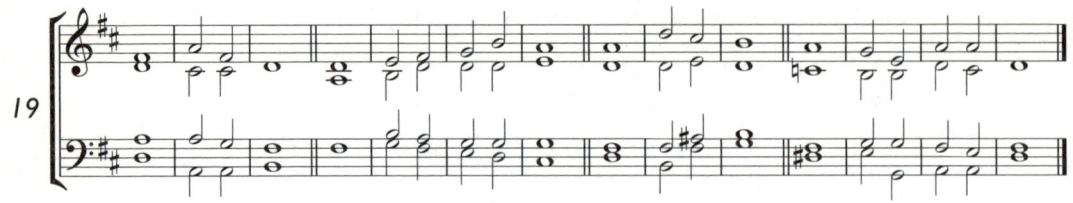

11 They press me hard, they surround me on ' every ' side, ♦
    watching how they may ' cast me ' to the ' ground,

12 Like a lion that is greedy ' for its ' prey, ♦
    like a young lion ' lurking in ' secret ' places.

13 Arise, Lord; confront them and ' cast them ' down; ♦
    deliver me from the ' wicked ' by your ' sword.

14 Deliver me, O Lord, ' by your ' hand ♦
    from those whose ' portion in ' life • is un'ending,

15 Whose bellies you ' fill with your ' treasure, ♦
    who are well supplied with children
        and ' leave their ' wealth • to their ' little ones.

16 As for me, I shall see your ' face in ' righteousness; ♦
    when I awake and behold your ' likeness, ' I shall be ' satisfied.

Psalm 18   Charles V. Stanford

1 I love you, O ' Lord my ' strength. ♦
   The Lord is my crag, my ' fortress and ' my de'liverer,

2 My God, my rock in ' whom I take ' refuge, ♦
   my shield, the horn of my sal'vation ' and my ' stronghold.

‡ 3 I cried to the Lord ' in my ' anguish ♦
   and I was ' saved ' from my ' enemies.

4 The cords of ' death en'twined me ♦
   and the torrents of des'truction ' over'whelmed me.

5 The cords of the Pit ' fastened a'bout me ♦
   and the ' snares of ' death en'tangled me.

6 In my distress I ' called upon the ' Lord ♦
   and cried ' out to my ' God for ' help.

7 He heard my voice ' in his ' temple ♦
   and my ' cry ' came to his ' ears.

8 The earth ' trembled and ' quaked; ♦
   the foundations of the mountains shook;
      they ' reeled be'cause he was ' angry.

9 Smoke rose from his nostrils
      and a consuming fire went ' out of his ' mouth; ♦
   burning ' coals ' blazed forth ' from him.

10 He parted the heavens ' and came ' down ♦
    and thick ' darkness was ' under his ' feet.

11 He rode upon the ' cherubim and ' flew; ♦
    he came ' flying • on the ' wings of the ' wind.

12 He made darkness his covering ' round a'bout him, ♦
    dark waters and thick ' clouds ' his pa'vilion.

13 From the brightness of his presence, ' through the ' clouds ♦
    burst ' hailstones and ' coals of ' fire.

14 The Lord also thundered ' out of ' heaven; ♦
    the Most High uttered his voice
       with ' hailstones and ' coals of ' fire.

15 He sent out his ' arrows and ' scattered them; ♦
    he hurled down ' lightnings and ' put them to ' flight.

16 The springs of the ' ocean were ' seen, ♦
    and the foun'dations • of the ' world un'covered

16a at your re'buke, O ' Lord, ♦
     at the blast of the ' breath of ' your dis'pleasure.

Charles V. Stanford

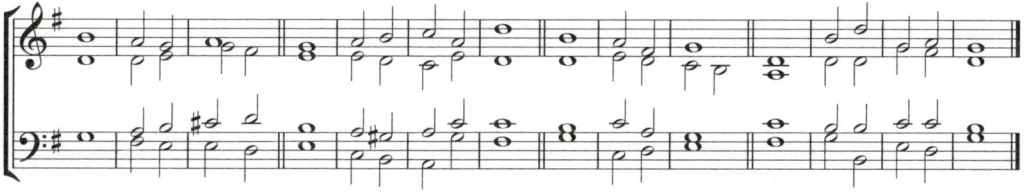

17 He reached down from on ' high and ' took me; ♦
    he drew me ' out of the ' mighty ' waters.

18 He delivered me from my ' strong ' enemy, ♦
    from foes that ' were too ' mighty ' for me.

19 They came upon me in the ' day of my ' trouble; ♦
    but the ' Lord was ' my up'holder.

20 He brought me out into a ' place of ' liberty; ♦
    he rescued me be'cause he de'lighted ' in me.

Charles V. Stanford

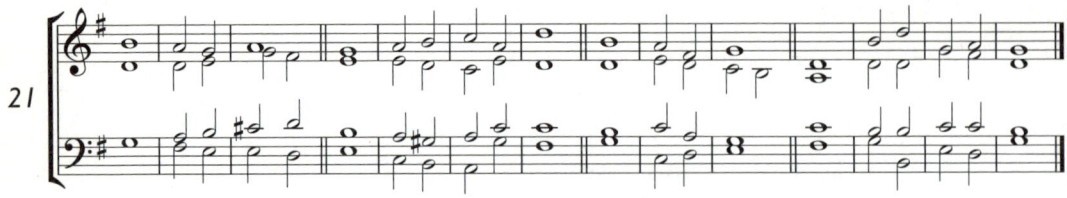

21

21 The Lord rewarded me after my ' righteous ' dealing; ♦
according to the cleanness of my ' hands he ' recom'pensed me,

22 Because I had kept the ' ways of the ' Lord ♦
and had not gone ' wickedly a'way from my ' God,

23 For I had an eye to ' all his ' laws, ♦
and did not cast ' out his com'mandments ' from me.

24 I was also whole'hearted be'fore him ♦
and ' kept myself ' from in'iquity;

25 Therefore the Lord rewarded me
 after my ' righteous ' dealing, ♦
and according to the cleanness of my ' hands ' in his ' sight.

26 With the faithful you ' show yourself ' faithful; ♦
with the ' true you ' show yourself ' true;

27 With the pure you ' show yourself ' pure, ♦
but with the crooked you ' show your'self per'verse.

28 For you will save a ' lowly ' people ♦
and bring down the ' high ' looks • of the ' proud.

29 You also shall ' light my ' candle; ♦
the Lord my God shall make my ' darkness ' to be ' bright.

30 By your help I shall run at an ' enemy ' host; ♦
with the help of my God ' I can leap ' over a ' wall.

Joseph Barnby

22

31 As for God, his way is perfect;
 the word of the Lord is ' tried • in the ' fire; ♦
he is a shield to ' all who ' trust in ' him.

32 For who is God ' but the ' Lord, ♦
and who is the ' rock ex'cept our ' God?

33 It is God who girds me a'bout with ' strength ♦
and ' makes my ' way ' perfect.

26 Psalm 18

34 He makes my ' feet like ' hinds' feet ♦
 so that I tread ' surely ' on the ' heights.

35 He teaches my ' hands to ' fight ♦
 and my arms to ' bend a ' bow of ' bronze.

36 You have given me the shield of ' your sal'vation; ♦
 your right hand upholds me
  and your ' grace has ' made me ' great.

37 You enlarge my ' strides be'neath me, ♦
 yet my ' feet ' do not ' slide.

38 I will pursue my enemies and ' over'take them, ♦
 nor turn again un'til I ' have des'troyed them.

39 I will smite them down so they ' cannot ' rise; ♦
 they shall ' fall be'neath my ' feet.

40 You have girded me with ' strength • for the ' battle; ♦
 you will cast ' down my ' enemies ' under me;

41 You will make my foes turn their ' backs up'on me ♦
 and I shall des'troy ' them that ' hate me.

42 They will cry out, but there shall be ' none to ' help them; ♦
 they will cry to the Lord, ' but he ' will not ' answer.

43 I shall beat them as small as the ' dust • on the ' wind; ♦
 I will cast them out as the ' mire ' in the ' streets.

44 You will deliver me from the ' strife • of the ' peoples; ♦
 you will ' make me the ' head • of the ' nations.

45 A people I have not known shall serve me;
  as soon as they hear me, they ' shall o'bey me; ♦
 strangers will ' humble them'selves be'fore me.

46 The foreign peoples will ' lose ' heart ♦
 and come ' trembling ' out of their ' strongholds.

Charles V. Stanford

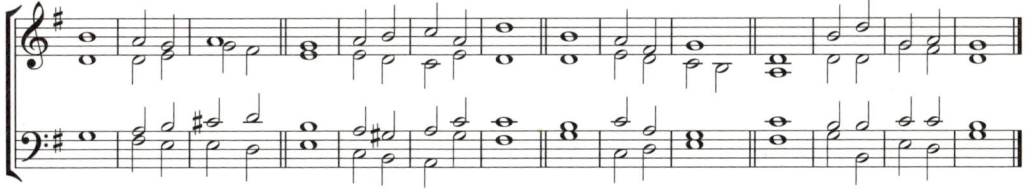

47 The Lord lives, and blessed ' be my ' rock! ♦
 Praised be the ' God of ' my sal'vation,

48 Even the ' God who ' vindicates me ♦
 and sub'dues the ' peoples ' under me!

Psalm 18

Charles V. Stanford

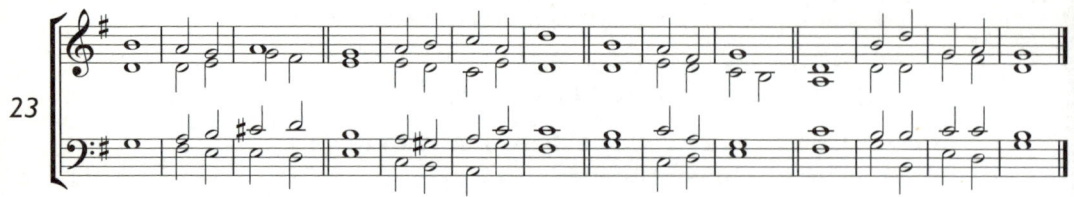

49 You that deliver me from my enemies,
   you will set me up a'bove my ' foes; ♦
   from the ' violent you ' will de'liver me;

50 Therefore will I give you thanks, O Lord, a'mong the ' nations ♦
   and sing ' praises ' to your ' name,

‡ 51 To the one who gives great victory ' to his ' king ♦
   and shows faithful love to his anointed,
   to David ' and his ' seed for ' ever.

Psalm 19

Thomas A. Walmisley

1 The heavens are telling the ' glory of ' God ♦
  and the ' firmament pro'claims his ' handiwork.

2 One day pours out its ' song • to an'other ♦
  and one night unfolds ' knowledge ' to an'other.

3 They have neither ' speech nor ' language ♦
  and their ' voices ' are not ' heard,

4 Yet their sound has gone out into ' all ' lands ♦
  and their ' words • to the ' ends of the ' world.

5 In them has he set a tabernacle ' for the ' sun, ♦
  that comes forth as a bridegroom out of his chamber
      and rejoices as a ' champion to ' run his ' course.

6 It goes forth from the end of the heavens
      and runs to the very ' end a'gain, ♦
  and there is nothing ' hidden ' from its ' heat.

7 The law of the Lord is perfect, re'viving the ' soul; ♦
  the testimony of the Lord is sure
      and gives ' wisdom ' to the ' simple.

28   Psalm 19

8 The statutes of the Lord are right and re'joice the ' heart; ♦
 the commandment of the Lord is pure
  and gives ' light ' to the ' eyes.

9 The fear of the Lord is clean and en'dures for ' ever; ♦
 the judgements of the Lord are true and ' righteous ' alto'gether.

10 More to be desired are they than gold,
  more than ' much fine ' gold, ♦
 sweeter also than honey, ' dripping ' from the ' honeycomb.

‡ 11 By them also is your ' servant ' taught ♦
 and in keeping them ' there is ' great re'ward.

12 Who can tell how often ' they of'fend? ♦
 O cleanse me ' from my ' secret ' faults!

13 Keep your servant also from pre'sumptuous ' sins ♦
 lest they get do'minion ' over ' me;

13a So shall I be ' unde'filed, ♦
 and ' innocent of ' great of'fence.

14 Let the words of my mouth and the meditation of my heart
  be acceptable ' in your ' sight, ♦
 O Lord, my ' strength and ' my re'deemer.

Psalm 20

Samuel Wesley

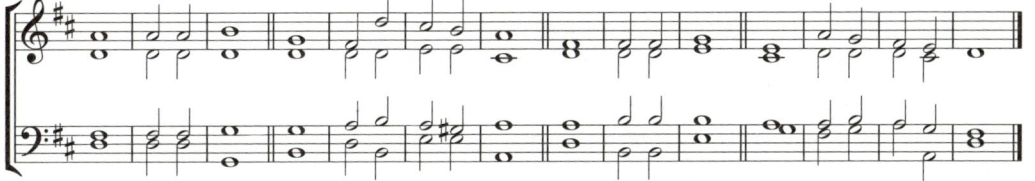

1 May the Lord hear you in the ' day of ' trouble, ♦
 the name of the ' God of ' Jacob de'fend you;

2 Send you ' help from his ' sanctuary ♦
 and ' strengthen you ' out of ' Zion;

3 Remember ' all your ' offerings ♦
 and ac'cept your ' burnt ' sacrifice;

4 Grant you your ' heart's de'sire ♦
 and ful'fil ' all your ' mind.

‡ 5 May we rejoice in your salvation
  and triumph in the ' name of our ' God; ♦
 may the Lord per'form all ' your pe'titions.

Samuel Wesley

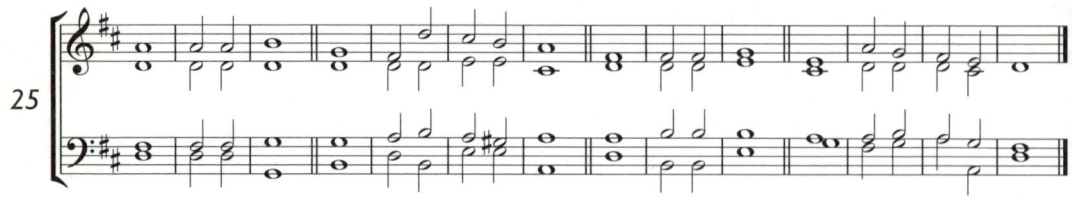

6 Now I know that the Lord will ' save his a'nointed; ♦
he will answer him from his holy heaven,
with the mighty ' strength of ' his right ' hand.

7 Some put their trust in chariots and ' some in ' horses, ♦
but we will call only on the ' name of the ' Lord our ' God.

8 They are brought ' down and ' fallen, ♦
but we are ' risen ' and stand ' upright.

9 O Lord, ' save the ' king ♦
and answer us ' when we ' call up'on you.

Psalm 21

Thomas A. Walmisley

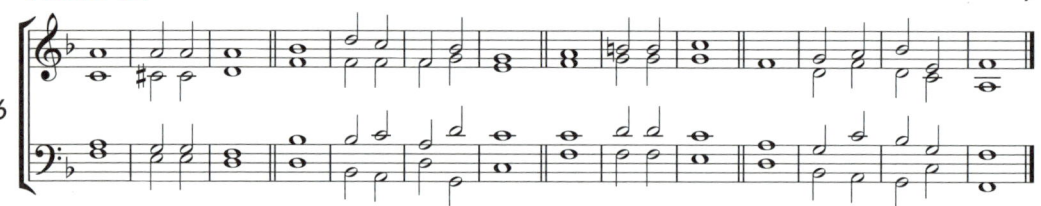

1 The king shall rejoice in your ' strength, O ' Lord; ♦
how greatly shall he re'joice in ' your sal'vation!

2 You have given him his ' heart's de'sire ♦
and have not de'nied • the re'quest of his ' lips.

3 For you come to meet him with ' blessings of ' goodness ♦
and set a crown of pure ' gold up'on his ' head.

4 He asked of you life ' and you ' gave it him, ♦
length of ' days, for ' ever and ' ever.

5 His honour is great because of ' your sal'vation; ♦
glory and majesty ' have you ' laid up'on him.

6 You have granted him ever'lasting fe'licity ♦
and will make him ' glad with ' joy • in your ' presence.

‡ 7 For the king puts his ' trust in the ' Lord; ♦
because of the loving-kindness of the Most High,
he shall ' not be ' over'thrown.

8 Your hand shall mark down ' all your ' enemies; ♦
   your right hand will ' find out ' those who ' hate you.

9 You will make them like a fiery oven
      in the ' time of your ' wrath; ♦
   the Lord will swallow them up in his anger
      ' and the ' fire will con'sume them.

10 Their fruit you will root ' out of the ' land ♦
   and their ' seed • from a'mong its in'habitants.

11 Because they intend ' evil a'gainst you ♦
   and devise wicked schemes ' which they ' cannot per'form,

12 You will ' put them to ' flight ♦
   when you ' aim your ' bow at their ' faces.

13 Be exalted, O Lord, in ' your own ' might; ♦
   we will make ' music and ' sing of your ' power.

Psalm 22

Luke Flintoft

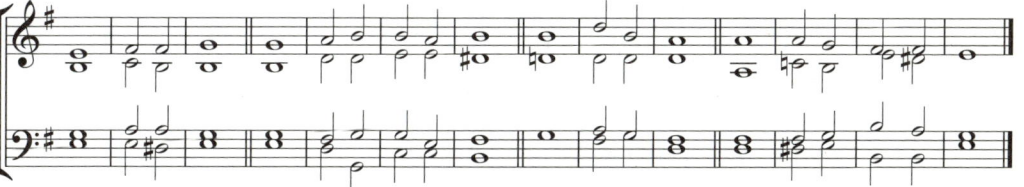

1 My God, my God, why have ' you for'saken me, ♦
   and are so far from my salvation,
      from the ' words of ' my dis'tress?

2 O my God, I cry in the daytime,
      but you ' do not ' answer; ♦
   and by night also, ' but I ' find no ' rest.

3 Yet you ' are the ' Holy One, ♦
   enthroned up'on the ' praises of ' Israel.

4 Our forebears ' trusted in ' you; ♦
   they ' trusted, and ' you de'livered them.

5 They cried out to you and ' were de'livered; ♦
   they put their trust in you ' and were ' not con'founded.

6 But as for me, I am a worm and ' no ' man, ♦
   scorned by all ' and des'pised • by the ' people.

7 All who see me ' laugh me to ' scorn; ♦
   they curl their lips and ' wag their ' heads, ' saying,

8 'He trusted in the Lord; ' let him de'liver him; ♦
   let him de'liver him, if ' he de'lights in him.'

Luke Flintoft

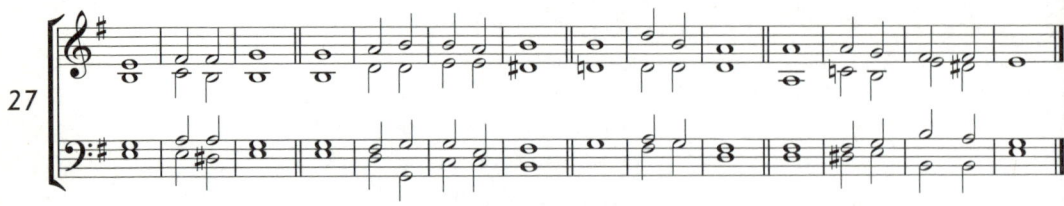

27

9   But it is you that took me ' out of the ' womb ♦
    and laid me safe up'on my ' mother's ' breast.

10 On you was I cast ever since ' I was ' born; ♦
    you are my God even ' from my ' mother's ' womb.

‡ 11 Be not far from me, for trouble is ' near at ' hand ♦
    and ' there is ' none to ' help.

12 Mighty oxen ' come a'round me; ♦
    fat bulls of Bashan close me ' in on ' every ' side.

13 They gape upon me ' with their ' mouths, ♦
    as it were a ' ramping • and a ' roaring ' lion.

14 I am poured out like water;
        all my bones are ' out of ' joint; ♦
    my heart has become like wax
        ' melting • in the ' depths of my ' body.

15 My mouth is dried up like a potsherd;
        my tongue ' cleaves to my ' gums; ♦
    you have ' laid me • in the ' dust of ' death.

16 For the hounds are all about me,
        the pack of evildoers close ' in on ' me; ♦
    they ' pierce my ' hands and my ' feet.

17 I can count ' all my ' bones; ♦
    they stand ' staring and ' looking up'on me.

18 They divide my ' garments a'mong them; ♦
    they cast ' lots ' for my ' clothing.

19 Be not far from ' me, O ' Lord; ♦
    you are my ' strength; ' hasten to ' help me.

20 Deliver my ' soul • from the ' sword, ♦
    my poor ' life • from the ' power of the ' dog.

21 Save me from the ' lion's ' mouth, ♦
    from the horns of wild oxen.
        ' You have ' answered ' me!

32   Psalm 22

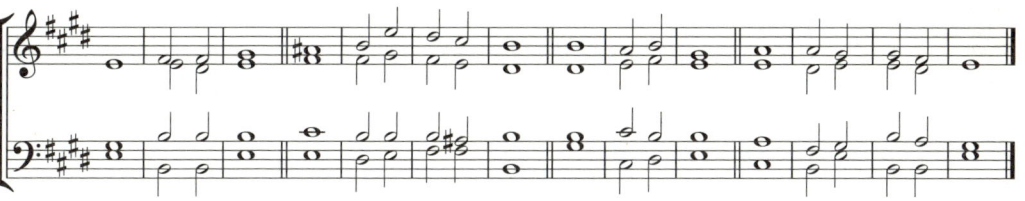

Matthew Camidge

22 I will tell of your ' name to my ' people; ♦
     in the midst of the congre'gation ' will I ' praise you.

23 Praise the Lord, ' you that ' fear him; ♦
     O seed of Jacob, glorify him;
         stand in awe of ' him, O ' seed of ' Israel.

24 For he has not despised nor abhorred the suffering of the poor;
         neither has he hidden his ' face ' from them; ♦
     but when they ' cried to ' him he ' heard them.

25 From you comes my praise in the great ' congre'gation; ♦
     I will perform my vows in the ' presence of ' those that ' fear you.

‡ 26 The poor shall ' eat • and be ' satisfied; ♦
     those who seek the Lord shall praise him;
         their ' hearts shall ' live for ' ever.

27 All the ends of the earth
         shall remember and ' turn to the ' Lord, ♦
     and all the families of the ' nations shall ' bow be'fore him.

28 For the kingdom ' is the ' Lord's ♦
     and he ' rules ' over the ' nations.

29 How can those who sleep in the earth
         bow ' down in ' worship, ♦
     or those who go down to the ' dust ' kneel be'fore him?

30 He has saved my life for himself;
         my des'cendants shall ' serve him; ♦
     this shall be told of the Lord for ' gene'rations to ' come.

‡ 31 They shall come and make known his salvation,
         to a people ' yet un'born, ♦
     declaring that ' he, the ' Lord, has ' done it.

Psalm 23
John Camidge, jun.

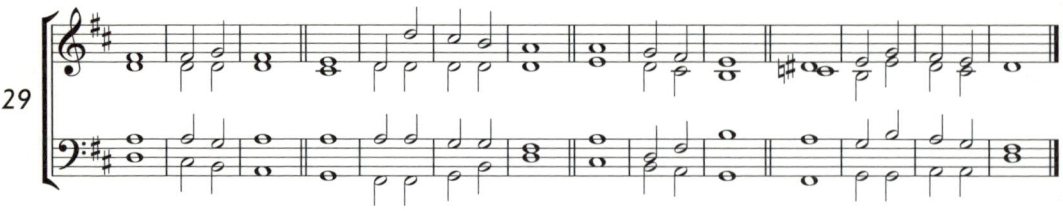

or

James Turle

1 The Lord ' is my ' shepherd; ♦
   therefore ' can I ' lack ' nothing.

2 He makes me lie down in ' green ' pastures ♦
   and leads me be'side ' still ' waters.

3 He shall re'fresh my ' soul ♦
   and guide me in the paths of righteousness ' for his ' name's ' sake.

4 Though I walk through the valley of the shadow of death,
      I will ' fear no ' evil; ♦
   for you are with me;
      your ' rod and your ' staff, they ' comfort me.

5 You spread a table before me
      in the presence of ' those who ' trouble me; ♦
   you have anointed my head with oil
      ' and my ' cup shall be ' full.

6 Surely goodness and loving mercy shall follow me
      all the ' days of my ' life, ♦
   and I will dwell in the ' house of the ' Lord for ' ever.

Psalm 24
Joseph Barnby

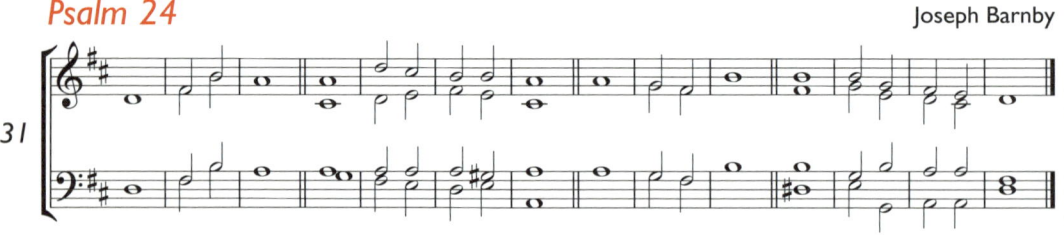

1 The earth is the Lord's and ' all that ' fills it, ♦
   the compass of the world and ' all who ' dwell there'in.

2 For he has founded it up'on the ' seas ♦
   and set it firm upon the ' rivers ' of the ' deep.

3 'Who shall ascend the ' hill of the ' Lord, ♦
  or who can rise ' up • in his ' holy ' place?'

4 'Those who have clean hands and a ' pure ' heart, ♦
  who have not lifted up their soul to an idol,
    nor ' sworn an ' oath • to a ' lie;

5 'They shall receive a ' blessing • from the ' Lord, ♦
  a just reward from the ' God of ' their sal'vation.'

6 Such is the company of ' those who ' seek him, ♦
  of those who seek your ' face, O ' God of ' Jacob.

7 Lift up your heads, O gates;
    be lifted up, you ever'lasting ' doors; ♦
  and the King of ' glory ' shall come ' in.

8 'Who is the ' King of ' glory?' ♦
  'The Lord, strong and mighty,
    the ' Lord • who is ' mighty in ' battle.'

9 Lift up your heads, O gates;
    be lifted up, you ever'lasting ' doors; ♦
  and the King of ' glory ' shall come ' in.

10 'Who is this ' King of ' glory?' ♦
   'The Lord of hosts,
     ' he • is the ' King of ' glory.'

Psalm 25

Frederick A. G. Ouseley

1 To you, O Lord, I lift up my soul;
    O my God, in ' you I ' trust; ♦
  let me not be put to shame;
    let not my ' enemies ' triumph ' over me.

2 Let none who look to you be ' put to ' shame, ♦
  but let the treacherous be ' shamed ' and frus'trated.

3 Make me to know your ' ways, O ' Lord, ♦
  and ' teach me ' your ' paths.

4 Lead me in your ' truth and ' teach me, ♦
  for you are the God of my salvation;
    for you have I ' hoped ' all the day ' long.

Frederick A. G. Ouseley

32

5 Remember, Lord, your com′passion and ′ love, ♦
   for they ′ are from ′ ever′lasting.

6 Remember not the sins of my youth
   or ′ my trans′gressions, ♦
   but think on me in your goodness, O Lord,
   ac′cording • to your ′ steadfast ′ love.

7 Gracious and upright ′ is the ′ Lord; ♦
   therefore shall he teach ′ sinners ′ in the ′ way.

8 He will guide the humble in ′ doing ′ right ♦
   and ′ teach his ′ way to the ′ lowly.

9 All the paths of the Lord are ′ mercy and ′ truth ♦
   to those who keep his ′ covenant ′ and his ′ testimonies.

10 For your name's ′ sake, O ′ Lord, ♦
   be merciful to my ′ sin, for ′ it is ′ great.

11 Who are those who ′ fear the ′ Lord? ♦
   Them will he teach in the ′ way that ′ they should ′ choose.

12 Their soul shall ′ dwell at ′ ease ♦
   and their offspring ′ shall in′herit the ′ land.

13 The hidden purpose of the Lord is for ′ those who ′ fear him ♦
   and ′ he will ′ show them his ′ covenant.

14 My eyes are ever ′ looking • to the ′ Lord, ♦
   for he shall pluck my ′ feet ′ out of the ′ net.

15 Turn to me and be ′ gracious ′ to me, ♦
   for I am alone ′ and brought ′ very ′ low.

16 The sorrows of my heart ′ have in′creased; ♦
   O bring me ′ out of ′ my dis′tress.

17 Look upon my ad′versity and ′ misery ♦
   and for′give me ′ all my ′ sin.

18 Look upon my enemies, for ′ they are ′ many ♦
   and they bear a ′ violent ′ hatred a′gainst me.

19 O keep my soul ′ and de′liver me; ♦
   let me not be put to shame, for I have ′ put my ′ trust in ′ you.

20,21 Let integrity and uprightness preserve me,
     for my hope has ′ been in ′ you. ♦
   Deliver ′ Israel, O ′ God,
     ′ out of ′ all his ′ troubles.

Psalm 25

Psalm 26

Edward J. Hopkins

1. Give judgement for me, O Lord,
    for I have ' walked with in'tegrity; ♦
   I have trusted in the ' Lord and ' have not ' faltered.

2. Test me, O ' Lord, and ' try me; ♦
   examine my ' heart ' and my ' mind.

3. For your love is be'fore my ' eyes; ♦
   I have ' walked ' in your ' truth.

4. I have not joined the company ' of the ' false, ♦
   nor con'sorted ' with the de'ceitful.

5. I hate the gathering of ' evil'doers ♦
   and I ' will not sit ' down • with the ' wicked.

6. I will wash my hands in ' innocence, O ' Lord, ♦
   that I may ' go a'bout your ' altar,

7. To make heard the ' voice of ' thanksgiving ♦
   and tell of ' all your ' wonderful ' deeds.

8. Lord, I love the house of your ' habi'tation ♦
   and the ' place • where your ' glory a'bides.

9. Sweep me not a'way with ' sinners, ♦
   nor my ' life ' with the ' blood•thirsty,

10. Whose hands are full of ' wicked ' schemes ♦
    and their ' right hand ' full of ' bribes.

11. As for me, I will ' walk with in'tegrity; ♦
    redeem me, Lord, ' and be ' merciful ' to me.

12. My ' foot stands ' firm; ♦
    in the great congregation ' I will ' bless the ' Lord.

Psalm 27

James Turle

34

1 The Lord is my light and my salvation;
    whom then ' shall I ' fear? ♦
The Lord is the strength of my life;
    of whom then ' shall I ' be a'fraid?

2 When the wicked, even my enemies and my foes,
    came upon me to ' eat up my ' flesh, ♦
they ' stumbled ' and ' fell.

3 Though a host encamp against me,
    my heart shall ' not be a'fraid, ♦
and though there rise up war against me,
    yet will I ' put my ' trust in ' him.

4 One thing have I asked of the Lord
    and that a'lone I ' seek: ♦
that I may dwell in the house of the Lord
    ' all the ' days of my ' life,

5 To behold the fair ' beauty • of the ' Lord ♦
    and to ' seek his ' will • in his ' temple.

6 For in the day of trouble
    he shall hide me ' in his ' shelter; ♦
in the secret place of his dwelling shall he hide me
    and set me ' high up'on a ' rock.

7 And now shall he ' lift up my ' head ♦
    above my ' enemies ' round a'bout me;

8 Therefore will I offer in his dwelling an oblation
    with ' great ' gladness; ♦
I will sing and make ' music ' to the ' Lord.

William Havergal

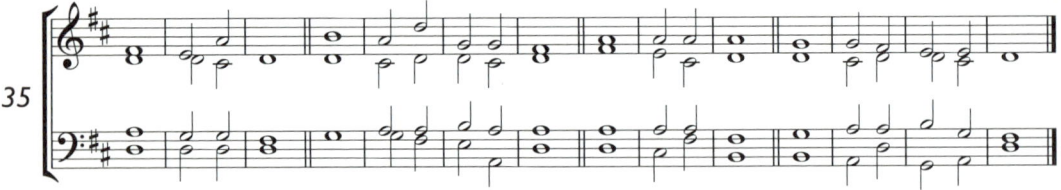

35

9 Hear my voice, O Lord, ' when I ' call; ♦
    have ' mercy up'on me and ' answer me.

10 My heart tells of your word, ' 'Seek my ' face.' ♦
    Your ' face, Lord, ' will I ' seek.

11 Hide ' not your ' face from me, ♦
   nor cast your ' servant a'way • in dis'pleasure.

12 You have ' been my ' helper; ♦
   leave me not, neither forsake me, O ' God of ' my sal'vation.

‡ 13 Though my father and my ' mother for'sake me, ♦
   the ' Lord will ' take me ' up.

14 Teach me your ' way, O ' Lord; ♦
   lead me on a level path,
      because of ' those who ' lie in ' wait for me.

15 Deliver me not into the ' will of my ' adversaries, ♦
   for false witnesses have risen up against me,
      and ' those who ' breathe out ' violence.

16 I believe that I shall see the ' goodness • of the ' Lord ♦
   in the ' land ' of the ' living.

17 Wait for the Lord;
      be strong and he shall ' comfort your ' heart; ♦
   wait ' patiently ' for the ' Lord.

Psalm 28

Samuel Wesley

1 To you I call, O Lord my rock;
      be not ' deaf • to my ' cry, ♦
   lest, if you do not hear me,
      I become like ' those who go ' down • to the ' Pit.

2 Hear the voice of my prayer when I cry ' out to ' you, ♦
   when I lift up my ' hands • to your ' holy of ' holies.

3 Do not snatch me away with the wicked,
      with the ' evil'doers, ♦
   who speak peaceably with their neighbours,
      while ' malice is ' in their ' hearts.

4 Repay them ac'cording • to their ' deeds ♦
   and according to the ' wickedness of ' their de'vices.

5 Reward them according to the ' work of their ' hands ♦
   and ' pay them their ' just de'serts.

6 They take no heed of the Lord's doings,
      nor of the ' works of his ' hands; ♦
   therefore shall he break them down
      ' and not ' build them ' up.

Samuel Wesley

7 Blessed ' be the ' Lord, ♦
for he has ' heard the ' voice of my ' prayer.

8 The Lord is my strength ' and my ' shield; ♦
my heart has trusted in ' him and ' I am ' helped;

‡ 9 Therefore my heart ' dances for ' joy ♦
and in my ' song ' will I ' praise him.

10 The Lord is the ' strength of his ' people, ♦
a safe ' refuge for ' his a'nointed.

11 Save your people and ' bless your in'heritance; ♦
shepherd them and ' carry ' them for ' ever.

Psalm 29

from Martin Luther

1 Ascribe to the Lord, you ' powers of ' heaven, ♦
ascribe to the ' Lord ' glory and ' strength.

2 Ascribe to the Lord the honour ' due • to his ' name; ♦
worship the ' Lord • in the ' beauty of ' holiness.

3 The voice of the Lord is upon the waters;
the God of ' glory ' thunders; ♦
the Lord is up'on the ' mighty ' waters.

4 The voice of the Lord is mighty in ' oper'ation; ♦
the voice of the Lord ' is a ' glorious ' voice.

5 The voice of the Lord ' breaks the ' cedar trees; ♦
the Lord ' breaks the ' cedars of ' Lebanon;

6 He makes Lebanon ' skip • like a ' calf ♦
and Sirion ' like a ' young wild ' ox.

7 The voice of the Lord splits the flash of lightning;
the voice of the Lord ' shakes the ' wilderness; ♦
the Lord ' shakes the ' wilderness of ' Kadesh.

8 The voice of the Lord makes the oak trees writhe
    and strips the ' forests ' bare; ♦
in his ' temple ' all cry, ' 'Glory!'

9 The Lord sits enthroned a'bove the ' water flood; ♦
the Lord sits enthroned as ' king for ' ever'more.

10 The Lord shall give ' strength to his ' people; ♦
the Lord shall give his ' people the ' blessing of ' peace.

Psalm 30

William Havergal

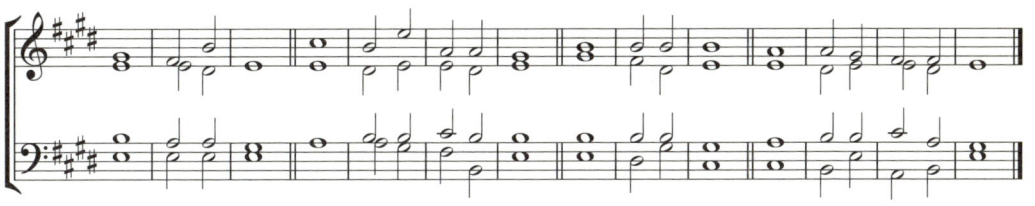

1 I will exalt you, O Lord,
    because you have ' raised me ' up ♦
and have not let my ' foes ' triumph ' over me.

2 O Lord my God, I cried ' out to ' you ♦
and ' you have ' healed ' me.

3 You brought me up, O Lord, ' from the ' dead; ♦
you restored me to life from among ' those that go ' down • to the ' Pit.

4 Sing to the Lord, you ' servants of ' his; ♦
give ' thanks to his ' holy ' name.

5 For his wrath endures but the twinkling of an eye,
    his favour ' for a ' lifetime. ♦
Heaviness may endure for a night,
    but ' joy comes ' in the ' morning.

6 In my prosperity I said,
    'I shall ' never be ' moved. ♦
You, Lord, of your goodness,
    have ' made my ' hill so ' strong.'

7 Then you ' hid your ' face from me ♦
and ' I was ' utterly dis'mayed.

8 To you, O ' Lord, I ' cried; ♦
to the Lord I ' made my ' suppli'cation:

9 'What profit is there in my blood,
    if I go ' down • to the ' Pit? ♦
Will the dust praise you ' or de'clare your ' faithfulness?

William Havergal

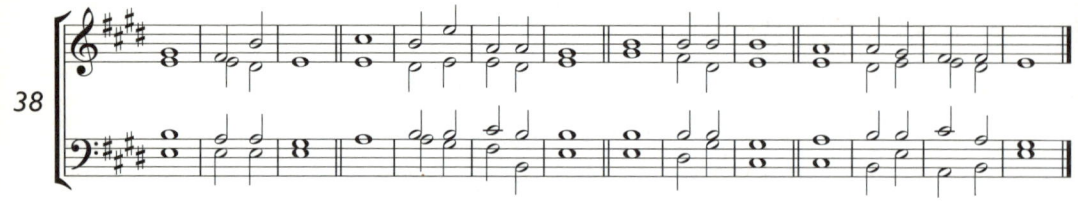

38

10 'Hear, O Lord, and have ' mercy up'on me; ♦
   O ' Lord, ' be my ' helper.'

11 You have turned my mourning ' into ' dancing; ♦
   you have put off my sackcloth and ' girded ' me with ' gladness;

12 Therefore my heart sings to ' you without ' ceasing; ♦
   O Lord my God, I will ' give you ' thanks for ' ever.

Psalm 31

Harry Bramma

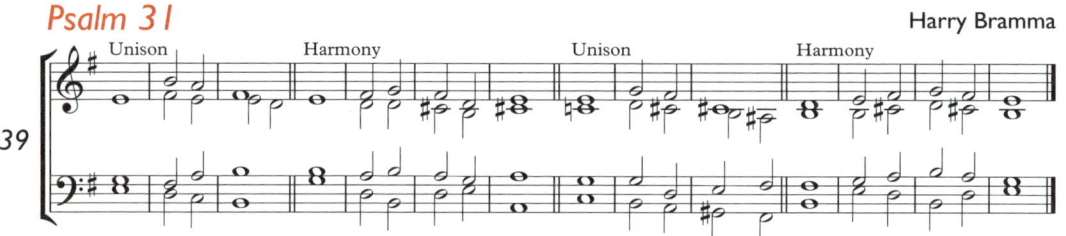

39

1 In you, O Lord, have I taken refuge;
   let me never be ' put to ' shame; ♦
   de'liver me ' in your ' righteousness.

2 Incline your ' ear to ' me; ♦
   make ' haste ' to de'liver me.

3 Be my strong rock, a fortress to save me,
   for you are my ' rock • and my ' stronghold; ♦
   guide me, and ' lead me ' for your ' name's sake.

4 Take me out of the net that they have laid ' secretly ' for me, ♦
   for ' you ' are my ' strength.

5 Into your hands I com'mend my ' spirit, ♦
   for you have redeemed me, O ' Lord ' God of ' truth.

6 I hate those who cling to ' worthless ' idols; ♦
   I ' put my ' trust • in the ' Lord.

7 I will be glad and re'joice in your ' mercy, ♦
   for you have seen my affliction
      and known my ' soul ' in ad'versity.

8 You have not shut me up in the ' hand of the ' enemy; ♦
   you have set my ' feet • in an ' open ' place.

9 Have mercy on me, Lord, for ' I am in ' trouble; ♦
　　my eye is consumed with sorrow,
　　　　my ' soul • and my ' body ' also.

10 For my life is wasted with grief, and my ' years with ' sighing; ♦
　　my strength fails me because of my affliction,
　　　　and my ' bones ' are con'sumed.

11 I have become a reproach to all my enemies
　　　　and even to my neighbours,
　　　　an object of dread to ' my ac'quaintances; ♦
　　when they ' see me • in the ' street they ' flee from me.

12 I am forgotten like one that is dead, ' out of ' mind; ♦
　　I have be'come • like a ' broken ' vessel.

13 For I have heard the whispering of the crowd;
　　　　fear is on ' every ' side; ♦
　　they scheme together against me,
　　　　and ' plot to ' take my ' life.

14 But my trust is in ' you, O ' Lord. ♦
　　I have ' said, 'You ' are my ' God.

15 'My times are ' in your ' hand; ♦
　　deliver me from the hand of my enemies,
　　　　and from ' those who ' persecute ' me.

16 'Make your face to ' shine up•on your ' servant, ♦
　　and save me ' for your ' mercy's ' sake.'

17 Lord, let me not be confounded
　　　　for I have ' called up'on you; ♦
　　but let the wicked be put to shame;
　　　　let them be ' silent ' in the ' grave.

18 Let the lying lips be ' put to ' silence ♦
　　that speak against the righteous
　　　　with ' arrogance, dis'dain • and con'tempt.

　　　　　　　　　　　　　　　　　　Thomas A. Walmisley

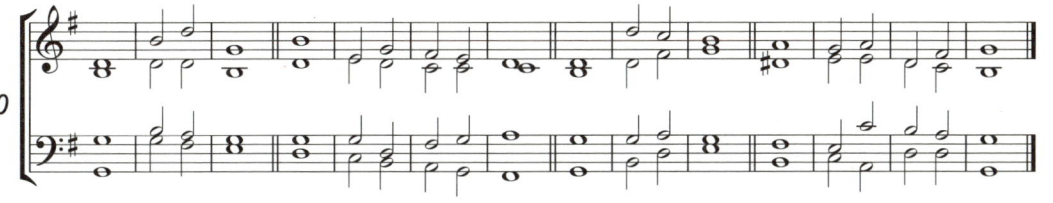

19 How abundant is your goodness, O Lord,
　　　　which you have laid up for ' those who ' fear you; ♦
　　which you have prepared in the sight of all
　　　　for those who ' put their ' trust in ' you.

20 You hide them in the shelter of your presence
　　　　from ' those who ' slander them; ♦
　　you keep them safe in your refuge ' from the ' strife of ' tongues.

Thomas A. Walmisley

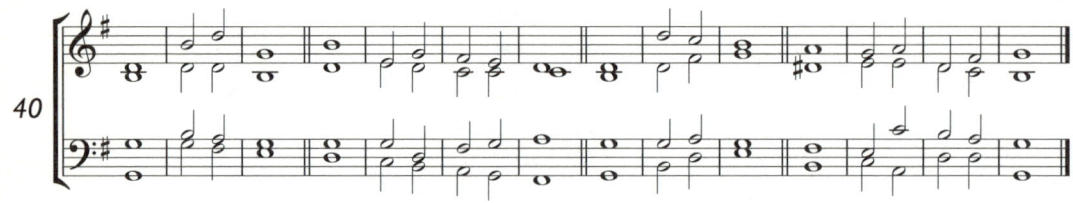

40

21 Blessed ' be the ' Lord! ♦
   For he has shown me his steadfast love
      when I was ' as a ' city be'sieged.

22 I had said in my alarm,
   'I have been cut off from the ' sight of your ' eyes.' ♦
   Nevertheless, you heard the voice of my prayer
      ' when I ' cried ' out to you.

23 Love the Lord, all ' you his ' servants; ♦
   for the Lord protects the faithful,
      but re'pays • to the ' full the ' proud.

24 Be strong and let your ' heart take ' courage, ♦
   all you who wait in ' hope ' for the ' Lord.

Psalm 32

George C. Martin

41

1 Happy the one whose transgression ' is for'given, ♦
   and ' whose ' sin is ' covered.

2 Happy the one to whom the Lord im'putes no ' guilt, ♦
   and in whose ' spirit there ' is no ' guile.

3 For I ' held my ' tongue; ♦
   my bones wasted away
      through my ' groaning ' all the day ' long.

4 Your hand was heavy upon me ' day and ' night; ♦
   my moisture was dried up ' like the ' drought in ' summer.

5 Then I acknowledged my ' sin to ' you ♦
   and my in'iquity I ' did not ' hide.

6 I said, 'I will confess my transgressions ' to the ' Lord,' ♦
   and you for'gave the ' guilt of my ' sin.

7 Therefore let all the faithful make their prayers to you
      in ' time of ' trouble; ♦
   in the great ' water flood, it ' shall not ' reach them.

8 You are a place for me to hide in;
    you pre'serve me from ' trouble; ♦
you sur'round me with ' songs • of de'liverance.

9 'I will instruct you and teach you
    in the way that ' you should ' go; ♦
I will ' guide you ' with my ' eye.

10 'Be not like horse and mule which have ' no • under'standing; ♦
whose mouths must be held with bit and bridle,
    or ' else • they will ' not stay ' near you.'

11 Great tribulations re'main for the ' wicked, ♦
but mercy embraces ' those who ' trust in the ' Lord.

12 Be glad, you righteous, and re'joice in the ' Lord; ♦
shout for joy, ' all who are ' true of ' heart.

Psalm 33

Noel Rawsthorne

1 Rejoice in the Lord, ' O you ' righteous, ♦
for it is good for the ' just to ' sing ' praises.

2 Praise the Lord ' with the ' lyre; ♦
on the ten-stringed ' harp ' sing his ' praise.

3 Sing for him a ' new ' song; ♦
play ' skilfully, with ' shouts of ' praise.

4 For the word of the ' Lord is ' true ♦
and ' all his ' works are ' sure.

‡ 5 He loves ' righteousness and ' justice; ♦
the earth is full of the loving'kindness ' of the ' Lord.

6 By the word of the Lord were the ' heavens ' made ♦
and all their ' host • by the ' breath of his ' mouth.

7 He gathers up the waters of the sea as ' in a ' waterskin ♦
and lays up the ' deep ' in his ' treasury.

8 Let all the earth ' fear the ' Lord; ♦
stand in awe of him, ' all who ' dwell in the ' world.

9 For he spoke, and ' it was ' done; ♦
he com'manded, and ' it stood ' fast.

Noel Rawsthorne

42

10 The Lord brings the counsel of the ' nations to ' naught; ♦
he frus'trates • the de'signs of the ' peoples.

11 But the counsel of the Lord shall en'dure for ' ever ♦
and the designs of his heart from gene'ration to ' gene'ration.

12 Happy the nation whose ' God • is the ' Lord ♦
and the people he has ' chosen ' for his ' own.

13 The Lord looks ' down from ' heaven ♦
and beholds ' all the ' children of ' earth.

14 From where he sits enthroned he ' turns his ' gaze ♦
on ' all who ' dwell on the ' earth.

15 He fashions ' all the ' hearts of them ♦
and under'stands ' all their ' works.

16 No king is saved by the ' might of his ' host; ♦
no warrior delivered ' by his ' great ' strength.

17 A horse is a vain hope ' for de'liverance; ♦
for all its ' strength it ' cannot ' save.

18 Behold, the eye of the Lord
is upon ' those who ' fear him, ♦
on those who wait in ' hope • for his ' steadfast ' love,

19 To deliver their ' soul from ' death ♦
and to ' feed them in ' time of ' famine.

20 Our soul waits longingly ' for the ' Lord; ♦
he is our ' help ' and our ' shield.

21 Indeed, our heart re'joices ' in him; ♦
in his holy name ' have we ' put our ' trust.

‡ 22 Let your loving-kindness, O Lord, ' be up'on us, ♦
as we have ' set our ' hope on ' you.

Psalm 34

C. Hubert H. Parry

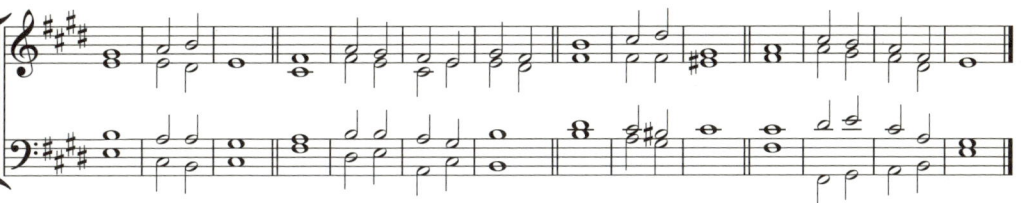

1 I will bless the ' Lord at ' all times; ♦
  his praise shall ' ever be ' in my ' mouth.

2 My soul shall glory ' in the ' Lord; ♦
  let the ' humble ' hear and be ' glad.

3 O magnify the ' Lord with ' me; ♦
  let us ex'alt his ' name to'gether.

4 I sought the Lord ' and he ' answered me ♦
  and de'livered me from ' all my ' fears.

5 Look upon him ' and be ' radiant ♦
  and your faces ' shall not ' be a'shamed.

6 This poor soul cried, and the ' Lord ' heard me ♦
  and ' saved me from ' all my ' troubles.

7 The angel ' of the ' Lord ♦
  encamps around those who ' fear him
     ' and de'livers them.

8 O taste and see that the ' Lord is ' gracious; ♦
  blessed is the ' one who ' trusts in ' him.

9 Fear the Lord, all ' you his ' holy ones, ♦
  for those who ' fear him ' lack ' nothing.

10 Lions may lack and ' suffer ' hunger, ♦
   but those who seek the Lord
      lack ' nothing ' that is ' good.

11 Come, my children, and ' listen to ' me; ♦
   I will ' teach • you the ' fear • of the ' Lord.

12 Who is there who de'lights in ' life ♦
   and longs for ' days • to en'joy good ' things?

13 Keep your ' tongue from ' evil ♦
   and your ' lips from ' lying ' words.

14 Turn from evil ' and do ' good; ♦
   seek ' peace ' and pur'sue it.

15 The eyes of the Lord are up'on the ' righteous ♦
   and his ears are ' open ' to their ' cry.

16 The face of the Lord is against ' those who do ' evil, ♦
   to root out the re'membrance • of them ' from the ' earth.

C. Hubert H. Parry

43

17 The righteous cry and the ' Lord ' hears them ♦
and delivers them ' out of ' all their ' troubles.

18 The Lord is near to the ' broken'hearted ♦
and will save ' those • who are ' crushed in ' spirit.

19 Many are the ' troubles • of the ' righteous; ♦
from them ' all • will the ' Lord de'liver them.

20 He keeps ' all their ' bones, ♦
so that not ' one of ' them is ' broken.

21 But evil shall ' slay the ' wicked ♦
and those who hate the ' righteous will ' be con'demned.

22 The Lord ransoms the ' life of his ' servants ♦
and will condemn ' none • who seek ' refuge ' in him.

Psalm 35

Jonathan Battishill

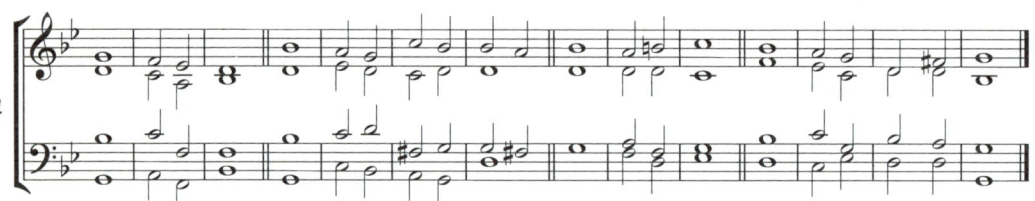

44

1 Contend, O Lord, with those that con'tend with ' me; ♦
fight against ' those that ' fight a'gainst me.

2 Take up ' shield and ' buckler ♦
and ' rise ' up to ' help me.

3 Draw the spear and bar the way
against those ' who pur'sue me; ♦
say to my soul, ' 'I am ' your sal'vation.'

4 Let those who seek after my life be shamed ' and dis'graced; ♦
let those who plot my ruin fall back ' and be ' put to con'fusion.

5 Let them be as chaff be'fore the ' wind, ♦
with the angel of the ' Lord ' thrusting them ' down.

6 Let their way be ' dark and ' slippery, ♦
with the ' angel • of the ' Lord pur'suing them.

7 For they have secretly spread a net for me with'out a ' cause; ♦
without any cause they have ' dug a ' pit for my ' soul.

8 Let ruin come upon them ˈ unaˈwares; ♦
   let them be caught in the net they laid;
      let them ˈ fall in it to ˈ their desˈtruction.

9 Then will my soul be joyful ˈ in the ˈ Lord ♦
   and ˈ glory in ˈ his salˈvation.

10 My very bones will say, 'Lord, ˈ who is ˈ like you? ♦
   You deliver the poor from those that are too strong for them,
      the poor and needy from ˈ those who ˈ would deˈspoil them.'

11 False witnesses rose ˈ up aˈgainst me; ♦
   they ˈ charged me with ˈ things I ˈ knew not.

12 They rewarded me ˈ evil for ˈ good, ♦
   to the desoˈlation ˈ of my ˈ soul.

13 But as for me, when they were sick I ˈ put on ˈ sackcloth ♦
   and ˈ humbled myˈself with ˈ fasting;

14 When my prayer returned empty ˈ to my ˈ bosom, ♦
   it was as though I ˈ grieved • for my ˈ friend or ˈ brother;

15 I behaved as one who ˈ mourns for his ˈ mother, ♦
   bowed down ˈ and brought ˈ very ˈ low.

16 But when I stumbled, they gathered in delight;
      they gathered toˈgether aˈgainst me; ♦
   as if they were strangers I did not know
      they ˈ tore at ˈ me without ˈ ceasing.

17 When I ˈ fell they ˈ mocked me; ♦
   they ˈ gnashed at me ˈ with their ˈ teeth.

18 O Lord, how long will ˈ you look ˈ on? ♦
   Rescue my soul from their ravages,
      and my poor ˈ life • from the ˈ young ˈ lions.

19 I will give you thanks in the great ˈ congreˈgation; ♦
   I will praise you ˈ in the ˈ mighty ˈ throng.

20 Do not let my treacherous foes reˈjoice ˈ over me, ♦
   or those who hate me without a cause
      ˈ mock me ˈ with their ˈ glances.

21 For they do not ˈ speak of ˈ peace, ♦
   but invent deceitful schemes
      against those that are ˈ quiet ˈ in the ˈ land.

22 They opened wide their mouths and deˈrided me, ˈ saying ♦
   'We have seen it ˈ with our ˈ very ˈ eyes.'

‡ 23 This you have seen, O Lord; do ˈ not keep ˈ silent; ♦
   go not ˈ far from ˈ me, O ˈ Lord.

Jonathan Battishill

44

24 Awake, arise, | to my | cause, ♦
    to my defence, my | God | and my | Lord!

25 Give me justice, O Lord my God,
        according | to your | righteousness; ♦
    let | them not | triumph | over me.

26 Let them not say to themselves,
        'Our | heart's de|sire!' ♦
    Let them not say, | 'We have | swallowed him | up.'

27 Let all who rejoice at my trouble be put to | shame and con|fusion; ♦
    let those who boast against me
        be | clothed with | shame • and dis|honour.

28 Let those who favour my cause re|joice and be | glad; ♦
    let them say always,
        'Great is the Lord, who de|lights • in his | servant's | well-being.'

29 So shall my tongue be | talking of your | righteousness ♦
    and of your | praise | all the day | long.

Psalm 36

Stanley Vann

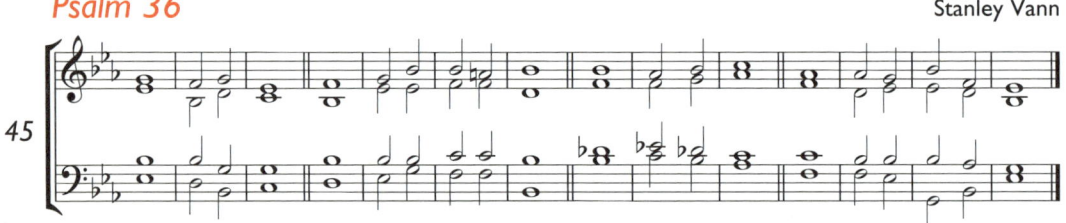

45

1 Sin whispers to the wicked, in the | depths of their | heart; ♦
    there is no fear of | God be|fore their | eyes.

2 They flatter themselves in their | own | eyes ♦
    that their abominable sin will | not be | found | out.

3 The words of their mouth are unrighteous and | full of de|ceit; ♦
    they have ceased to act wisely | and to | do | good.

4 They think out mischief upon their beds
        and have set themselves in | no good | way; ♦
    nor do they ab|hor | that which is | evil.

5 Your love, O Lord, reaches ' to the ' heavens ♦
   and your ' faithfulness ' to the ' clouds.

6 Your righteousness stands like the strong mountains,
      your justice like the ' great ' deep; ♦
   you, Lord, shall ' save both ' man and ' beast.

7 How precious is your loving ' mercy, O ' God! ♦
   All mortal flesh shall take refuge
      under the ' shadow ' of your ' wings.

8 They shall be satisfied with the abundance ' of your ' house; ♦
   they shall drink from the ' river of ' your de'lights.

9 For with you is the ' well of ' life ♦
   and in your ' light shall ' we see ' light.

10 O continue your loving-kindness to ' those who ' know you ♦
   and your righteousness to ' those who are ' true of ' heart.

11 Let not the foot of pride ' come a'gainst me, ♦
   nor the hand of the un'godly ' thrust me a'way.

12 There are they fallen, ' all who work ' wickedness. ♦
   They are cast down and shall ' not be ' able to ' stand.

Psalm 37

Thomas Attwood

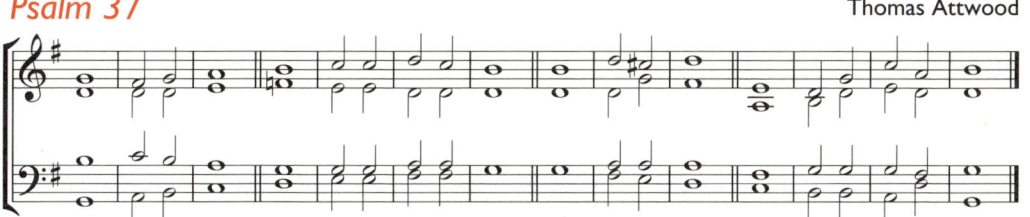

1 Fret not because of ' evil'doers; ♦
   be not ' jealous of ' those • who do ' wrong.

2 For they shall soon ' wither like ' grass ♦
   and like the green ' herb ' fade a'way.

3 Trust in the Lord and be ' doing ' good; ♦
   dwell in the land ' and be ' nourished with ' truth.

4 Let your delight be ' in the ' Lord ♦
   and he will ' give you your ' heart's de'sire.

5 Commit your way to the Lord and ' put your ' trust in him, ♦
   and ' he will ' bring it to ' pass.

6 He will make your righteousness as ' clear as the ' light ♦
   and your just ' dealing ' as the ' noonday.

Thomas Attwood

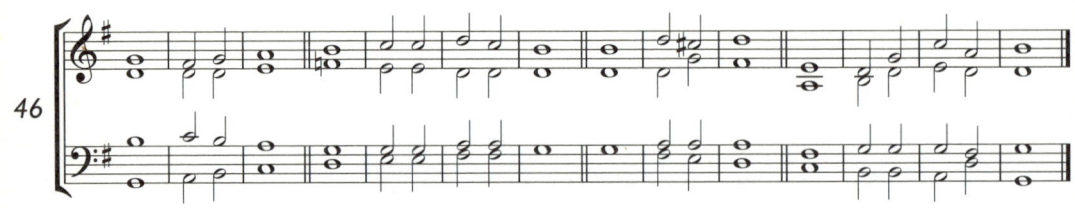

46

7 Be still before the ' Lord and ' wait for him; ♦
do not fret over those that prosper
    as they ' follow their ' evil ' schemes.

8 Refrain from anger and a'bandon ' wrath; ♦
do not fret, ' lest • you be ' moved to do ' evil.

9 For evildoers ' shall be cut ' off, ♦
but those who wait upon the Lord ' shall pos'sess the ' land.

10 Yet a little while and the wicked shall ' be no ' more; ♦
you will search for their ' place and ' find them ' gone.

11 But the lowly shall pos'sess the ' land ♦
and shall de'light • in a'bundance of ' peace.

12 The wicked plot a'gainst the ' righteous ♦
and ' gnash at them ' with their ' teeth.

13 The Lord shall ' laugh at the ' wicked, ♦
for he ' sees that their ' day is ' coming.

14 The wicked draw their sword and bend their bow
    to strike down the ' poor and ' needy, ♦
to slaughter ' those who ' walk in ' truth.

15 Their sword shall go through their ' own ' heart ♦
and their ' bows ' shall be ' broken.

16 The little that the ' righteous ' have ♦
is better than great ' riches ' of the ' wicked.

17 For the arms of the wicked ' shall be ' broken, ♦
but the ' Lord up'holds the ' righteous.

18 The Lord knows the ' days of the ' godly, ♦
and their in'heritance shall ' stand for ' ever.

19 They shall not be put to shame in the ' perilous ' time, ♦
and in days of famine ' they shall ' have e'nough.

20 But the ' wicked shall ' perish; ♦
like the glory of the meadows
    the enemies of the Lord shall vanish;
' they shall ' vanish like ' smoke.

21 The wicked borrow and ' do not re'pay, ♦
but the ' righteous are ' generous in ' giving.

22 For those who are blest by God shall pos'sess the ' land, ♦
but those who are cursed by him ' shall be ' rooted ' out.

Edward J. Hopkins

23 When your steps are guided ' by the ' Lord ♦
and you de'light ' in his ' way,

24 Though you stumble, you shall ' not fall ' headlong, ♦
for the Lord ' holds you ' fast • by the ' hand.

25 I have been young and ' now am ' old, ♦
yet never have I seen the righteous forsaken,
    or their ' children ' begging their ' bread.

26 All the day long they are ' generous in ' lending, ♦
and their children ' also ' shall be ' blest.

27 Depart from evil ' and do ' good ♦
and you ' shall a'bide for ' ever.

28 For the Lord loves the ' thing • that is ' right ♦
and will ' not for'sake his ' faithful ones.

29 The unjust shall be des'troyed for ' ever, ♦
and the offspring of the wicked ' shall be ' rooted ' out.

30 The righteous shall pos'sess the ' land ♦
and ' dwell in ' it for ' ever.

31 The mouth of the righteous ' utters ' wisdom, ♦
and their tongue ' speaks the ' thing • that is ' right.

32 The law of their God is ' in their ' heart ♦
and their ' footsteps ' shall not ' slide.

33 The wicked ' spy on the ' righteous ♦
and ' seek oc'casion to ' slay them.

34 The Lord will not leave them ' in their ' hand, ♦
nor let them be con'demned when ' they are ' judged.

35 Wait upon the Lord and ' keep his ' way; ♦
he will raise you up to possess the land,
    and when the wicked are up'rooted, ' you shall ' see it.

36 I myself have seen the wicked in ' great ' power ♦
and flourishing like a ' tree in ' full ' leaf.

‡ 37 I went by and lo, ' they were ' gone; ♦
I sought them, but ' they could ' nowhere be ' found.

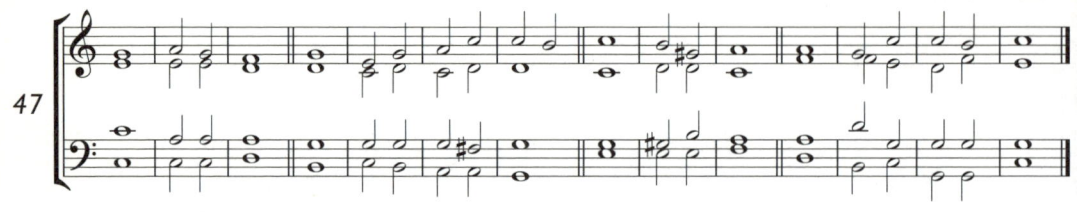

38 Keep innocence and heed the ' thing • that is ' right, ♦
for that will ' bring you ' peace • at the ' last.

39 But the sinners shall ' perish to'gether, ♦
and the posterity of the wicked ' shall be ' rooted ' out.

40 The salvation of the righteous ' comes from the ' Lord; ♦
he is their stronghold ' in the ' time of ' trouble.

41 The Lord shall stand by them ' and de'liver them; ♦
he shall deliver them from the wicked and shall save them,
  because they have ' put their ' trust in ' him.

Psalm 38

Andrew Russell

1 Rebuke me not, O Lord, ' in your ' anger, ♦
neither chasten me ' in your ' heavy dis'pleasure.

2 For your arrows ' have stuck ' fast in me ♦
and your hand ' presses ' hard up'on me.

3 There is no health in my flesh
    because of your ' indig'nation; ♦
there is no peace in my ' bones be'cause of my ' sin.

4 For my iniquities have gone ' over my ' head; ♦
their weight is a ' burden too ' heavy to ' bear.

5 My wounds ' stink and ' fester ♦
be'cause of ' my ' foolishness.

6 I am utterly bowed down and brought ' very ' low; ♦
I go about ' mourning ' all the day ' long.

7 My loins are filled with ' searing ' pain; ♦
there ' is no ' health in my ' flesh.

8 I am feeble and ' utterly ' crushed; ♦
I roar aloud because of the dis'quiet ' of my ' heart.

9 O Lord, you know all ' my de'sires ♦
  and my sighing ' is not ' hidden ' from you.

10 My heart is pounding, my ' strength has ' failed me; ♦
  the light of my ' eyes is ' gone ' from me.

11 My friends and companions stand apart from ' my af'fliction; ♦
  my ' neighbours ' stand afar ' off.

12 Those who seek after my ' life lay ' snares for me; ♦
  and those who would harm me whisper evil
    and mutter ' slander ' all the day ' long.

13 But I am like one who is ' deaf and ' hears not, ♦
  like one that is dumb, who ' does not ' open his ' mouth.

14 I have become like one who ' does not ' hear ♦
  and from whose ' mouth comes ' no re'tort.

15 For in you, Lord, have I ' put my ' trust; ♦
  you will ' answer me, O ' Lord my ' God.

16 For I said, 'Let them not ' triumph ' over me, ♦
  those who exult over me ' when my ' foot ' slips.'

17 Truly, I am on the ' verge of ' falling ♦
  and my ' pain is ' ever ' with me.

18 I will con'fess • my in'iquity ♦
  and be ' sorry ' for my ' sin.

19 Those that are my enemies without any ' cause are ' mighty, ♦
  and those who hate me ' wrongfully are ' many in ' number.

20 Those who repay evil for good ' are a'gainst me, ♦
  because the ' good is ' what I ' seek.

21 Forsake me ' not, O ' Lord; ♦
  be not ' far from me, ' O my ' God.

22 Make ' haste to ' help me, ♦
  O ' Lord of ' my sal'vation.

Psalm 39

John Goss
from Jeremiah Clarke

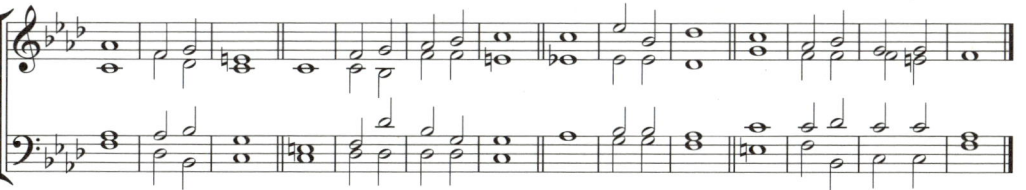

1 I said, 'I will keep watch ' over my ' ways, ♦
  so that I of'fend not ' with my ' tongue.

2 'I will guard my ' mouth • with a ' muzzle, ♦
  while the ' wicked are ' in my ' sight.'

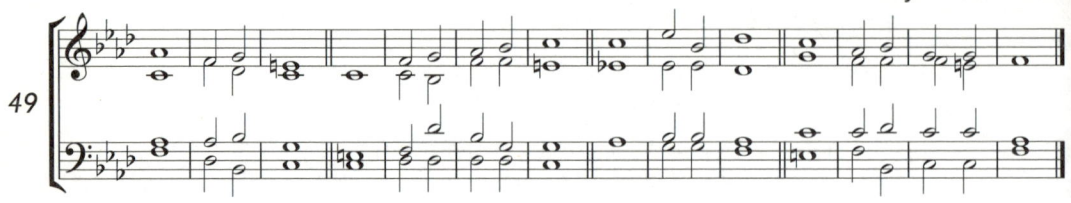

John Goss
from Jeremiah Clarke

3 So I held my tongue ' and said ' nothing; ♦
    I kept silent ' but to ' no a'vail.

4 My distress increased, my heart grew ' hot with'in me; ♦
    while I mused, the fire was kindled
        and I ' spoke out ' with my ' tongue:

5 'Lord, let me know my end and the ' number • of my ' days, ♦
    that I may ' know how ' short my ' time is.

6 'You have made my days but a handsbreadth,
        and my lifetime is as nothing ' in your ' sight; ♦
    truly, even those who stand ' upright are ' but a ' breath.

‡ 7 'We walk about like a shadow
        and in vain we ' are in ' turmoil; ♦
    we heap up riches and ' cannot tell ' who will ' gather them.

8 'And now, ' what is my ' hope? ♦
    Truly my ' hope is ' even in ' you.

9 'Deliver me from ' all my trans'gressions ♦
    and do not ' make me the ' taunt • of the ' fool.'

10 I fell silent and did not ' open my ' mouth, ♦
    for surely ' it was ' your ' doing.

11 Take a'way your ' plague from me; ♦
    I am con'sumed • by the ' blows of your ' hand.

12 With rebukes for sin you punish us;
        like a moth you con'sume our ' beauty; ♦
    truly, ' everyone is ' but a ' breath.

13 Hear my prayer, O Lord, and give ' ear to my ' cry; ♦
    hold ' not your ' peace • at my ' tears.

14 For I am but a ' stranger with ' you, ♦
    a wayfarer, as ' all my ' forebears ' were.

15 Turn your gaze from me, that I may be ' glad a'gain, ♦
    before I go my ' way and ' am no ' more.

Psalm 40

Noel Rawsthorne

1 I waited patiently ' for the ' Lord; ♦
  he inclined to ' me and ' heard my ' cry.

2 He brought me out of the roaring pit,
     out of the ' mire and ' clay; ♦
  he set my feet upon a rock and ' made my ' footing ' sure.

3 He has put a new song in my mouth,
     a song of ' praise • to our ' God; ♦
  many shall see and fear
     and ' put their ' trust in the ' Lord.

4 Blessed is the one who ' trusts in the ' Lord, ♦
  who does not turn to the ' proud that ' follow a ' lie.

5 Great are the wonders you have done, O Lord my God.
     How great ' your de'signs for us! ♦
  There is none that ' can be com'pared with ' you.

6 If I were to pro'claim them and ' tell of them ♦
  they would be more than I am ' able ' to ex'press.

7 Sacrifice and offering you do ' not de'sire ♦
  but my ' ears ' you have ' opened;

8 Burnt offering and sacrifice for sin you have ' not re'quired; ♦
  then ' said I: ' 'Lo, I ' come.

9 'In the scroll of the book it is written of me
     that I should do your will, ' O my ' God; ♦
  I delight to do it: your ' law • is with'in my ' heart.'

10 I have declared your righteousness in the great ' congre'gation; ♦
   behold, I did not restrain my lips,
      and ' that, O ' Lord, you ' know.

11 Your righteousness I have not hidden ' in my ' heart; ♦
   I have spoken of your ' faithfulness and ' your sal'vation;

11a I have not concealed your loving'kindness and ' truth ♦
    from the ' great ' congre'gation.

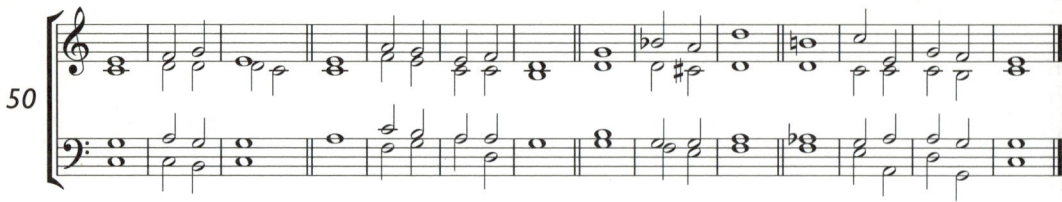

Noel Rawsthorne

12 Do not withhold your compassion from ' me, O ' Lord; ♦
   let your love and your ' faithfulness ' always pre'serve me,

13 For innumerable troubles have come about me;
      my sins have overtaken me so that I ' cannot look ' up; ♦
   they are more in number than the hairs of my head,
      ' and my ' heart ' fails me.

14 Be pleased, O Lord, ' to de'liver me; ♦
   O ' Lord, make ' haste to ' help me.

15 Let them be ashamed and altogether dismayed
      who seek after my life ' to des'troy it; ♦
   let them be driven back and put to ' shame
      who ' wish me ' evil.

16 Let those who heap ' insults up'on me ♦
   be ' desolate be'cause of their ' shame.

17 Let all who seek you rejoice in you ' and be ' glad; ♦
   let those who love your salvation say ' always,
      'The ' Lord is ' great.'

18 Though I am ' poor and ' needy, ♦
   the ' Lord ' cares for ' me.

19 You are my helper and ' my de'liverer; ♦
   O my ' God, make ' no de'lay.

Psalm 41

George M. Garrett

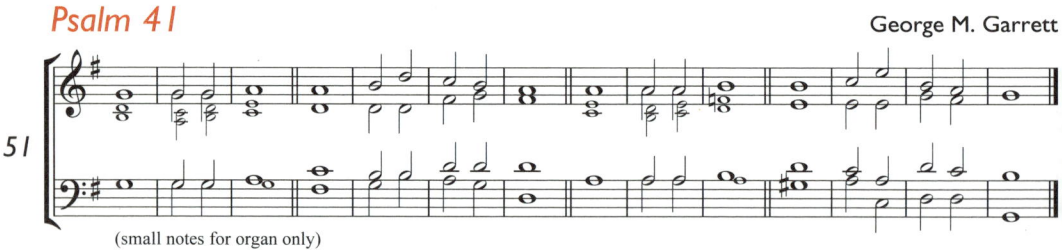

(small notes for organ only)

1 Blessed are those who consider the ' poor and ' needy; ♦
   the Lord will deliver them ' in the ' time of ' trouble.

2 The Lord preserves them and restores their life,
      that they may be happy ' in the ' land; ♦
   he will not hand them ' over • to the ' will of their ' enemies.

3 The Lord sustains them ' on their ' sickbed; ♦
   their sickness, ' Lord, you ' will re'move.

4 And so I said, 'Lord, be ' merciful ' to me; ♦
   heal me, for ' I have ' sinned a'gainst you.'

John Stainer

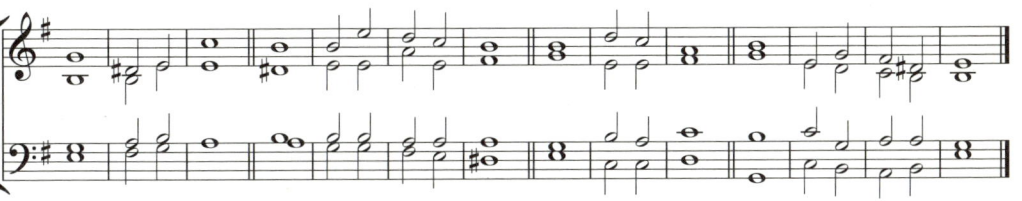

5 My enemies speak ' evil a'bout me, ♦
   asking when I shall ' die and my ' name ' perish.

6 If they come to see me, they utter ' empty ' words; ♦
   their heart gathers mischief;
      when they go ' out, they ' tell it a'broad.

7 All my enemies whisper to'gether a'gainst me, ♦
   against me ' they de'vise ' evil,

8 Saying that a deadly thing ' has laid ' hold on me, ♦
   and that I will not rise a'gain from ' where I ' lie.

‡ 9 Even my bosom friend, whom I trusted,
      who ' ate of my ' bread, ♦
   has lifted ' up his ' heel a'gainst me.

George M. Garrett

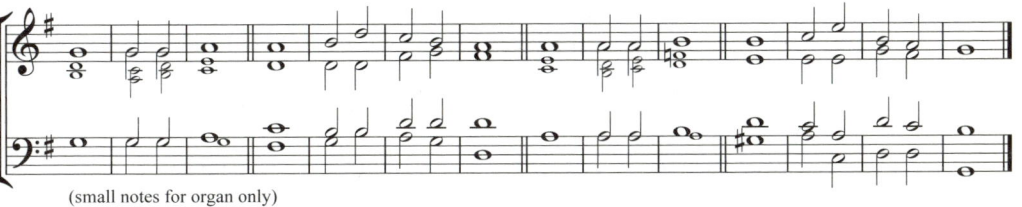

(small notes for organ only)

10 But you, O Lord, be ' merciful ' to me ♦
    and raise me up, ' that I ' may re'ward them.

11 By this I ' know that you ' favour me, ♦
   that my enemy ' does not ' triumph ' over me.

12 Because of my integrity ' you up'hold me ♦
   and will set me be'fore your ' face for ' ever.

13 Blessed be the ' Lord • God of ' Israel, ♦
   from everlasting to everlasting. A'men and ' A'men.

Psalm 41

Psalm 42

Luke Flintoft

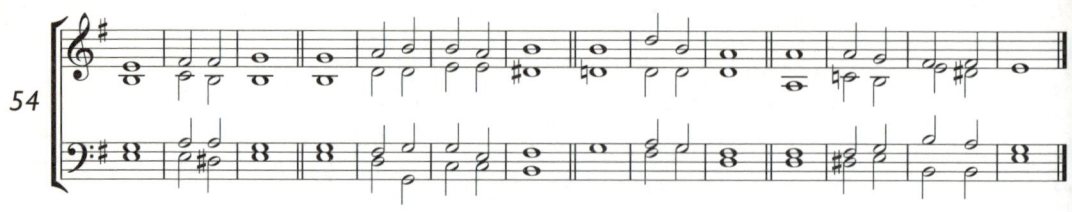

54

1 As the deer ' longs for the ' water brooks, ♦
   so longs my ' soul for ' you, O ' God.

2 My soul is athirst for God, even for the ' living ' God; ♦
   when shall I come be'fore the ' presence of ' God?

3 My tears have been my bread ' day and ' night, ♦
   while all day long they say to me, ' 'Where is ' now your ' God?'

4 Now when I think on these things, I pour ' out my ' soul: ♦
   how I went with the multitude
       and led the procession ' to the ' house of ' God,

‡ 5 With the voice of ' praise and ' thanksgiving, ♦
   among ' those who ' kept ' holy day.

6 *Why are you so full of heaviness, ' O my ' soul,* ♦
   and why are you ' so dis'quieted with'in me?

7 *O put your ' trust in ' God;* ♦
   for I will yet give him thanks,
       who is the help of my ' countenance, ' and my ' God.

8 My soul is ' heavy with'in me; ♦
   therefore I will remember you from the land of Jordan,
       and from Hermon ' and the ' hill of ' Mizar.

9 Deep calls to deep in the ' thunder • of your ' waterfalls; ♦
   all your breakers and ' waves ' have gone ' over me.

10 The Lord will grant his loving-kindness ' in the ' daytime; ♦
   through the night his song will be with me,
       a ' prayer • to the ' God of my ' life.

11 I say to God my rock,
       'Why have ' you for'gotten me, ♦
   and why go I so heavily, ' while the ' enemy op'presses me?'

‡ 12 As they crush my bones, my ' enemies ' mock me; ♦
   while all day long they say to me, ' 'Where is ' now your ' God?'

13 *Why are you so full of heaviness, ' O my ' soul,* ♦
   and why are you ' so dis'quieted with'in me?

14 *O put your ' trust in ' God;* ♦
   for I will yet give him thanks,
       who is the help of my ' countenance, ' and my ' God.

Psalm 43
Luke Flintoft

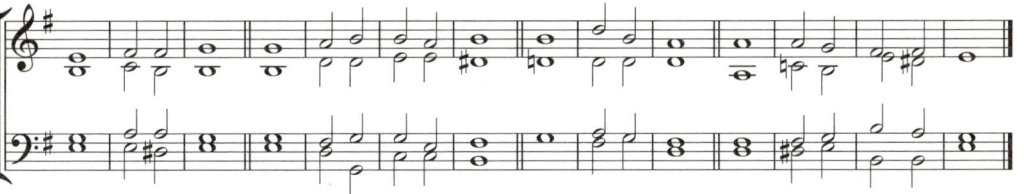

1 Give judgement for me, O God,
    and defend my cause against an un′godly ′ people; ♦
  deliver me from the de′ceitful ′ and the ′ wicked.

2 For you are the God of my refuge;
    why have you ′ cast me ′ from you, ♦
  and why go I so heavily, ′ while the ′ enemy op′presses me?

3 O send out your light and your truth, that ′ they may ′ lead me, ♦
  and bring me to your holy ′ hill and ′ to your ′ dwelling,

4 That I may go to the altar of God,
    to the God of my ′ joy and ′ gladness; ♦
  and on the lyre I will give thanks to ′ you, O ′ God my ′ God.

5 *Why are you so full of heaviness, ′ O my ′ soul, ♦*
  and why are you ′ so dis′quieted with′in me?

6 *O put your ′ trust in ′ God; ♦*
  for I will yet give him thanks,
    who is the help of my ′ countenance, ′ and my ′ God.

Psalm 44
James Turle

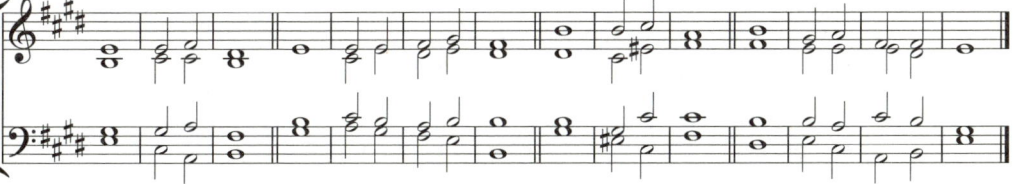

1 We have heard with our ears, O God, our ′ forebears have ′ told us, ♦
  all that you did in their ′ days, in ′ time of ′ old;

2 How with your hand you drove out nations and ′ planted us ′ in, ♦
  and broke the power of ′ peoples and ′ set us ′ free.

3 For not by their own sword did our ancestors ′ take the ′ land ♦
  nor ′ did their ′ own arm ′ save them,

4 But your right hand, your arm, and the ′ light of your ′ countenance, ♦
  because ′ you were ′ gracious ′ to them.

James Turle

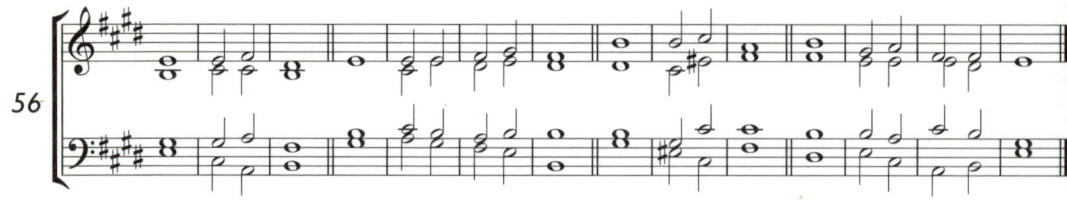

5 You are my King ' and my ' God, ♦
  who com'manded sal'vation for ' Jacob.

6 Through you we drove ' back our ' adversaries; ♦
  through your name ' we trod ' down our ' foes.

7 For I did not ' trust in my ' bow; ♦
  it was not my ' own ' sword that ' saved me;

8 It was you that saved us ' from our ' enemies ♦
  and ' put our ' adversaries to ' shame.

‡ 9 We gloried in God ' all the day ' long, ♦
  and were ' ever ' praising your ' name.

Henry Stonex

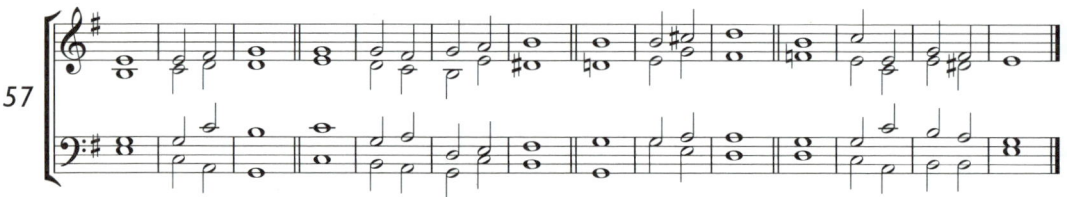

10 But now you have rejected us and ' brought us to ' shame, ♦
   and ' go not ' out • with our ' armies.

11 You have made us turn our ' backs • on our ' enemies, ♦
   and our ' enemies ' have de'spoiled us.

12 You have made us like ' sheep • to be ' slaughtered, ♦
   and have ' scattered us a'mong the ' nations.

13 You have sold your people ' for a ' pittance ♦
   and made no ' profit ' on their ' sale.

14 You have made us the ' taunt of our ' neighbours, ♦
   the scorn and derision of ' those • that are ' round a'bout us.

15 You have made us a byword a'mong the ' nations; ♦
   among the ' peoples they ' wag their ' heads.

16 My confusion is ' daily be'fore me, ♦
   and ' shame has ' covered my ' face,

17 At the taunts of the slanderer ' and re'viler, ♦
   at the sight of the ' enemy ' and a'venger.

18 All this has come upon us,
   though we have ' not for'gotten you ♦
   and have ' not played ' false • to your ' covenant.

19 Our hearts have ' not turned ' back, ♦
   nor our ' steps gone ' out of your ' way,

20 Yet you have crushed us in the ' haunt of ' jackals, ♦
   and covered us ' with the ' shadow of ' death.

21 If we have forgotten the ' name of our ' God, ♦
   or stretched out our hands to ' any ' strange ' god,

22 Will not God ' search it ' out? ♦
   For he knows the ' secrets ' of the ' heart.

23 But for your sake are we killed ' all the day ' long, ♦
   and are counted as ' sheep ' for the ' slaughter.

24 Rise up! Why ' sleep, O ' Lord? ♦
   Awake, and do ' not re'ject us for ' ever.

25 Why do you ' hide your ' face ♦
   and forget our ' grief ' and op'pression?

26 Our soul is bowed ' down • to the ' dust; ♦
   our ' belly ' cleaves • to the ' earth.

27 Rise up, O ' Lord, to ' help us ♦
   and redeem us for the ' sake of your ' steadfast ' love.

Psalm 45

William Hawes

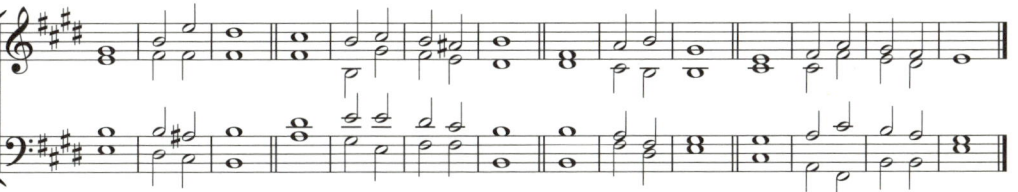

1 My heart is astir with ' gracious ' words; ♦
   as I make my song for the king,
      my tongue is the ' pen • of a ' ready ' writer.

2 You are the ' fairest of ' men; ♦
   full of grace are your lips,
      for ' God has ' blest you for ' ever.

3 Gird your sword upon your ' thigh, O ' mighty one; ♦
   gird on your ' majes'ty and ' glory.

4 Ride on and prosper in the ' cause of ' truth ♦
   and for the sake of hu'mili'ty and ' righteousness.

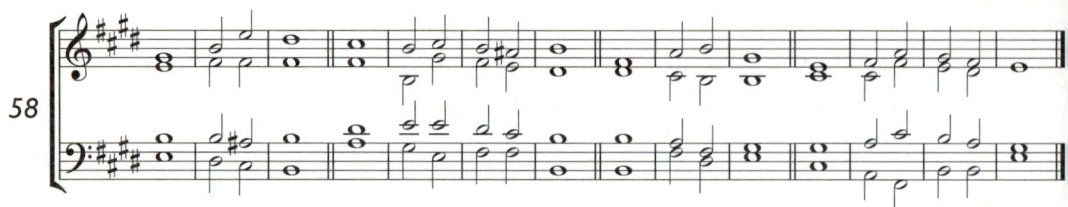

William Hawes

5 Your right hand will teach you ' terrible ' things; ♦
your arrows will be sharp in the heart of the king's enemies,
    so that ' peoples ' fall be'neath you.

6 Your throne is ' God's throne, for ' ever; ♦
the sceptre of your ' kingdom • is the ' sceptre of ' righteousness.

7 You love righteousness and ' hate in'iquity; ♦
therefore God, your God, has anointed you
    with the oil of ' gladness a'bove your ' fellows.

8 All your garments are fragrant with myrrh, ' aloes and ' cassia; ♦
from ivory palaces the music of ' strings ' makes you ' glad.

‡ 9 Kings' daughters are among your ' honourable ' women; ♦
at your right hand stands the ' queen in ' gold of ' Ophir.

10 Hear, O daughter; consider and in'cline your ' ear; ♦
forget your own people ' and your ' father's ' house.

11 So shall the king have ' pleasure • in your ' beauty; ♦
he is your ' lord, so ' do him ' honour.

12 The people of Tyre shall ' bring you ' gifts; ♦
the richest of the ' people shall ' seek your ' favour.

13 The king's daughter is all ' glorious with'in; ♦
her clothing is em'broidered ' cloth of ' gold.

14 She shall be brought to the king in ' raiment of ' needlework; ♦
after her the ' virgins • that are ' her com'panions.

15 With joy and gladness shall ' they be ' brought ♦
and enter into the ' palace ' of the ' king.

16 'Instead of your fathers ' you shall have ' sons, ♦
whom you shall make princes ' over ' all the ' land.

17 'I will make your name to be remembered through ' all • gene'rations; ♦
therefore shall the peoples ' praise you for ' ever and ' ever.'

64   *Psalm 45*

Psalm 46

from Martin Luther

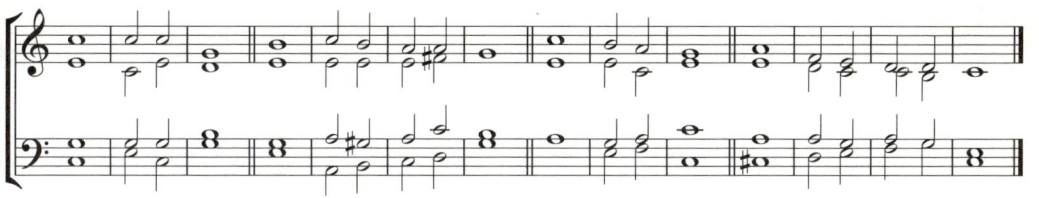

1 God is our ′ refuge and ′ strength, ♦
  a very ′ present ′ help in ′ trouble;

2 Therefore we will not fear, though the ′ earth be ′ moved, ♦
  and though the mountains ′ tremble • in the ′ heart of the ′ sea;

‡ 3 Though the waters ′ rage and ′ swell, ♦
  and though the mountains ′ quake • at the ′ towering ′ seas.

4 There is a river whose streams make glad the ′ city of ′ God, ♦
  the holy place of the ′ dwelling • of the ′ Most ′ High.

5 God is in the midst of her;
    therefore shall she ′ not be re′moved; ♦
  God shall ′ help her • at the ′ break of ′ day.

6 The nations are in uproar and the ′ kingdoms are ′ shaken, ♦
  but God utters his voice and the ′ earth shall ′ melt a′way.

7 *The Lord of ′ hosts is ′ with us; ♦*
  the God of ′ Jacob ′ is our ′ stronghold.

8 Come and behold the ′ works • of the ′ Lord, ♦
  what destruction he has ′ wrought up′on the ′ earth.

9 He makes wars to cease in ′ all the ′ world; ♦
  he shatters the bow and snaps the spear
    and burns the ′ chariots ′ in the ′ fire.

10 'Be still, and know that ′ I am ′ God; ♦
  I will be exalted among the nations;
    I will be ex′alted ′ in the ′ earth.'

11 *The Lord of ′ hosts is ′ with us; ♦*
  the God of ′ Jacob ′ is our ′ stronghold.

Psalm 47 — James Turle

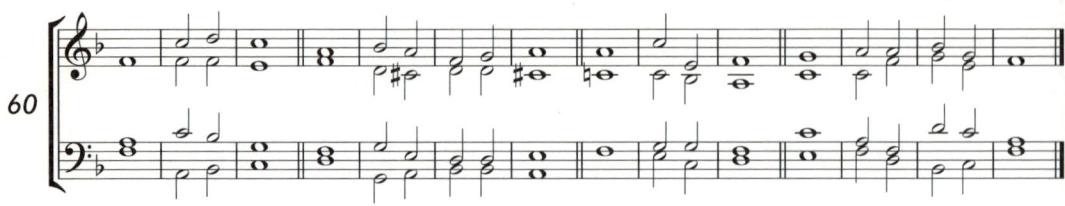

60

1 Clap your hands together, | all you | peoples; ♦
  O sing to | God with | shouts of | joy.

2 For the Lord Most High | is to be | feared; ♦
  he is the great | King • over | all the | earth.

3 He subdued the | peoples | under us ♦
  and the | nations | under our | feet.

4 He has chosen our | heritage | for us, ♦
  the pride of | Jacob, | whom he | loves.

5 God has gone up with a | merry | noise, ♦
  the | Lord • with the | sound of the | trumpet.

6 O sing praises to | God, sing | praises; ♦
  sing | praises • to our | King, sing | praises.

7 For God is the King of | all the | earth; ♦
  sing | praises with | all your | skill.

8 God reigns | over the | nations; ♦
  God has taken his seat up'on his | holy | throne.

9 The nobles of the peoples are | gathered to'gether ♦
  with the | people • of the | God of | Abraham.

10 For the powers of the earth be'long to | God ♦
   and he is | very | highly ex'alted.

Psalm 48 — George M. Garrett

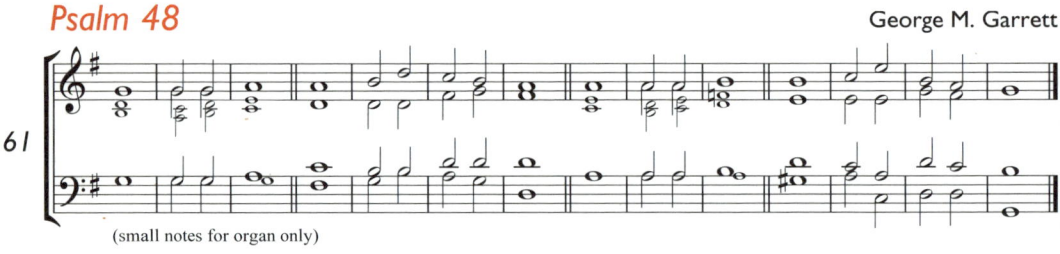

61

(small notes for organ only)

1 Great is the Lord and | highly • to be | praised, ♦
  in the | city | of our | God.

2 His holy mountain is fair and | lifted | high, ♦
  the | joy of | all the | earth.

66   Psalm 47

3 On Mount Zion, the di'vine ' dwelling place, ♦
   stands the ' city • of the ' great ' king.

4 In her palaces God has ' shown him'self ♦
   to ' be a ' sure ' refuge.

5 For behold, the kings of the ' earth as'sembled ♦
   and ' swept ' forward to'gether.

6 They saw, and ' were dumb'founded; ♦
   dis'mayed, they ' fled in ' terror.

7 Trembling seized them there;
      they writhed like a ' woman in ' labour, ♦
   as when the east wind ' shatters the ' ships of ' Tarshish.

8 As we had heard, so have we seen
      in the city of the Lord of hosts, the ' city • of our ' God: ♦
   God has es'tablished ' her for ' ever.

9 We have waited on your loving'kindness, O ' God, ♦
   in the ' midst ' of your ' temple.

10 As with your name, O God,
      so your praise reaches to the ' ends of the ' earth; ♦
   your right ' hand is ' full of ' justice.

11 Let Mount Zion rejoice and the daughters of ' Judah be ' glad, ♦
   be'cause of your ' judgements, O ' Lord.

12 Walk about Zion and go round about her;
      count ' all her ' towers; ♦
   consider well her ' bulwarks; pass ' through her ' citadels,

‡ 13 That you may tell those who come after
      that such is our God for ' ever and ' ever. ♦
   It is he that shall be our ' guide for ' ever'more.

Psalm 49

Stephen Elvey

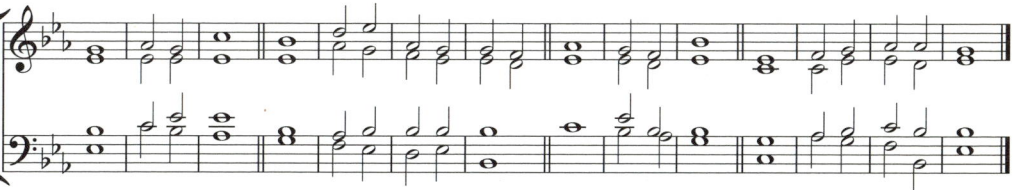

1 Hear this, ' all you ' peoples; ♦
   listen, all ' you that ' dwell • in the ' world,

2 You of low or ' high de'gree, ♦
   both ' rich and ' poor to'gether.

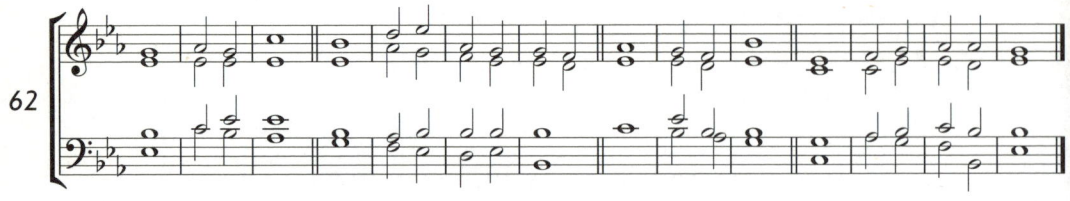

Stephen Elvey

3 My mouth shall ' speak of ' wisdom ♦
and my heart shall ' meditate on ' under'standing.

4 I will incline my ' ear • to a ' parable; ♦
I will unfold my ' riddle ' with the ' lyre.

5 Why should I fear in ' evil ' days, ♦
when the ' malice • of my ' foes sur'rounds me,

6 Such as ' trust • in their ' goods ♦
and glory in the a'bundance ' of their ' riches?

7 For no one can indeed ' ransom an'other ♦
or pay to ' God the ' price of de'liverance.

8 To ransom a soul ' is too ' costly; ♦
there is ' no price ' one could ' pay for it,

‡ 9 So that they might ' live for ' ever, ♦
and ' never ' see the ' grave.

10 For we see that the wise die also;
with the foolish and ' ignorant they ' perish ♦
and ' leave their ' riches to ' others.

11 Their tomb is their home for ever,
their dwelling through ' all • gene'rations, ♦
though they call their lands ' after their ' own ' names.

12 Those who have honour, but lack ' under'standing, ♦
are ' like the ' beasts that ' perish.

13 Such is the way of those who ' boast in them'selves, ♦
the end of those who de'light in their ' own ' words.

14 Like a flock of sheep they are destined to die;
' death is their ' shepherd; ♦
they go ' down ' straight • to the ' Pit.

15 Their beauty shall ' waste a'way, ♦
and the land of the ' dead shall ' be their ' dwelling.

16 But God shall ' ransom my ' soul; ♦
from the grasp of ' death ' will he ' take me.

17 Be not afraid if ' some grow ' rich ♦
and the ' glory • of their ' house in'creases,

18 For they will carry nothing away ' when they ' die, ♦
   nor will their ' glory ' follow ' after them.

19 Though they count themselves happy ' while they ' live ♦
   and ' praise you for ' your suc'cess,

20 They shall enter the company ' of their ' ancestors ♦
   who will ' nevermore ' see the ' light.

21 Those who have honour, but lack ' under'standing, ♦
   are ' like the ' beasts that ' perish.

Psalm 50

John Harper

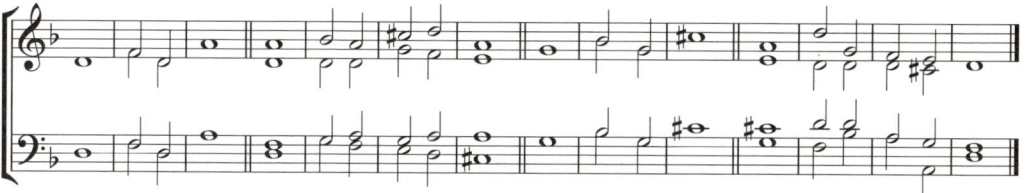

1 The Lord, the most mighty ' God, has ' spoken ♦
   and called the world from the rising of the ' sun ' to its ' setting.

2 Out of Zion, perfect in beauty, ' God shines ' forth; ♦
   our God comes ' and will ' not keep ' silence.

3 Consuming fire goes ' out be'fore him ♦
   and a mighty ' tempest ' stirs a'bout him.

4 He calls the ' heaven a'bove, ♦
   and the earth, that ' he may ' judge his ' people:

5 'Gather to ' me my ' faithful, ♦
   who have ' sealed my ' covenant with ' sacrifice.'

6 Let the heavens de'clare his ' righteousness, ♦
   for ' God him'self is ' judge.

7 Hear, O my people, and ' I will ' speak: ♦
   'I will testify against you, O Israel;
      for ' I am ' God, your ' God.

8 'I will not reprove you ' for your ' sacrifices, ♦
   for your burnt ' offerings are ' always be'fore me.

9 'I will take no bull ' out of your ' house, ♦
   nor ' he-goat ' out of your ' folds,

10 'For all the beasts of the ' forest are ' mine, ♦
   the cattle up'on a ' thousand ' hills.

11 'I know every ' bird of the ' mountains ♦
   and the ' insect • of the ' field is ' mine.

12 'If I were hungry, I ' would not ' tell you, ♦
   for the whole world is ' mine and ' all that ' fills it.

John Harper

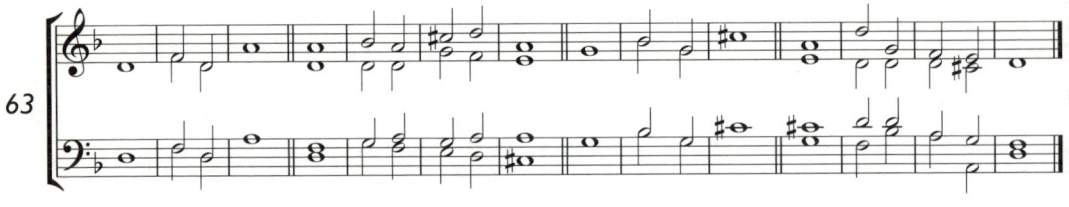

13 'Do you think I eat the ' flesh of ' bulls, ♦
or ' drink the ' blood of ' goats?

14 'Offer to God a ' sacrifice of ' thanksgiving ♦
and fulfil your ' vows to ' God Most ' High.

‡ 15 'Call upon me in the ' day of ' trouble; ♦
I will deliver ' you and ' you shall ' honour me.'

16 But to the ' wicked, says ' God: ♦
'Why do you recite my statutes
  and take my ' covenant up'on your ' lips,

17 'Since you re'fuse to be ' disciplined ♦
and have ' cast my ' words be'hind you?

18 'When you saw a thief, ' you made ' friends with him ♦
and you ' threw in your ' lot • with ad'ulterers.

19 'You have loosed your ' lips for ' evil ♦
and ' harnessed your ' tongue • to de'ceit.

‡ 20 'You sit and speak evil ' of your ' brother; ♦
you slander your ' own ' mother's ' son.

21 'These things have you done, and should ' I keep ' silence? ♦
Did you think that I am even ' such a ' one as your'self?

22 'But no, I ' must re'prove you, ♦
and set before your eyes the ' things that ' you have ' done.

23 'You that forget God, con'sider this ' well, ♦
lest I tear you apart and ' there is ' none • to de'liver you.

24 'Whoever offers me the sacrifice of thanksgiving ' honours ' me ♦
and to those who keep my way
  will I ' show • the sal'vation of ' God.'

Psalm 51

Matthew Camidge

or

Joseph Barnby

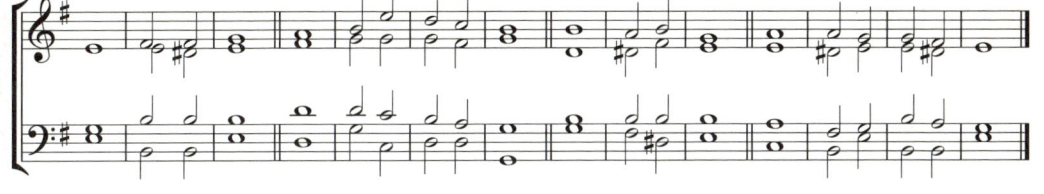

1 Have mercy on me, O God, in ' your great ' goodness; ♦
   according to the abundance of your compassion
      ' blot out ' my of'fences.

2 Wash me thoroughly ' from my ' wickedness ♦
   and ' cleanse me ' from my ' sin.

3 For I ac'knowledge my ' faults ♦
   and my ' sin is ' ever be'fore me.

4 Against you only ' have I ' sinned ♦
   and done what is ' evil ' in your ' sight,

‡ 5 So that you are justified ' in your ' sentence ♦
   and ' righteous ' in your ' judgement.

6 I have been wicked even ' from my ' birth, ♦
   a sinner ' when my ' mother con'ceived me.

7 Behold, you desire truth ' deep with'in me ♦
   and shall make me understand wisdom
      ' in the ' depths of my ' heart.

8 Purge me with hyssop and I ' shall be ' clean; ♦
   wash me and I ' shall be ' whiter than ' snow.

9 Make me hear of ' joy and ' gladness, ♦
   that the bones you have ' broken ' may re'joice.

10 Turn your ' face from my ' sins ♦
   and ' blot out ' all my mis'deeds.

11 Make me a clean ' heart, O ' God, ♦
   and re'new a right ' spirit with'in me.

12 Cast me not a'way from your ' presence ♦
   and take not your ' holy ' spirit ' from me.

13 Give me again the joy of ' your sal'vation ♦
   and sustain me ' with your ' gracious ' spirit;

‡ 14 Then shall I teach your ' ways • to the ' wicked ♦
   and sinners ' shall re'turn to ' you.

Matthew Camidge

Joseph Barnby

15 Deliver me from my guilt, O God,
    the God of ' my sal'vation, ♦
    and my ' tongue shall ' sing of your ' righteousness.

16 O Lord, ' open my ' lips ♦
    and my ' mouth shall pro'claim your ' praise.

17 For you desire no sacrifice, ' else • I would ' give it; ♦
    you take no de'light in ' burnt ' offerings.

18 The sacrifice of God is a ' broken ' spirit; ♦
    a broken and contrite heart, O God, ' you will ' not des'pise.

19 O be favourable and ' gracious to ' Zion; ♦
    build ' up the ' walls of Je'rusalem.

20 Then you will accept sacrifices offered in righteousness,
    the burnt offerings ' and ob'lations; ♦
    then shall they offer up ' bulls ' on your ' altar.

Psalm 52

Joseph Barnby

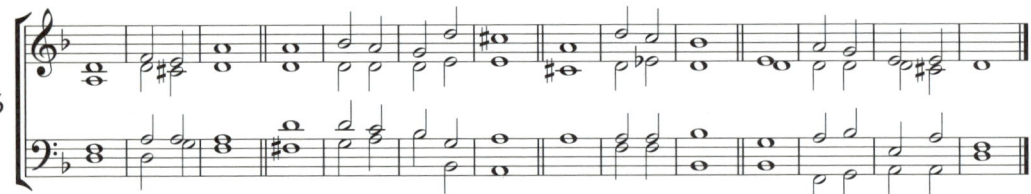

1 Why do you glory in ' evil, you ' tyrant, ♦
    while the goodness of ' God en'dures con'tinually?

2 You plot destruction, ' you de'ceiver; ♦
    your tongue is ' like a ' sharpened ' razor.

3 You love evil ' rather than ' good, ♦
    falsehood ' rather • than the ' word of ' truth.

4 You love all ' words that ' hurt, ♦
   O ' you de'ceitful ' tongue.

‡ 5 Therefore God shall utterly ' bring you ' down; ♦
   he shall take you and pluck you out of your tent
      and root you ' out of the ' land • of the ' living.

6 The righteous shall ' see this and ' tremble; ♦
   they shall ' laugh you to ' scorn, and ' say:

7 'This is the one who did not take ' God • for a ' refuge, ♦
   but trusted in great riches ' and re'lied upon ' wickedness.'

8 But I am like a spreading olive tree in the ' house of ' God; ♦
   I trust in the goodness of ' God for ' ever and ' ever.

9 I will always give thanks to you for ' what you have ' done; ♦
   I will hope in your name, for your ' faithful ' ones de'light in it.

Psalm 53

C. Hylton Stewart

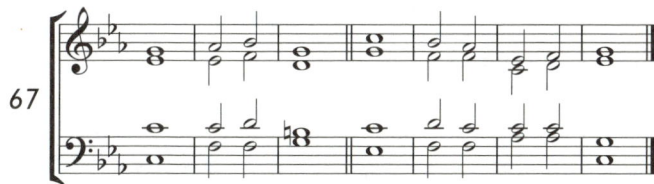

67

1 The fool has said in his heart, 'There ' is no ' God.' ♦
   Corrupt are they, and abominable in their wickedness;
      there is ' no one ' that does ' good.

2 God has looked down from heaven upon the ' children of ' earth, ♦
   to see if there is anyone who is ' wise and ' seeks after ' God.

‡ 3 They are all gone out of the way;
   all alike have be'come cor'rupt; ♦
   there is no one that does ' good, ' no not ' one.

4 Have they no knowledge, those ' evil'doers, ♦
   who eat up my people as if they ate bread,
      and ' do not ' call upon ' God?

5 There shall they be in great fear,
   such fear as ' never ' was; ♦
   for God will scatter the ' bones of ' the un'godly.

6 They will be ' put to ' shame, ♦
   because ' God ' has re'jected them.

7 O that Israel's salvation would ' come • out of ' Zion! ♦
   When God restores the fortunes of his people
      then will Jacob re'joice and ' Israel be ' glad.

Psalm 54

John Goss

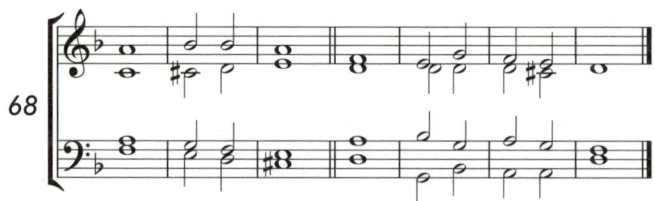

68

1 Save me, O God, | by your | name ♦
  and | vindi•cate me | by your | power.

2 Hear my | prayer, O | God; ♦
  give | heed • to the | words of my | mouth.

‡ 3 For strangers have risen up against me,
      and the ruthless seek | after my | life; ♦
    they have | not set | God be'fore them.

4 Behold, | God is my | helper; ♦
  it is the | Lord • who up'holds my | life.

5 May evil rebound on those who | lie in | wait for me; ♦
  des'troy them | in your | faithfulness.

6 An offering of a free heart | will I | give you ♦
  and praise your name, O | Lord, for | it is | gracious.

7 For he has delivered me out of | all my | trouble, ♦
  and my eye has seen the | downfall | of my | enemies.

Psalm 55

Charles V. Stanford

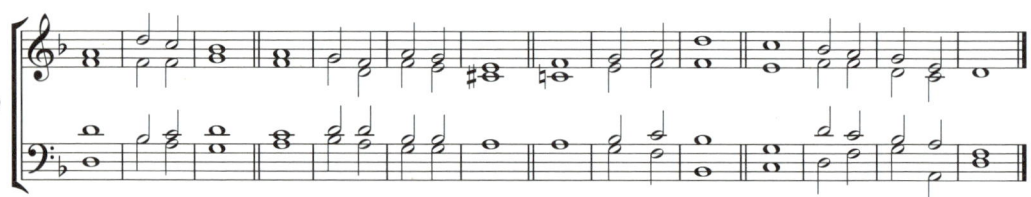

69

1 Hear my | prayer, O | God; ♦
  hide not your'self from | my pe'tition.

2 Give heed to | me and | answer me; ♦
  I am | restless in | my com'plaining.

3 I am alarmed at the | voice of the | enemy ♦
  and at the | clamour | of the | wicked;

4 For they would bring down | evil up'on me ♦
  and are | set a'gainst me in | fury.

5 My heart is dis'quieted with'in me, ♦
  and the terrors of | death have | fallen up'on me.

6 Fearfulness and trembling are | come up'on me, ♦
  and a horrible | dread has | over'whelmed me.

7 And I said: 'O that I had ' wings • like a ' dove, ♦
 for then would I fly a'way and ' be at ' rest.

8 'Then would I flee ' far a'way ♦
 and make my ' lodging ' in the ' wilderness.

9 'I would make ' haste to es'cape ♦
 from the ' stormy ' wind and ' tempest.'

10 Confuse their tongues, O Lord, ' and di'vide them, ♦
 for I have seen violence and ' strife ' in the ' city.

11 Day and night they go a'bout • on her ' walls; ♦
 mischief and ' trouble are ' in her ' midst.

12 Wickedness ' walks in her ' streets; ♦
 oppression and guile ' never ' leave her ' squares.

13 For it was not an open enemy ' that re'viled me, ♦
 for ' then I ' could have ' borne it;

14 Nor was it my adversary that puffed himself ' up a'gainst me, ♦
 for then I ' would have ' hid myself ' from him.

15 But it was even you, one ' like my'self, ♦
 my companion and my ' own fa'miliar ' friend.

16 We took sweet ' counsel to'gether ♦
 and walked with the multitude ' in the ' house of ' God.

‡ 17 Let death come suddenly upon them;
 let them go down a'live • to the ' Pit; ♦
 for wickedness inhabits their ' dwellings, their ' very ' hearts.

Thomas A. Walmisley

18 As for me, I will ' call upon ' God ♦
 and the ' Lord ' will de'liver me.

19 In the evening and morning and at noonday
 I will pray and make my ' suppli'cation, ♦
 and ' he shall ' hear my ' voice.

20 He shall redeem my soul in peace
 from the battle ' waged a'gainst me, ♦
 for ' many have ' come up'on me.

21 God, who is enthroned of old,
 will hear and ' bring them ' down; ♦
 they will not repent, for they ' have no ' fear of ' God.

Psalm 55

Thomas A. Walmisley

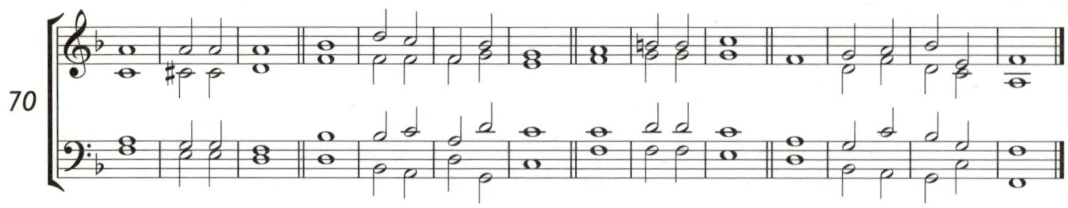

22 My companion stretched out his hands a'gainst his ' friend ♦
and has ' broken ' his ' covenant;

23 His speech was softer than butter, though war was ' in his ' heart; ♦
his words were smoother than oil, yet ' are they ' naked ' swords.

24 Cast your burden upon the Lord and he ' will sus'tain you, ♦
and will not let the ' righteous ' fall for ' ever.

25 But those that are bloodthirsty and de'ceitful, O ' God, ♦
you will bring ' down • to the ' pit of des'truction.

‡ 26 They shall not live out ' half their ' days, ♦
but my trust shall ' be in ' you, O ' Lord.

Psalm 56

Jonathan Battishill

1 Have mercy on me, O God, for they ' trample ' over me; ♦
all day long ' they as'sault • and op'press me.

2 My adversaries trample over me ' all the day ' long; ♦
many are they that ' make proud ' war a'gainst me.

3 In the day of my fear I put my ' trust in ' you, ♦
in ' God whose ' word I ' praise.

4 In God I trust, and ' will not ' fear, ♦
for ' what can ' flesh ' do to me?

5 All day long they ' wound me with ' words; ♦
their every '.thought • is to ' do me ' evil.

6 They stir up trouble; they ' lie in ' wait; ♦
marking my ' steps, they ' seek my ' life.

7 Shall they escape for ' all their ' wickedness? ♦
In anger, O God, ' cast the ' peoples ' down.

8 You have counted up my groaning;
   put my tears ' into your ' bottle; ♦
are they not ' written ' in your ' book?

Jonathan Battishill

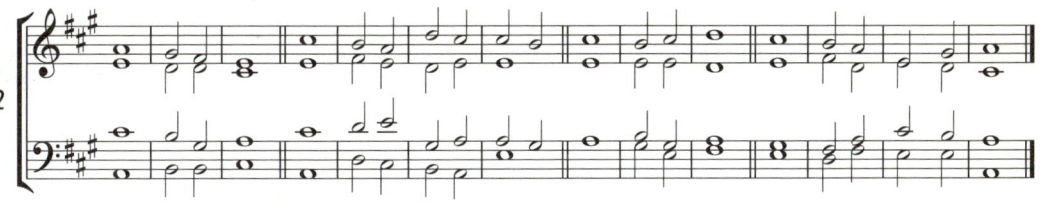

9 Then shall my enemies turn back
    on the day when I ' call up'on you; ♦
    this I know, for ' God is ' on my ' side.

10 In God whose word I praise,
    in the Lord whose ' word I ' praise, ♦
    in God I trust and will not fear:
      ' what can ' flesh ' do to me?

11 To you, O God, will I ful'fil my ' vows; ♦
    to you will I pre'sent my ' offerings of ' thanks,

12 For you will deliver my soul from death
    and my ' feet from ' falling, ♦
    that I may walk before ' God • in the ' light of the ' living.

Psalm 57

Kellow J. Pye

1 Be merciful to me, O God, be ' merciful to ' me, ♦
    for my ' soul takes ' refuge in ' you;

2 In the shadow of your wings will ' I take ' refuge ♦
    until the storm of des'truction ' has passed ' by.

3 I will call upon the ' Most High ' God, ♦
    the God who ful'fils his ' purpose ' for me.

4 He will send from heaven and save me
    and rebuke those that would ' trample up'on me; ♦
    God will send forth his ' love ' and his ' faithfulness.

5 I lie in the ' midst of ' lions, ♦
    people whose teeth are spears and arrows,
      and their ' tongue a ' sharp ' sword.

6 Be exalted, O God, a'bove the ' heavens, ♦
    and your glory ' over ' all the ' earth.

Kellow J. Pye

    7 They have laid a ' net for my ' feet; ♦
        my ' soul is ' pressed ' down;

   7a they have dug a ' pit be'fore me ♦
        and will ' fall • into ' it them'selves.

    8 My heart is ready, O God, my ' heart is ' ready; ♦
        I will ' sing and ' give you ' praise.

    9 Awake, my soul; awake, ' harp and ' lyre, ♦
        that ' I • may a'waken the ' dawn.

   10 I will give you thanks, O Lord, a'mong the ' peoples; ♦
        I will sing praise to ' you a'mong the ' nations.

   11 For your loving-kindness is as ' high as the ' heavens, ♦
        and your faithfulness ' reaches ' to the ' clouds.

‡ 12 Be exalted, O God, a'bove the ' heavens, ♦
        and your glory ' over ' all the ' earth.

Psalm 58

Joseph Barnby

    1 Do you indeed speak ' justly, you ' mighty? ♦
        Do you ' rule the ' peoples with ' equity?

    2 With unjust heart you act through'out the ' land; ♦
        your ' hands ' mete out ' violence.

    3 The wicked are estranged, even ' from the ' womb; ♦
        those who speak falsehood go a'stray ' from their ' birth.

    4 They are as venomous ' as a ' serpent; ♦
        they are like the deaf ' adder which ' stops its ' ears,

‡ 5 Which does not heed the ' voice of the ' charmers, ♦
        and is deaf to the ' skilful ' weaver of ' spells.

6 Break, O God, their ' teeth in their ' mouths; ♦
smash the ' fangs of these ' lions, O ' Lord.

7 Let them vanish like water that ' runs a'way; ♦
let them ' wither like ' trodden ' grass.

8 Let them be as the slimy ' track of the ' snail, ♦
like the untimely birth that ' never ' sees the ' sun.

9 Before ever their pots feel the ' heat of the ' thorns, ♦
green or blazing, ' let them be ' swept a'way.

10 The righteous will be glad when they ' see God's ' vengeance; ♦
they will bathe their ' feet • in the ' blood of the ' wicked.

11 So that people will say,
  'Truly, there is a harvest ' for the ' righteous; ♦
truly, there is a God who ' judges ' in the ' earth.'

Psalm 59
Joseph Barnby

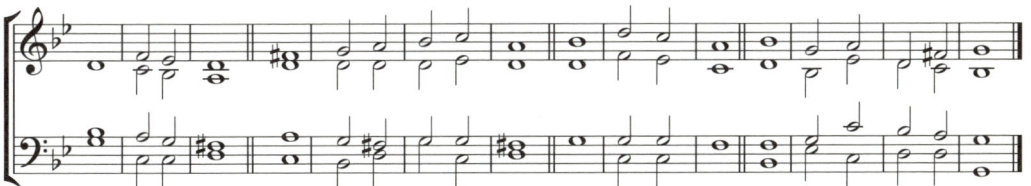

1 Rescue me from my enemies, ' O my ' God; ♦
set me high above ' those that rise ' up a'gainst me.

2 Save me from the ' evil'doers ♦
and from ' murderous ' foes de'liver me.

3 For see how they lie in ' wait • for my ' soul ♦
and the mighty ' stir up ' trouble a'gainst me.

4 Not for any fault or sin of ' mine, O ' Lord; ♦
for no offence, they run and pre'pare them'selves for ' war.

5 Rouse yourself, come to my ' aid and ' see; ♦
for you are the Lord of ' hosts, the ' God of ' Israel.

6 Awake, and judge ' all the ' nations; ♦
show no mercy ' to the ' evil ' traitors.

7 They return at nightfall and ' snarl like ' dogs ♦
and ' prowl a'bout the ' city.

8 They pour out evil words with their mouths;
  swords are ' on their ' lips; ♦
'For ' who', they ' say, 'can ' hear us?'

9 But you ' laugh at them, O ' Lord; ♦
you hold all the ' nations ' in de'rision.

10 For you, O my strength, ' will I ' watch; ♦
you, O God, ' are my ' strong ' tower.

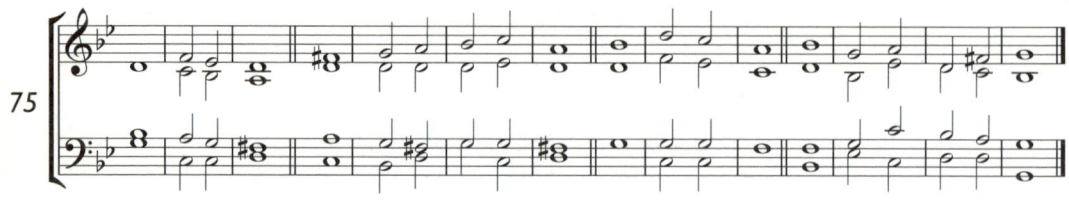
Joseph Barnby

75

11 My God in his steadfast ' love will ' come to me; ♦
    he will let me behold the ' downfall ' of my ' enemies.

12 Slay them not, lest my ' people for'get; ♦
    send them reeling by your might
        and bring them ' down, O ' Lord our ' shield.

13 For the sins of their mouth, for the ' words of their ' lips, ♦
    let them be ' taken ' in their ' pride.

14 For the cursing and falsehood ' they have ' uttered, ♦
    consume them in wrath, consume them ' till they ' are no ' more.

15 And they shall know that God ' rules in ' Jacob, ♦
    and ' to the ' ends of the ' earth.

16 And still they return at nightfall and ' snarl like ' dogs ♦
    and ' prowl a'bout the ' city.

17 Though they forage for ' something • to de'vour, ♦
    and ' howl • if they ' are not ' filled,

18 Yet will I ' sing of your ' strength ♦
    and every morning ' praise your ' steadfast ' love;

19 For you have ' been my ' stronghold, ♦
    my refuge ' in the ' day of my ' trouble.

20 To you, O my strength, ' will I ' sing; ♦
    for you, O God, are my refuge,
        my ' God of ' steadfast ' love.

Psalm 60

James Turle

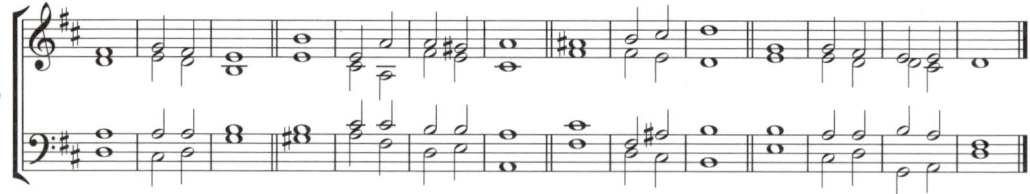

76

1 O God, you have cast us ' off and ' broken us; ♦
   you have been angry; re'store us • to your'self a'gain.

2 You have shaken the earth and ' torn it a'part; ♦
   heal its ' wounds, ' for it ' trembles.

3 You have made your people drink ' bitter ' things; ♦
   we reel from the ' deadly ' wine • you have ' given us.

Psalm 60

4 You have made those who ' fear you to ' flee, ♦
to es'cape • from the ' range of the ' bow.

‡ 5 That your beloved may ' be de'livered, ♦
save us by ' your right ' hand and ' answer us.

6 God has spoken ' in his ' holiness: ♦
'I will triumph and divide Shechem,
    and share ' out the ' valley of ' Succoth.

7 'Gilead is mine and Ma'nasseh is ' mine; ♦
Ephraim is my ' helmet and ' Judah my ' sceptre.

‡ 8 'Moab shall be my washpot;
    over Edom will I ' cast my ' sandal; ♦
across Philistia ' will I ' shout in ' triumph.'

9 Who will lead me into the ' strong ' city? ♦
Who will ' bring me ' into ' Edom?

10 Have you not cast us ' off, O ' God? ♦
Will you no longer ' go forth ' with our ' troops?

11 Grant us your help a'gainst the ' enemy, ♦
for ' earthly ' help • is in ' vain.

12 Through God will we ' do great ' acts, ♦
for it is he that ' shall tread ' down our ' enemies.

Psalm 61

Samuel Wesley

1 Hear my ' crying, O ' God, ♦
and ' listen ' to my ' prayer.

2 From the end of the earth I call to you with ' fainting ' heart; ♦
O set me on the ' rock • that is ' higher than ' I.

3 For ' you are my ' refuge, ♦
a strong ' tower a'gainst the ' enemy.

4 Let me dwell in your ' tent for ' ever ♦
and take refuge under the ' cover ' of your ' wings.

5 For you, O God, will ' hear my ' vows; ♦
you will grant the request of ' those who ' fear your ' name.

6 You will add length of days to the ' life of the ' king, ♦
that his years may endure through'out all ' gene'rations.

Samuel Wesley

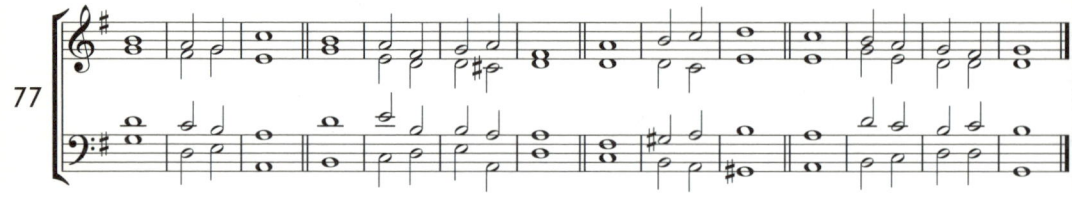

77

7 May he sit enthroned before ′ God for ′ ever; ♦
  may steadfast ′ love and ′ truth watch ′ over him.

8 So will I always sing ′ praise to your ′ name, ♦
  and day by ′ day ful′fil my ′ vows.

Psalm 62

John Stainer
from Beethoven

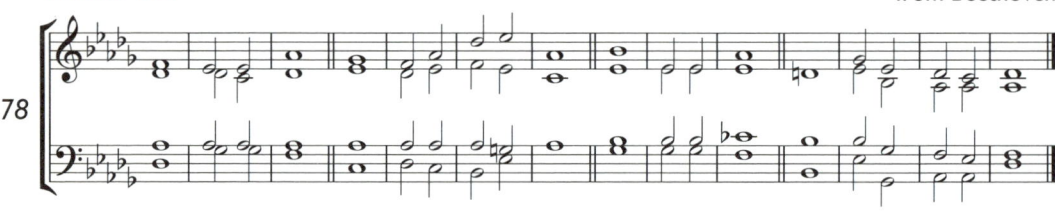

78

1 On God alone my soul in ′ stillness ′ waits; ♦
  from ′ him comes ′ my sal′vation.

2 He alone is my rock and ′ my sal′vation, ♦
  my stronghold, so that ′ I shall ′ never be ′ shaken.

3 How long will all of you assail me ′ to des′troy me, ♦
  as you would a tottering wall ′ or a ′ leaning ′ fence?

4 They plot only to thrust me down from my place of honour;
      lies are their ′ chief de′light; ♦
  they bless with their mouth, but ′ in their ′ heart they ′ curse.

5 Wait on God alone in stillness, ′ O my ′ soul; ♦
  for in ′ him ′ is my ′ hope.

6 He alone is my rock and ′ my sal′vation, ♦
  my stronghold, so that ′ I shall ′ not be ′ shaken.

7 In God is my strength ′ and my ′ glory; ♦
  God is my strong rock; in ′ him ′ is my ′ refuge.

8 Put your trust in him ′ always, my ′ people; ♦
  pour out your hearts before him, for ′ God ′ is our ′ refuge.

9 The peoples are but a breath,
      the whole human ′ race • a de′ceit; ♦
  on the scales they are alto′gether ′ lighter than ′ air.

10 Put no trust in oppression; in robbery take no ′ empty ′ pride; ♦
  though wealth increase, ′ set not your ′ heart up′on it.

11 God spoke once, and twice have I ' heard the ' same, ♦
    that ' power be'longs to ' God.

12 Steadfast love belongs to ' you, O ' Lord, ♦
    for you repay everyone ac'cording ' to their ' deeds.

Psalm 63

Joseph Barnby

1 O God, you are my God; ' eagerly I ' seek you; ♦
   my ' soul • is a'thirst for ' you.

2 My flesh ' also ' faints for you, ♦
   as in a dry and thirsty ' land • where there ' is no ' water.

3 So would I gaze upon you in your ' holy ' place, ♦
   that I might behold your ' power ' and your ' glory.

4 Your loving-kindness is better than ' life it'self ♦
   and ' so my ' lips shall ' praise you.

5 I will bless you as ' long as I ' live ♦
   and lift up my ' hands ' in your ' name.

6 My soul shall be satisfied, as with ' marrow and ' fatness, ♦
   and my mouth shall ' praise you with ' joyful ' lips,

7 When I remember you up'on my ' bed ♦
   and meditate on you in the ' watches ' of the ' night.

8 For you have ' been my ' helper ♦
   and under the shadow of your ' wings will ' I re'joice.

9 My ' soul ' clings to you; ♦
   your ' right hand shall ' hold me ' fast.

10 But those who seek my soul ' to des'troy it ♦
    shall go ' down • to the ' depths of the ' earth;

11 Let them fall by the ' edge of the ' sword ♦
    and be'come a ' portion for ' jackals.

12 But the king shall rejoice in God;
    all those who swear by him ' shall be ' glad, ♦
    for the mouth of those who speak ' lies ' shall be ' stopped.

Psalm 64

John L. Hopkins

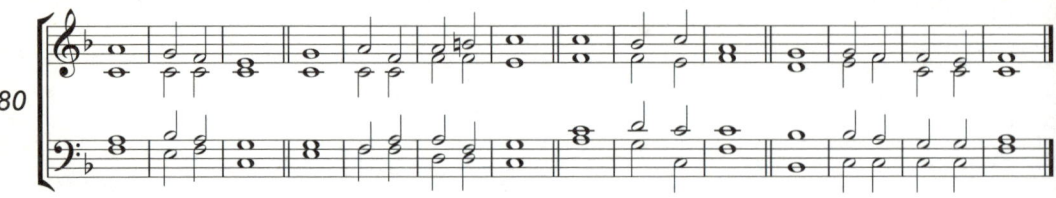

80

1 Hear my voice, O God, in ' my com'plaint; ♦
preserve my ' life from ' fear of the ' enemy.

2 Hide me from the conspiracy ' of the ' wicked, ♦
from the ' gathering of ' evil'doers.

3 They sharpen their ' tongue • like a ' sword ♦
and aim their ' bitter ' words like ' arrows,

4 That they may shoot at the ' blameless from ' hiding places; ♦
suddenly they ' shoot, and ' are not ' seen.

5 They hold fast to their ' evil ' course; ♦
they talk of laying snares, ' saying, ' 'Who will ' see us?'

6 They search out wickedness and lay a ' cunning ' trap, ♦
for deep are the ' inward ' thoughts of the ' heart.

7 But God will shoot at them with his ' swift ' arrow, ♦
and ' suddenly ' they shall be ' wounded.

8 Their own tongues shall ' make them ' fall, ♦
and all who see them shall ' wag their ' heads in ' scorn.

9 All peoples shall fear and tell what ' God has ' done, ♦
and they will ' ponder ' all his ' works.

10 The righteous shall rejoice in the Lord
and put their ' trust in ' him, ♦
and all that are true of ' heart ' shall ex'ult.

Psalm 65

Thomas Attwood

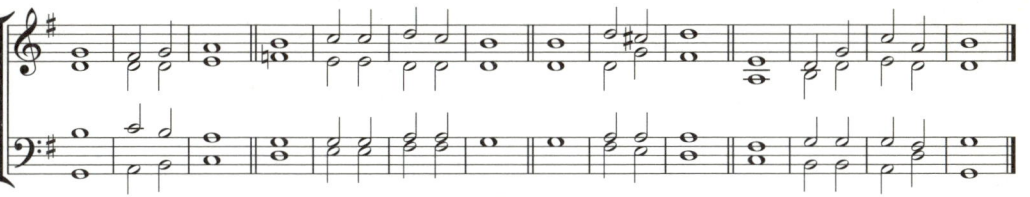

1 Praise is due to you, O ' God, in ' Zion; ♦
   to you that answer ' prayer shall ' vows be ' paid.

2 To you shall all flesh come to con'fess their ' sins; ♦
   when our misdeeds prevail against us,
      ' you will ' purge them a'way.

3 Happy are they whom you choose
      and draw to your ' courts to ' dwell there. ♦
   We shall be satisfied with the blessings of your house,
      ' even • of your ' holy ' temple.

4 With wonders you will answer us in your righteousness,
      O God of ' our sal'vation, ♦
   O hope of all the ends of the earth
      and ' of the ' farthest ' seas.

5 In your strength you set ' fast the ' mountains ♦
   and are ' girded a'bout with ' might.

6 You still the ' raging • of the ' seas, ♦
   the roaring of their waves and the ' clamour ' of the ' peoples.

‡ 7 Those who dwell at the ends of the earth
      tremble ' at your ' marvels; ♦
   the gates of the morning and ' evening ' sing your ' praise.

8 You visit the ' earth and ' water it; ♦
   you ' make it ' very ' plenteous.

9 The river of God is ' full of ' water; ♦
   you prepare grain for your people,
      for ' so you pro'vide • for the ' earth.

10 You drench the furrows and ' smooth out the ' ridges; ♦
    you soften the ground with ' showers and ' bless its ' increase.

11 You crown the ' year with your ' goodness, ♦
    and your ' paths • over'flow with ' plenty.

12 May the pastures of the wilderness ' flow with ' goodness ♦
    and the ' hills be ' girded with ' joy.

13 May the meadows be clothed with ' flocks of ' sheep ♦
    and the valleys stand so thick with corn
       that ' they shall ' laugh and ' sing.

Psalm 66

Edward J. Hopkins

82

1 Be joyful in God, ' all the ' earth; ♦
    sing the glory of his name;
        sing the ' glory ' of his ' praise.

2 Say to God, 'How awesome ' are your ' deeds! ♦
    Because of your great strength
        your ' enemies shall ' bow be'fore you.

3 'All the ' earth shall ' worship you, ♦
    sing to you, sing ' praise ' to your ' name.'

4 Come now and behold the ' works of ' God, ♦
    how wonderful he is in his ' dealings with ' human'kind.

5 He turned the sea into dry land;
    the river they passed ' through on ' foot; ♦
    there ' we re'joiced in ' him.

6 In his might he rules for ever;
    his eyes keep watch ' over the ' nations; ♦
    let no ' rebel rise ' up a'gainst him.

7 Bless our God, ' O you ' peoples; ♦
    make the voice of his ' praise ' to be ' heard,

8 Who holds our ' souls in ' life ♦
    and suffers ' not our ' feet to ' slip.

9 For you, O ' God, have ' proved us; ♦
    you have ' tried us as ' silver is ' tried.

10 You brought us ' into the ' snare; ♦
    you laid heavy ' burdens up'on our ' backs.

‡ 11 You let enemies ride over our heads;
    we went through ' fire and ' water; ♦
    but you brought us out ' into a ' place of ' liberty.

12 I will come into your house with burnt offerings
    and will ' pay you my ' vows, ♦
    which my lips uttered
        and my mouth promised ' when I ' was in ' trouble.

13 I will offer you fat burnt sacrifices with the ' smoke of ' rams; ♦
    I will ' sacrifice ' oxen and ' goats.

14 Come and listen, all ' you who fear ' God, ♦
    and I will tell you what ' he has ' done for my ' soul.

15 I called out to him ' with my ' mouth ♦
    and his ' praise was ' on my ' tongue.

16 If I had nursed evil ' in my ' heart, ♦
    the ' Lord would ' not have ' heard me,

17 But in truth ' God has ' heard me; ♦
    he has ' heeded the ' voice of my ' prayer.

‡ 18 Blessed be God, who has not ' rejected my ' prayer, ♦
    nor withheld his ' loving ' mercy ' from me.

Psalm 67

James Nares

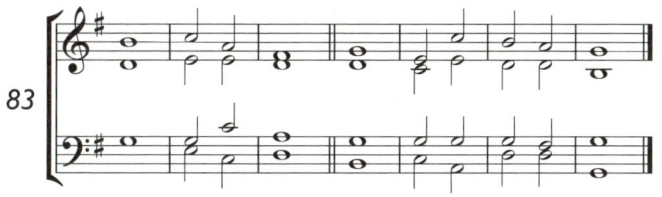

83

1 God be gracious to ' us and ' bless us ♦
   and make his ' face to ' shine up'on us,

2 That your way may be ' known upon ' earth, ♦
   your saving ' power a'mong all ' nations.

‡ 3 *Let the peoples ' praise you, O ' God;* ♦
   let ' all the ' peoples ' praise you.

4 O let the nations re'joice and be ' glad, ♦
   for you will judge the peoples righteously
      and ' govern the ' nations • upon ' earth.

5 *Let the peoples ' praise you, O ' God;* ♦
   let ' all the ' peoples ' praise you.

6 Then shall the earth bring ' forth her ' increase, ♦
   and God, our ' own ' God, will ' bless us.

7 God ' will ' bless us, ♦
   and all the ' ends of the ' earth shall ' fear him.

Psalm 68

Timothy Rogers

84

1 Let God arise and let his ' enemies be ' scattered; ♦
    let those that ' hate him ' flee be'fore him.

2 As the smoke vanishes, so may they ' vanish a'way; ♦
    as wax melts at the fire,
        so let the wicked ' perish • at the ' presence of ' God.

3 But let the righteous be glad and re'joice before ' God; ♦
    let ' them make ' merry with ' gladness.

4 Sing to God, sing praises to his name;
        exalt him who ' rides • on the ' clouds. ♦
    The Lord is his ' name; re'joice be'fore him.

5 Father of the fatherless, de'fender of ' widows, ♦
    God in his ' holy ' habi'tation!

6 God gives the solitary a home
        and brings forth prisoners to ' songs of ' welcome, ♦
    but the rebellious in'habit a ' burning ' desert.

7 O God, when you went forth be'fore your ' people, ♦
    when you ' marched ' through the ' wilderness,

8 The earth shook and the heavens dropped down rain,
        at the presence of God, the ' Lord of ' Sinai, ♦
    at the presence of ' God, the ' God of ' Israel.

9 You sent down a gracious ' rain, O ' God; ♦
    you refreshed your in'heritance when ' it was ' weary.

10 Your people ' came to ' dwell there; ♦
    in your goodness, O God, ' you pro'vide • for the ' poor.

11 The Lord ' gave the ' word; ♦
    great was the company of ' women who ' bore the ' tidings:

11a 'Kings and their armies they ' flee, they ' flee!' ♦
    and women at home ' are di'viding the ' spoil.

12 Though you stayed a'mong the ' sheepfolds, ♦
    see now a dove's wings covered with silver
        and its ' feathers with ' green ' gold.

13 When the Almighty ' scattered the ' kings, ♦
    it was like ' snowflakes ' falling on ' Zalmon.

14 You mighty mountain, great ' mountain of ' Bashan! ♦
You towering ' mountain, great ' mountain of ' Bashan!

15 Why look with envy, you towering mountains,
at the mount which God has ' desired • for his ' dwelling, ♦
the place where the ' Lord will ' dwell for ' ever?

16 The chariots of God are twice ten thousand,
even ' thousands • upon ' thousands; ♦
the Lord is among them, the Lord of ' Sinai in ' holy ' power.

17 You have gone up on high and led ' captivity ' captive; ♦
you have received tribute,
even from those who rebelled,
that you may ' reign as ' Lord and ' God.

Thomas Attwood

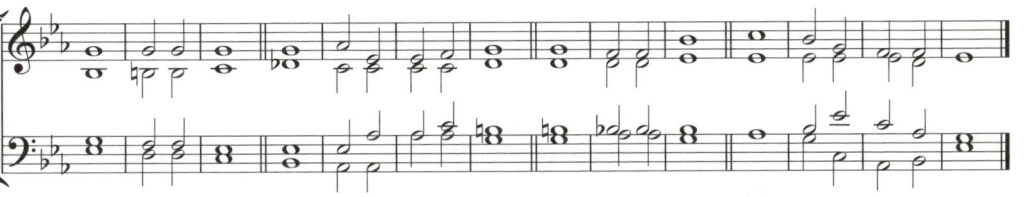

18 Blessed be the Lord who bears our burdens ' day by ' day, ♦
for ' God is ' our sal'vation.

19 God is for us the God of ' our sal'vation; ♦
God is the Lord who ' can de'liver from ' death.

‡ 20 God will smite the ' head of his ' enemies, ♦
the hairy scalp of ' those who ' walk in ' wickedness.

21 The Lord has said, 'From the ' heights of ' Bashan, ♦
from the depths of the ' sea • will I ' bring them ' back,

22 'Till you dip your ' foot in ' blood ♦
and the tongue of your ' dogs • has a ' taste of your ' enemies.'

23 We see your solemn ' processions, O ' God, ♦
your processions into the sanctuary, my ' God ' and my ' King.

24 The singers go before, the musicians ' follow ' after, ♦
in the midst of ' maidens ' playing on ' timbrels.

25 In your companies, ' bless your ' God; ♦
bless the Lord, you that ' are • of the ' fount of ' Israel.

26 At the head there is Benjamin, least of the tribes,
the princes of Judah in ' joyful ' company, ♦
the princes of ' Zebu'lun and ' Naphtali.

Thomas Attwood

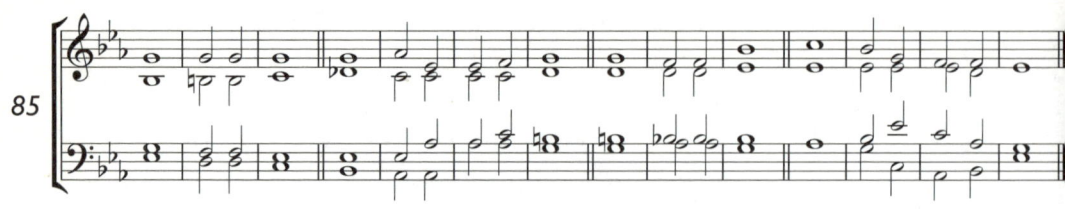

85

27 Send forth your ' strength, O ' God; ♦
establish, O God, what ' you have ' wrought in ' us.

28 For your temple's sake ' in Je'rusalem ♦
kings shall ' bring their ' gifts to ' you.

29 Drive back with your word the wild ' beast of the ' reeds, ♦
the herd of the ' bull-like, the ' brutish ' hordes.

30 Trample down those who ' lust • after ' silver; ♦
scatter the ' peoples • that de'light in ' war.

‡ 31 Vessels of bronze shall be ' brought from ' Egypt; ♦
Ethiopia will stretch ' out her ' hands to ' God.

32 Sing to God, you ' kingdoms • of the ' earth; ♦
make music in ' praise ' of the ' Lord;

33 He rides on the ancient ' heaven of ' heavens ♦
and sends forth his ' voice, a ' mighty ' voice.

34 Ascribe power to God, whose splendour is ' over ' Israel, ♦
whose ' power • is a'bove the ' clouds.

35 How terrible is God in his ' holy ' sanctuary, ♦
the God of Israel, who gives power and strength to his ' people!
' Blessed be ' God.

Psalm 69

James Turle

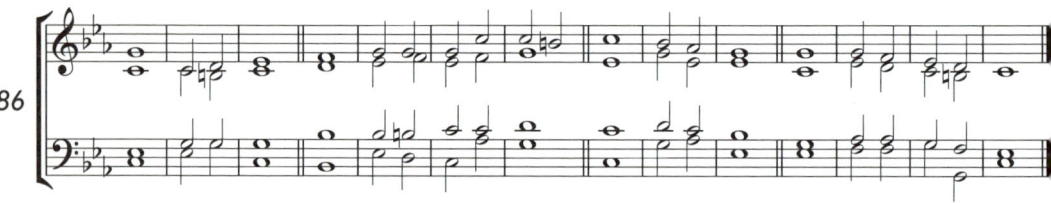

86

1 Save me, ' O ' God, ♦
for the waters have come up, ' even ' to my ' neck.

2 I sink in deep mire where there ' is no ' foothold; ♦
I have come into deep waters ' and the ' flood sweeps ' over me.

3 I have grown weary with crying; my ' throat is ' raw; ♦
my eyes have failed from ' looking so ' long • for my ' God.

4 Those who hate me with'out • any ' cause ♦
are more than the ' hairs ' of my ' head;

5 Those who would des'troy me are ' mighty; ♦
my enemies accuse me falsely:
    must I now give ' back • what I ' never ' stole?

6 O God, you ' know my ' foolishness, ♦
and my ' faults • are not ' hidden ' from you.

7 Let not those who hope in you
    be put to shame through me, Lord ' God of ' hosts; ♦
let not those who seek you be disgraced because of ' me,
    O ' God of ' Israel.

8,9 For your sake have I suffered reproach;
    shame has ' covered my ' face. ♦
I have become a stranger to my kindred,
    an alien ' to my ' mother's ' children.

10 Zeal for your house has ' eaten me ' up; ♦
the scorn of those who ' scorn you has ' fallen up'on me.

11 I humbled my'self with ' fasting, ♦
but that was ' turned to ' my re'proach.

12 I put on ' sackcloth ' also ♦
and be'came a ' byword a'mong them.

13 Those who sit at the gate ' murmur a'gainst me, ♦
and the ' drunkards make ' songs a'bout me.

Samuel Wesley

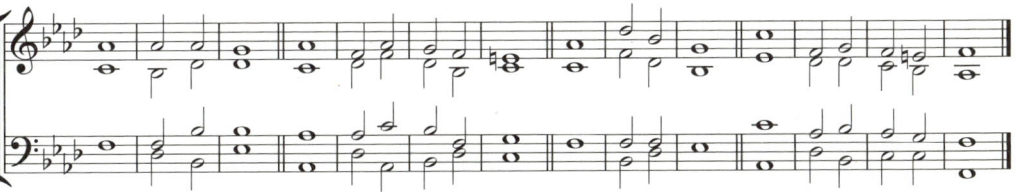

14 But as for me, I make my prayer to ' you, O ' Lord; ♦
at an ac'ceptable ' time, O ' God.

15 Answer me, O God, in the abundance ' of your ' mercy ♦
and ' with your ' sure sal'vation.

16 Draw me out of the mire, ' that I ' sink not; ♦
let me be rescued from those who hate me
    and ' out of the ' deep ' waters.

17 Let not the water flood drown me,
    neither the deep ' swallow me ' up; ♦
let not the Pit ' shut its ' mouth up'on me.

18 Answer me, Lord, for your loving'kindness is ' good; ♦
turn to me in the ' multitude ' of your ' mercies.

19 Hide not your ' face • from your ' servant; ♦
be swift to answer me, ' for I ' am in ' trouble.

Samuel Wesley

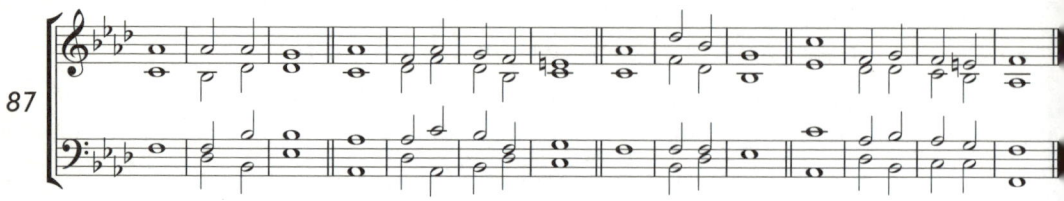

20 Draw near to my ' soul • and re'deem me; ♦
   de'liver me be'cause of my ' enemies.

21 You know my reproach, my shame and ' my dis'honour; ♦
   my adversaries are ' all ' in your ' sight.

22 Reproach has broken my heart; I am ' full of ' heaviness. ♦
   I looked for some to have pity, but there was no one,
      neither ' found I ' any to ' comfort me.

23 They gave me ' gall to ' eat, ♦
   and when I was thirsty, they ' gave me ' vinegar to ' drink.

James Turle

24 Let the table before them ' be a ' trap ♦
   and their ' sacred ' feasts a ' snare.

25 Let their eyes be darkened, that they ' cannot ' see, ♦
   and give them continual ' trembling ' in their ' loins.

26 Pour out your indig'nation up'on them, ♦
   and let the heat of your ' anger ' over'take them.

27 Let their ' camp be ' desolate, ♦
   and let there be ' no one to ' dwell • in their ' tents.

‡ 28 For they persecute the one whom ' you have ' stricken, ♦
   and increase the sorrows of ' him whom ' you have ' pierced.

29 Lay to their charge ' guilt upon ' guilt, ♦
   and let them not re'ceive your ' vindi'cation.

30 Let them be wiped out of the ' book of the ' living ♦
   and not be ' written a'mong the ' righteous.

Samuel Wesley

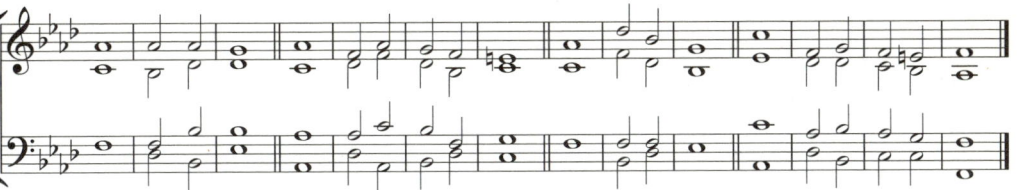

31 As for me, I am ' poor • and in ' misery; ♦
   your saving help, O ' God, will ' lift me ' up.

32 I will praise the name of ' God • with a ' song; ♦
   I will pro'claim his ' greatness with ' thanksgiving.

33 This will please the Lord more than an ' offering of ' oxen, ♦
   more than ' bulls with ' horns and ' hooves.

34 The humble shall ' see • and be ' glad; ♦
   you who seek ' God, your ' heart shall ' live.

35 For the Lord ' listens • to the ' needy, ♦
   and his own who are imprisoned ' he does ' not des'pise.

36 Let the heavens and the ' earth ' praise him, ♦
   the seas and ' all that ' moves ' in them;

37 For God will save Zion and rebuild the ' cities of ' Judah; ♦
   they shall live there and ' have it ' in pos'session.

38 The children of his servants ' shall in'herit it, ♦
   and they that love his ' name shall ' dwell there'in.

Psalm 70

Richard Goodson

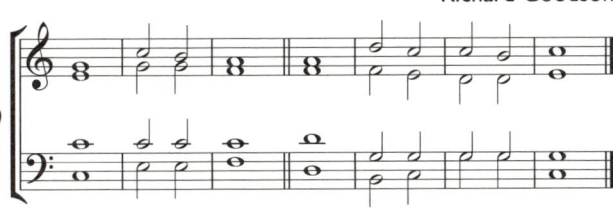

90

1 O God, make ' speed to ' save me; ♦
  O ' Lord, make ' haste to ' help me.

2 Let those who seek my life
     be put to ' shame and con'fusion; ♦
  let them be turned back and dis'graced
     who ' wish me ' evil.

3 Let those who ' mock and de'ride me ♦
  turn ' back be'cause of their ' shame.

4 But let all who seek you rejoice and be ' glad in ' you; ♦
  let those who love your salvation say ' always, ' 'Great is the ' Lord!'

Richard Goodson

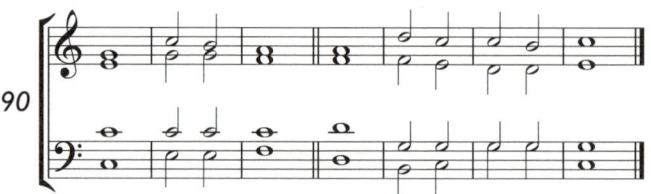

90

5 As for me, I am ' poor and ' needy; ♦
come to me ' quickly, ' O ' God.

6 You are my help and ' my de'liverer; ♦
O ' Lord, do ' not de'lay.

Psalm 71

John Soaper

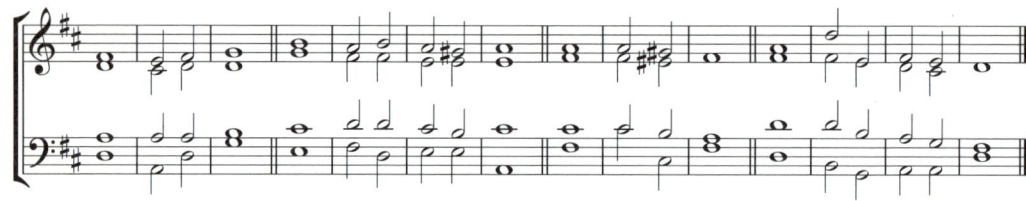

91

1 In you, O Lord, do ' I seek ' refuge; ♦
let me ' never be ' put to ' shame.

2 In your righteousness, deliver me and ' set me ' free; ♦
incline your ' ear to ' me and ' save me.

3 Be for me a stronghold to which I may ' ever re'sort; ♦
send out to save me, for ' you are my ' rock • and my ' fortress.

4 Deliver me, my God, from the ' hand of the ' wicked, ♦
from the grasp of the evil'doer ' and the op'pressor.

5 For you are my hope, ' O Lord ' God, ♦
my confidence, ' even ' from my ' youth.

6 Upon you have I leaned from my birth,
when you drew me from my ' mother's ' womb; ♦
my praise ' shall be ' always of ' you.

7 I have become a ' portent to ' many, ♦
but you are my ' refuge ' and my ' strength.

8 Let my mouth be ' full of your ' praise ♦
and your ' glory ' all the day ' long.

9 Do not cast me away in the time of ' old ' age; ♦
forsake me ' not • when my ' strength ' fails.

10 For my enemies are ' talking a'gainst me, ♦
and those who lie in wait for my ' life take ' counsel to'gether.

11 They say, 'God has forsaken him;
pur'sue him and ' take him, ♦
be'cause • there is ' none • to de'liver him.'

94   Psalm 71

12 O God, ' be not ' far from me; ♦
    come quickly to ' help me, ' O my ' God.

‡ 13 Let those who are against me
        be put to ' shame and dis'grace; ♦
    let those who seek to do me evil
        be ' covered with ' scorn • and re'proach.

'Trent'

14 But as for me I will ' hope con'tinually ♦
    and will ' praise you ' more and ' more.

15 My mouth shall tell of your righteousness
        and salvation ' all the day ' long, ♦
    for I ' know no ' end of the ' telling.

16 I will begin with the mighty works of the ' Lord ' God; ♦
    I will recall your ' righteousness, ' yours a'lone.

17 O God, you have taught me since ' I was ' young, ♦
    and to this day I ' tell • of your ' wonderful ' works.

18 Forsake me not, O God,
        when I am ' old and grey-'headed, ♦
    till I make known your deeds to the next generation
        and your power to ' all that ' are to ' come.

19 Your righteousness, O God, ' reaches • to the ' heavens; ♦
    in the great things you have done, ' who is like ' you, O ' God?

20 What troubles and adversities ' you have ' shown me, ♦
    and yet you will turn and refresh me
        and bring me from the ' deep of the ' earth a'gain.

21 In'crease my ' honour; ♦
    turn a'gain ' and comfort ' me.

22 Therefore will I praise you upon the harp
        for your faithfulness, ' O my ' God; ♦
    I will sing to you with the lyre, O ' Holy ' One of ' Israel.

23 My lips will sing ' out • as I ' play to you, ♦
    and so will my ' soul, which ' you have re'deemed.

‡ 24 My tongue also will tell of your righteousness ' all the day ' long, ♦
    for they shall be shamed and disgraced
        who ' sought to ' do me ' evil.

Psalm 71

Psalm 72   Edward J. Hopkins

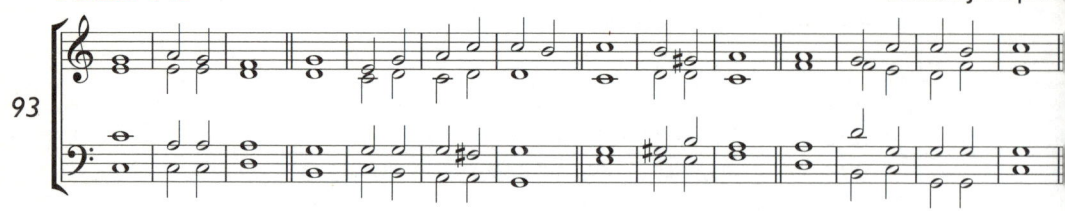

93

1 Give the king your ' judgements, O ' God, ♦
   and your righteousness ' to the ' son of a ' king.

2 Then shall he judge your ' people ' righteously ♦
   and your ' poor ' with ' justice.

3 May the mountains ' bring forth ' peace, ♦
   and the little hills ' righteousness ' for the ' people.

4 May he defend the poor a'mong the ' people, ♦
   deliver the children of the ' needy and ' crush • the op'pressor.

5 May he live as long as the sun and ' moon en'dure, ♦
   from one gene'ration ' to an'other.

6 May he come down like rain upon the ' mown ' grass, ♦
   like the ' showers that ' water the ' earth.

‡ 7 In his time shall ' righteousness ' flourish, ♦
   and abundance of peace
       till the ' moon shall ' be no ' more.

8 May his dominion extend from ' sea to ' sea ♦
   and from the River ' to the ' ends of the ' earth.

9 May his foes ' kneel be'fore him ♦
   and his ' enemies ' lick the ' dust.

10 The kings of Tarshish and of the isles ' shall pay ' tribute; ♦
   the kings of Sheba and ' Seba ' shall bring ' gifts.

11 All kings shall fall ' down be'fore him; ♦
   all ' nations shall ' do him ' service.

12 For he shall deliver the ' poor that cry ' out, ♦
   the needy and ' those who ' have no ' helper.

13 He shall have pity on the ' weak and ' poor; ♦
   he shall pre'serve the ' lives of the ' needy.

14 He shall redeem their lives from op'pression and ' violence, ♦
   and dear shall their ' blood be ' in his ' sight.

15 Long may he live;
       unto him may be given ' gold from ' Sheba; ♦
   may prayer be made for him continually
       and may they ' bless him ' all the day ' long.

16 May there be abundance of grain on the earth,
     standing thick up'on the ' hilltops; ♦
may its fruit flourish like Lebanon
     and its grain ' grow • like the ' grass of the ' field.

17 May his name remain for ever
     and be established as long as the ' sun en'dures; ♦
may all nations be blest in ' him
     and ' call him ' blessed.

18 Blessed be the Lord, the ' God of ' Israel, ♦
     who a'lone does ' wonderful ' things.

19 And blessed be his glorious ' name for ' ever. ♦
May all the earth be filled with his ' glory.
     A'men. A'men.

Psalm 73

Matthew Camidge

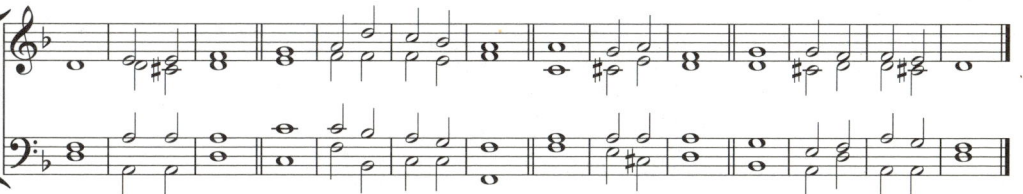

1 Truly, God is ' loving to ' Israel, ♦
     to those ' who are ' pure in ' heart.

2 Nevertheless, my feet were ' almost ' gone; ♦
     my ' steps had ' well-nigh ' slipped.

3 For I was ' envious • of the ' proud; ♦
     I saw the ' wicked in ' such pros'perity;

4 For they ' suffer no ' pains ♦
     and their ' bodies are ' sleek and ' sound;

5 They come to no mis'fortune like ' other folk; ♦
     nor are they ' plagued as ' others ' are;

6 Therefore pride ' is their ' necklace ♦
     and violence ' wraps them ' like a ' cloak.

7 Their iniquity ' comes from with'in; ♦
     the conceits of their ' hearts ' over'flow.

8 They scoff, and speak ' only of ' evil; ♦
     they talk of op'pression ' from on ' high.

9 They set their mouth a'gainst the ' heavens, ♦
     and their tongue ' ranges ' round the ' earth;

10 And so the ' people ' turn to them ♦
     and ' find in ' them no ' fault.

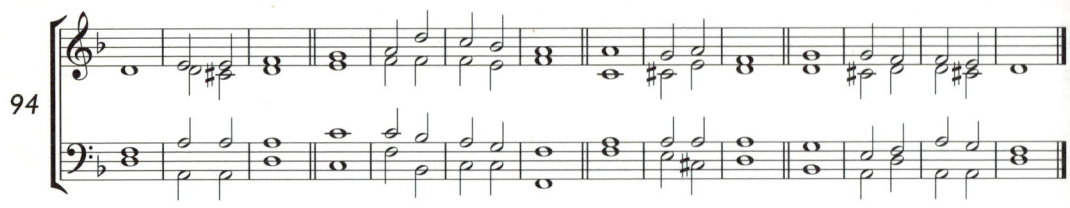

Matthew Camidge

11 They say, ' 'How should ' God know? ♦
   Is there knowledge ' in the ' Most ' High?'

12 Behold, ' these are the ' wicked; ♦
   ever at ease, ' they in'crease their ' wealth.

13 Is it in vain that I ' cleansed my ' heart ♦
   and ' washed my ' hands in ' innocence?

14 All day long have ' I been ' stricken ♦
   and ' chastened ' every ' morning.

15 If I had said, 'I will ' speak as ' they do,' ♦
   I should have betrayed the gene'ration ' of your ' children.

16 Then thought I to ' under'stand this, ♦
   but it ' was too ' hard for ' me,

17 Until I entered the ' sanctuary of ' God ♦
   and under'stood the ' end of the ' wicked:

18 How you set them in ' slippery ' places; ♦
   you ' cast them ' down • to des'truction.

19 How suddenly do they ' come to des'truction, ♦
   perish and ' come to a ' fearful ' end!

20 As with a dream ' when one a'wakes, ♦
   so, Lord, when you arise you ' will des'pise their ' image.

21 When my heart be'came em'bittered ♦
   and ' I was ' pierced • to the ' quick,

22 I was but ' foolish and ' ignorant; ♦
   I was like a brute ' beast in ' your ' presence.

23 Yet I am ' always ' with you; ♦
   you hold me ' by my ' right ' hand.

24 You will guide me ' with your ' counsel ♦
   and ' afterwards re'ceive me with ' glory.

25 Whom have I in ' heaven but ' you? ♦
   And there is nothing upon earth that I de'sire •
      in com'parison with ' you.

26 Though my flesh and my ' heart ' fail me, ♦
   God is the strength of my heart ' and my ' portion for ' ever.

27 Truly, those who for'sake you will ' perish; ♦
you will put to silence the ' faithless ' who be'tray you.

28 But it is good for me to draw ' near to ' God; ♦
in the Lord God have I made my refuge,
that I may ' tell of ' all your ' works.

Psalm 74

John Stainer

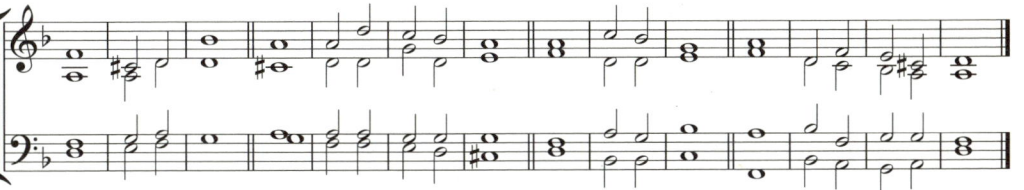

1 O God, why have you 'utterly dis'owned us? ♦
Why does your anger burn
a'gainst the ' sheep of your ' pasture?

2 Remember your congregation that you ' purchased of ' old, ♦
the tribe you redeemed for your own possession,
and Mount ' Zion ' where you ' dwelt.

3 Hasten your steps towards the ' endless ' ruins, ♦
where the enemy has laid ' waste ' all your ' sanctuary.

4 Your adversaries roared in the ' place • of your ' worship; ♦
they set up their ' banners as ' tokens of ' victory.

5 Like men brandishing axes on high in a ' thicket of ' trees, ♦
all her carved work they smashed ' down with ' hatchet and ' hammer.

6 They set fire to your ' holy ' place; ♦
they defiled the dwelling place of your name
and ' razed it ' to the ' ground.

7 They said in their heart, 'Let us make havoc of them ' alto'gether,' ♦
and they burned down all the sanctuaries of ' God ' in the ' land.

8 There are no signs to see, not one ' prophet ' left, ♦
not one a'mong us who ' knows how ' long.

9 How long, O God, will the ' adver•sary ' scoff? ♦
Shall the enemy blas'pheme your ' name for ' ever?

10 Why have you with'held your ' hand ♦
and hidden your ' right hand ' in your ' bosom?

Edmund Chipp

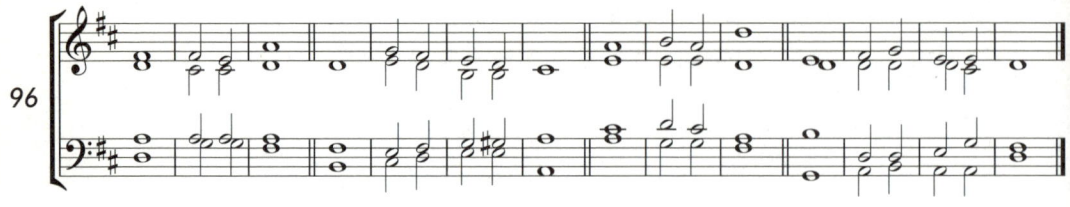

11 Yet God is my ' king • from of ' old, ♦
    who did deeds of sal'vation • in the ' midst of the ' earth.

12 It was you that divided the ' sea • by your ' might ♦
    and shattered the heads of the ' dragons ' on the ' waters;

13 You alone crushed the ' heads of Le'viathan ♦
    and gave him to the ' beasts • of the ' desert for ' food.

14 You cleft the rock for ' fountain and ' flood; ♦
    you dried up ' ever'flowing ' rivers.

15 Yours is the day, yours ' also the ' night; ♦
    you es'tablished the ' moon • and the ' sun.

16 You set all the ' bounds of the ' earth; ♦
    you ' fashioned both ' summer and ' winter.

17 Remember now, Lord, how the ' enemy ' scoffed, ♦
    how a foolish ' people des'pised your ' name.

18 Do not give to wild beasts the ' soul of your ' turtle dove; ♦
    forget not the ' lives of your ' poor for ' ever.

19 Look upon ' your cre'ation, ♦
    for the earth is full of darkness,
        ' full of the ' haunts of ' violence.

20 Let not the oppressed turn a'way a'shamed, ♦
    but let the poor and ' needy ' praise your ' name.

21 Arise, O God, maintain your ' own ' cause; ♦
    remember how fools re'vile you ' all the day ' long.

22 Forget not the ' clamour • of your ' adversaries, ♦
    the tumult of your enemies ' that as'cends con'tinually.

Psalm 75

John Foster

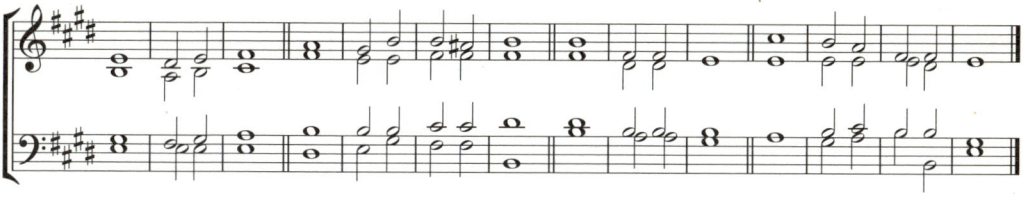

1 We give you thanks, O God, we ' give you ' thanks, ♦
for your name is near, as your ' wonderful ' deeds de'clare.

2 'I will seize the ap'pointed ' time; ♦
I, the ' Lord, will ' judge with ' equity.

3 'Though the earth reels and ' all that ' dwell in her, ♦
it is I that ' hold her ' pillars ' steady.

4 'To the boasters I say, ' "Boast no ' longer," ♦
and to the wicked, ' "Do not ' lift up your ' horn.

5 '"Do not lift up your ' horn on ' high; ♦
do not ' speak • with a ' stiff ' neck." '

6 For neither from the east ' nor from the ' west, ♦
nor yet from the ' wilderness comes ' exal'tation.

7 But God a'lone is ' judge; ♦
he puts down one and ' raises ' up an'other.

8 For in the hand of the Lord there ' is a ' cup, ♦
well mixed and ' full of ' foaming ' wine.

‡ 9 He pours it out for all the ' wicked • of the ' earth; ♦
they shall ' drink it, and ' drain the ' dregs.

10 But I will re'joice for ' ever ♦
and make ' music • to the ' God of ' Jacob.

11 All the horns of the wicked ' will I ' break, ♦
but the horns of the ' righteous shall ' be ex'alted.

Psalm 76

Walter Parratt

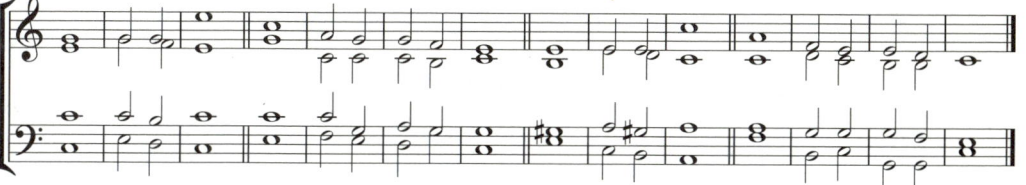

1 In Judah ' God is ' known; ♦
his ' name is ' great in ' Israel.

2 At Salem ' is his ' tabernacle, ♦
and his ' dwelling ' place in ' Zion.

Walter Parratt

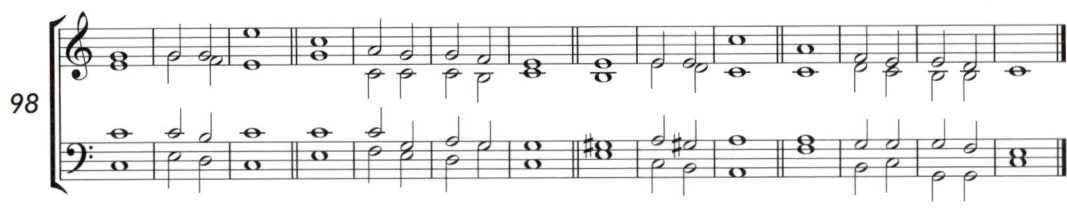

3 There broke he the flashing ' arrows • of the ' bow, ♦
   the shield, the ' sword • and the ' weapons of ' war.

4 In the light of splendour ' you ap'peared, ♦
   glorious ' from the e'ternal ' mountains.

5 The boastful were plundered; they have ' slept their ' sleep; ♦
   none of the ' warriors can ' lift their ' hand.

6 At your rebuke, O ' God of ' Jacob, ♦
   both ' horse and ' chariot fell ' stunned.

7 Terrible are ' you in ' majesty: ♦
   who can stand before your ' face when ' you are ' angry?

8 You caused your judgement to be ' heard from ' heaven; ♦
   the earth ' trembled ' and was ' still,

9 When God a'rose to ' judgement, ♦
   to ' save • all the ' meek upon ' earth.

10 You crushed the ' wrath of the ' peoples ♦
   and ' bridled the ' wrathful ' remnant.

11 Make a vow to the Lord your ' God and ' keep it; ♦
   let all who are round about him bring gifts
       to him that is ' worthy ' to be ' feared.

12 He breaks down the ' spirit of ' princes ♦
   and strikes ' terror • in the ' kings of the ' earth.

Psalm 77

Luke Flintoft

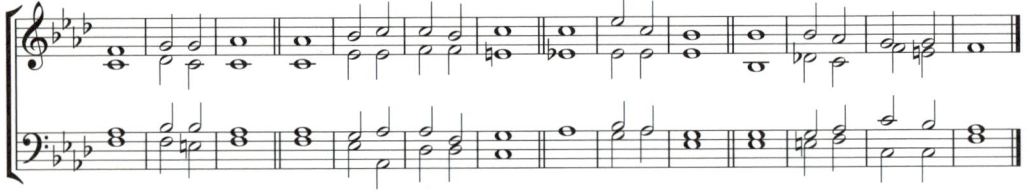

1 I cry a'loud to ' God; ♦
   I cry aloud to ' God and ' he will ' hear me.

2 In the day of my trouble I have ' sought the ' Lord; ♦
   by night my hand is stretched out and does not tire;
       my ' soul re'fuses ' comfort.

3 I think upon God ' and I ' groan; ♦
   I ponder, ' and my ' spirit ' faints.

4 You will not let my ' eyelids ' close; ♦
  I am so troubled ' that I ' cannot ' speak.

5 I consider the ' days of ' old; ♦
  I re'member the ' years long ' past;

6 I commune with my ' heart • in the ' night; ♦
  my spirit ' searches for ' under'standing.

7 Will the Lord cast us ' off for ' ever? ♦
  Will he ' no more ' show us his ' favour?

8 Has his loving mercy clean ' gone for ' ever? ♦
  Has his promise come to an ' end for ' ever'more?

9 Has God for'gotten • to be ' gracious? ♦
  Has he shut up his com'passion ' in dis'pleasure?

10 And I said, 'My ' grief is ' this: ♦
   that the right hand of the Most ' High has ' lost its ' strength.'

James Turle

11 I will remember the ' works of the ' Lord ♦
   and call to mind your ' wonders of ' old ' time.

12 I will meditate on ' all your ' works ♦
   and ' ponder your ' mighty ' deeds.

13 Your way, O ' God, is ' holy; ♦
   who is so ' great a ' god as ' our God?

14 You are the ' God who worked ' wonders ♦
   and declared your ' power a'mong the ' peoples.

15 With a mighty arm you re'deemed your ' people, ♦
   the ' children of ' Jacob and ' Joseph.

16 The waters saw you, O God;
      the waters saw you and ' were a'fraid; ♦
   the ' depths ' also were ' troubled.

17 The clouds poured out water; the ' skies ' thundered; ♦
   your arrows ' flashed on ' every ' side;

18 The voice of your thunder was in the whirlwind;
      your lightnings ' lit up the ' ground; ♦
   the ' earth ' trembled and ' shook.

19 Your way was in the sea, and your paths in the ' great ' waters, ♦
   but your ' footsteps ' were not ' known.

20 You led your ' people like ' sheep ♦
   by the ' hand of ' Moses and ' Aaron.

Psalm 77

Psalm 78

John Camidge Junior

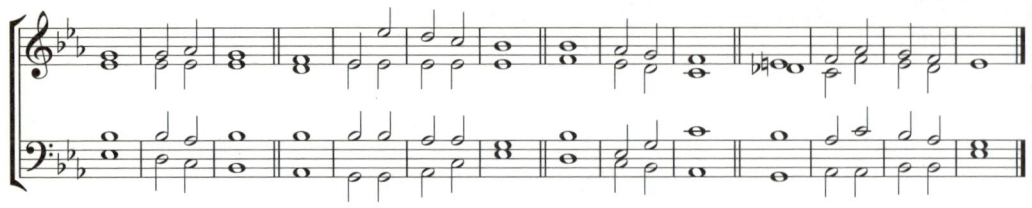

1 Hear my teaching, ' O my ' people; ♦
   incline your ' ears • to the ' words of my ' mouth.

2 I will open my ' mouth • in a ' parable; ♦
   I will pour forth ' mysteries ' from of ' old,

3 Such as we have ' heard and ' known, ♦
   which our ' forebears ' have ' told us.

4 We will not hide from their children,
      but will recount to gene'rations to ' come, ♦
   the praises of the Lord and his power
      and the ' wonderful ' works • he has ' done.

5 He laid a solemn charge on Jacob
      and made it a ' law in ' Israel, ♦
   which he com'manded them to ' teach their ' children,

6 That the generations to come might know,
      and the children ' yet un'born, ♦
   that they in turn might ' tell it ' to their ' children;

7 So that they might put their ' trust in ' God ♦
   and not forget the deeds of ' God,
      but ' keep • his com'mandments,

8 And not be like their forebears,
      a stubborn and rebellious ' gene'ration, ♦
   a generation whose heart was not steadfast,
      and whose spirit ' was not ' faithful to ' God.

9 The people of Ephraim, ' armed • with the ' bow, ♦
   turned ' back • in the ' day of ' battle;

10 They did not keep the ' covenant of ' God ♦
   and re'fused to ' walk in his ' law;

11 They forgot what ' he had ' done ♦
   and the ' wonders ' he had ' shown them.

12 For he did marvellous things in the ' sight of their ' forebears, ♦
   in the land of Egypt, ' in the ' field of ' Zoan.

13 He divided the sea and ' let them pass ' through; ♦
   he made the ' waters stand ' still • in a ' heap.

14 He led them with a ' cloud by ' day ♦
   and all the night ' through • with a ' blaze of ' fire.

15 He split the hard ' rocks • in the ' wilderness ♦
 and gave them drink as ' from the ' great ' deep.

16 He brought streams ' out of the ' rock ♦
 and made ' water gush ' out like ' rivers.

John Goss

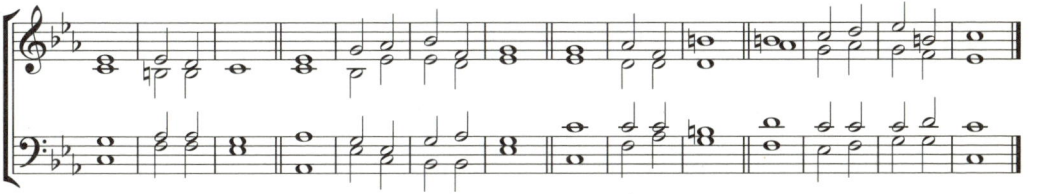

17 Yet for all this they sinned ' more a'gainst him ♦
 and defied the Most ' High ' in the ' wilderness.

18 They tested ' God • in their ' hearts ♦
 and de'manded ' food • for their ' craving.

19 They spoke against ' God and ' said, ♦
 'Can God prepare a ' table ' in the ' wilderness?

20 'He struck the rock indeed, so that the waters gushed out
  and the streams ' over'flowed, ♦
 but can he give bread or provide ' meat ' for his ' people?'

21 When the Lord heard this, he was ' full of ' wrath; ♦
 a fire was kindled against Jacob
  and his ' anger went ' out against ' Israel,

22 For they had no ' faith in ' God ♦
 and put no ' trust in his ' saving ' help.

23 So he commanded the ' clouds a'bove ♦
 and ' opened the ' doors of ' heaven.

24 He rained down upon them ' manna to ' eat ♦
 and ' gave them the ' grain of ' heaven.

25 So mortals ate the ' bread of ' angels; ♦
 he ' sent them ' food in ' plenty.

26 He caused the east wind to ' blow • in the ' heavens ♦
 and led out the ' south wind ' by his ' might.

27 He rained flesh upon them as ' thick as ' dust ♦
 and winged fowl ' like the ' sand of the ' sea.

28 He let it fall in the ' midst of their ' camp ♦
 and ' round a'bout their ' tents.

‡ 29 So they ate and ' were well ' filled, ♦
 for he ' gave them what ' they de'sired.

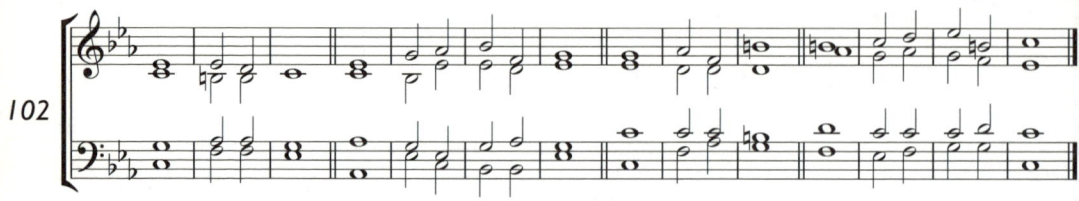

John Goss

102

30 But they did not ' stop their ' craving; ♦
    their ' food was ' still in their ' mouths,

31 When the anger of God ' rose a'gainst them, ♦
    and slew their strongest men
        and ' felled the ' flower of ' Israel.

32 But for all this, they ' sinned yet ' more ♦
    and put no ' faith in his ' wonderful ' works.

33 So he brought their days to an end ' like a ' breath ♦
    and their ' years in ' sudden ' terror.

34 Whenever he slew them, ' they would ' seek him; ♦
    they would repent and ' earnestly ' search for ' God.

35 They remembered that ' God • was their ' rock ♦
    and the ' Most High ' God • their re'deemer.

36 Yet they did but flatter him ' with their ' mouth ♦
    and dis'sembled ' with their ' tongue.

37 Their heart was not ' steadfast to'wards him, ♦
    neither were they ' faithful ' to his ' covenant.

38 But he was so merciful that he forgave their misdeeds
        and did ' not des'troy them; ♦
    many a time he turned back his wrath
        and did not suffer his whole dis'pleasure ' to be ' roused.

39 For he remembered that they ' were but ' flesh, ♦
    a wind that passes ' by and ' does not re'turn.

Edgar Day

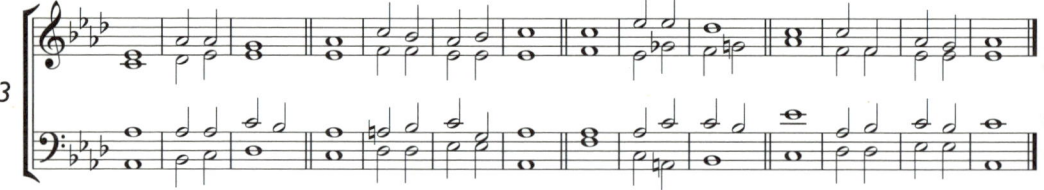

103

40 How often they rebelled against him ' in the ' wilderness ♦
    and ' grieved him ' in the ' desert!

41 Again and again they ' tempted ' God ♦
    and provoked the ' Holy ' One of ' Israel.

42 They did not re'member his ' power ♦
    in the day when he re'deemed them ' from the ' enemy;

43 How he had wrought his ' signs in ' Egypt ♦
   and his ' wonders • in the ' field of ' Zoan.

44 He turned their ' rivers • into ' blood, ♦
   so that they ' could not ' drink of their ' streams.

45 He sent swarms of flies among them, ' which de'voured them, ♦
   and ' frogs which ' brought them ' ruin.

46 He gave their ' produce • to the ' caterpillar, ♦
   the ' fruit of their ' toil • to the ' locust.

47 He destroyed their ' vines with ' hailstones ♦
   and their ' sycamore ' trees • with the ' frost.

48 He delivered their ' cattle to ' hailstones ♦
   and their ' flocks ' – to ' thunderbolts.

49 He set loose on them his ' blazing ' anger: ♦
   fury, displeasure and trouble,
       a ' troop of des'troying ' angels.

50 He made a way for his anger
       and spared not their ' souls from ' death, ♦
   but gave their life ' over ' to the ' pestilence.

51 He smote the ' firstborn of ' Egypt, ♦
   the first fruits of their ' strength • in the ' tents of ' Ham.

52 But he led out his ' people like ' sheep ♦
   and guided them in the ' wilderness ' like a ' flock.

53 He led them to safety and they were ' not a'fraid, ♦
   but the ' sea • over'whelmed their ' enemies.

54 He brought them to his ' holy ' place, ♦
   the mountain which his ' right hand ' took • in pos'session.

55 He drove out the nations before them
       and shared out to them ' their in'heritance; ♦
   he settled the tribes of ' Israel ' in their ' tents.

John Goss

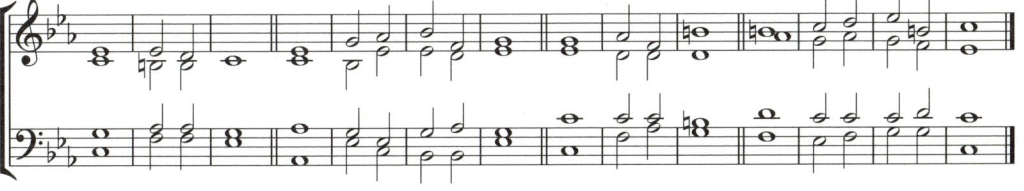

56 Yet still they tested God Most High
       and re'belled a'gainst him, ♦
   and ' would not ' keep his com'mandments.

57 They turned back and fell away ' like their ' forebears, ♦
   starting aside ' like an ' unstrung ' bow.

‡ 58 They grieved him ' with their ' hill altars ♦
   and provoked him to dis'pleasure ' with their ' idols.

John Goss

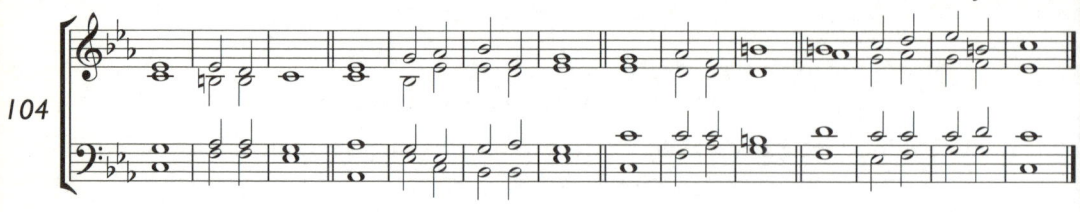
104

59 God heard and was ' greatly ' angered, ♦
and ' utterly re'jected ' Israel.

60 He forsook the ' tabernacle at ' Shiloh, ♦
the ' tent • of his ' presence on ' earth.

61 He gave the ark of his strength ' into cap'tivity, ♦
his splendour ' into the ' adver•sary's ' hand.

62 He delivered his ' people • to the ' sword ♦
and ' raged a'gainst his in'heritance.

63 The fire con'sumed their young ' men; ♦
there was ' no one • to la'ment their ' maidens.

64 Their priests ' fell • by the ' sword, ♦
and their ' widows made ' no • lamen'tation.

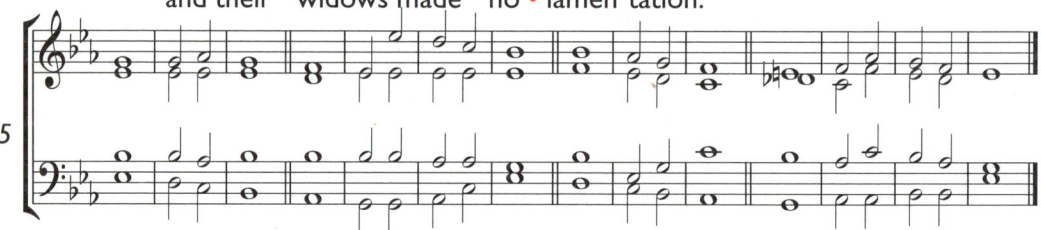
105

65 Then the Lord woke as ' out of ' sleep, ♦
like a warrior who had been ' over'come with ' wine.

66 He struck his enemies ' from be'hind ♦
and put them ' to per'petual ' shame.

67 He rejected the ' tent of ' Joseph ♦
and chose ' not the ' tribe of ' Ephraim,

68 But he chose the ' tribe of ' Judah ♦
and the hill of ' Zion, ' which he ' loved.

69 And there he built his sanctuary like the ' heights of ' heaven, ♦
like the ' earth • which he ' founded for ' ever.

70 He chose David ' also, his ' servant, ♦
and ' took him a'way • from the ' sheepfolds.

71 From following the ewes with their ' lambs he ' took him, ♦
that he might shepherd Jacob his people
   and ' Israel ' his in'heritance.

72 So he shepherded them with a de'voted ' heart ♦
and with ' skilful ' hands he ' guided them.

Psalm 79

Henry Stonex

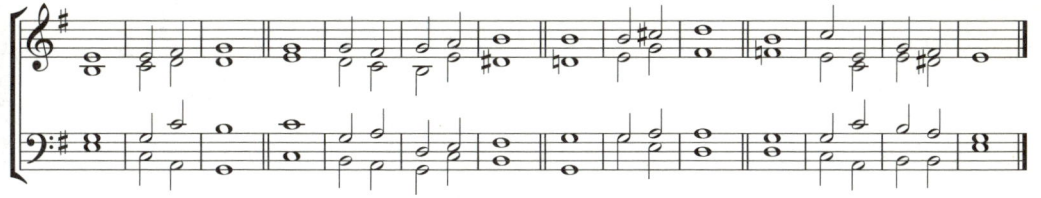

1 O God, the heathen have come ' into your ' heritage; ♦
  your holy temple have they defiled
      and made Je'rusalem a ' heap of ' stones.

2 The dead bodies of your servants they have given
      to be food for the ' birds of the ' air, ♦
  and the flesh of your ' faithful • to the ' beasts of the ' field.

3 Their blood have they shed like water
      on every ' side of Je'rusalem, ♦
  and ' there was ' no one to ' bury them.

4 We have become the ' taunt of our ' neighbours, ♦
  the scorn and derision of ' those that are ' round a'bout us.

5 Lord, how long will you be ' angry, for ' ever? ♦
  How long will your jealous ' fury ' blaze like ' fire?

6 Pour out your wrath upon the nations that ' have not ' known you, ♦
  and upon the kingdoms that have not ' called up'on your ' name.

7 For they have de'voured ' Jacob ♦
  and ' laid ' waste his ' dwelling place.

8 Remember not against us our ' former ' sins; ♦
  let your compassion make haste to meet us,
      for ' we are brought ' very ' low.

9 Help us, O God of our salvation, for the ' glory • of your ' name; ♦
  deliver us, and wipe away our sins ' for your ' name's ' sake.

10 Why should the ' heathen ' say, ♦
   'Where is ' now ' their ' God?'

11 Let vengeance for your servants' ' blood • that is ' shed ♦
   be known among the ' nations ' in our ' sight.

12 Let the sorrowful sighing of the prisoners ' come be'fore you, ♦
   and by your mighty arm
       preserve those ' who are con'demned to ' die.

13 May the taunts with which our neighbours ' taunted you, ' Lord, ♦
   return ' sevenfold ' into their ' bosom.

14 But we that are your people and the sheep of your pasture
       will give you ' thanks for ' ever, ♦
   and tell of your praise from gene'ration to ' gene'ration.

Psalm 80

Stanley Vann

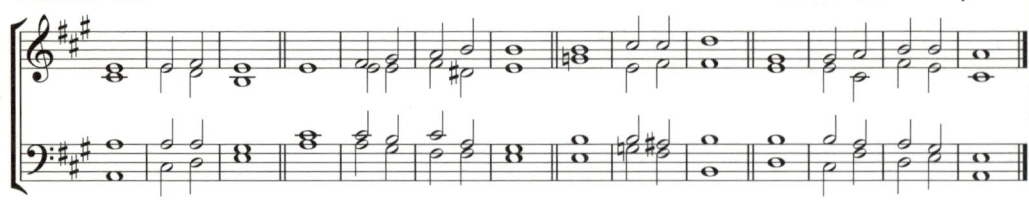

1 Hear, O ' Shepherd of ' Israel, ♦
  you that led ' Joseph ' like a ' flock;

2 Shine forth, you that are enthroned up'on the ' cherubim, ♦
  before Ephraim, ' Benjamin ' and Ma'nasseh.

3 Stir up your ' mighty ' strength ♦
  and ' come to ' our sal'vation.

4 *Turn us a'gain, O ' God;* ♦
  show the light of your countenance, ' and we ' shall be ' saved.

5 O Lord ' God of ' hosts, ♦
  how long will you be ' angry • at your ' people's ' prayer?

6 You feed them with the ' bread of ' tears; ♦
  you give them a'bundance of ' tears to ' drink.

7 You have made us the de'rision • of our ' neighbours, ♦
  and our ' enemies ' laugh us to ' scorn.

8 *Turn us again, O ' God of ' hosts;* ♦
  show the light of your countenance, ' and we ' shall be ' saved.

9 You brought a ' vine • out of ' Egypt; ♦
  you drove ' out the ' nations and ' planted it.

10 You made ' room a'round it, ♦
   and when it had taken ' root, it ' filled the ' land.

11 The hills were ' covered • with its ' shadow ♦
   and the cedars of ' God ' by its ' boughs.

12 It stretched out its ' branches • to the ' Sea ♦
   and its ' tendrils ' to the ' River.

13 Why then have you broken ' down its ' wall, ♦
   so that all who pass ' by pluck ' off its ' grapes?

14 The wild boar out of the wood ' tears it ' off, ♦
   and all the ' insects • of the ' field de'vour it.

15 Turn again, O ' God of ' hosts, ♦
   look down from ' heaven ' and be'hold;

16 Cherish this vine which your ' right hand has ' planted, ♦
   and the branch that you ' made so ' strong for your'self.

17 Let those who burnt it with fire, who ' cut it ' down, ♦
    perish ' at the re'buke • of your ' countenance.

18 Let your hand be upon the ' man • at your ' right hand, ♦
    the son of man you ' made so ' strong • for your'self.

19 And so will we ' not go ' back from you; ♦
    give us life, and we shall ' call up'on your ' name.

20 *Turn us again, O Lord ' God of ' hosts; ♦*
    show the light of your countenance, ' and we ' shall be ' saved.

Psalm 81

Henry T. Smart

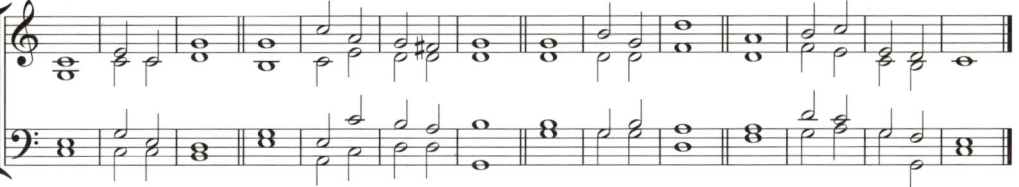

1 Sing merrily to ' God our ' strength, ♦
  shout for ' joy • to the ' God of ' Jacob.

2 Take up the song and ' sound the ' timbrel, ♦
  the tuneful ' lyre ' with the ' harp.

3 Blow the trumpet at the ' new ' moon, ♦
  as at the full moon, up'on our ' solemn ' feast day.

4 For this is a ' statute for ' Israel, ♦
  a ' law • of the ' God of ' Jacob,

‡ 5 The charge he laid on the ' people of ' Joseph, ♦
  when they came ' out of the ' land of ' Egypt.

Noel Rawsthorne

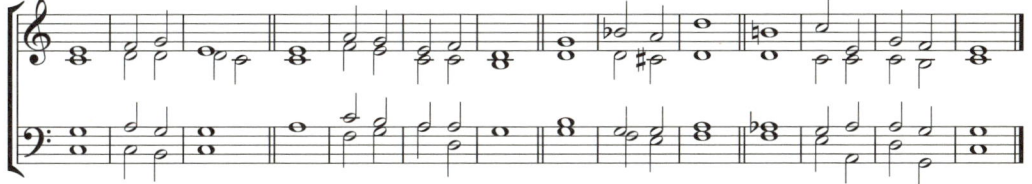

6 I heard a voice I did not ' know, that ' said: ♦
  'I eased their shoulder from the burden;
     their hands were set ' free from ' bearing the ' load.

7 'You called upon me in trouble and ' I de'livered you; ♦
  I answered you from the secret place of thunder
     and proved you ' at the ' waters of ' Meribah.

Noel Rawsthorne

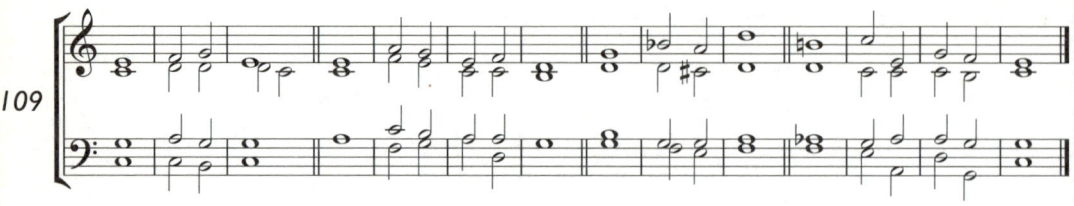

109

8 'Hear, O my people, and I ' will ad ' monish you: ♦
O Israel, if you ' would but ' listen to ' me!

9 'There shall be no strange ' god a ' mong you; ♦
you shall not ' worship a ' foreign ' god.

‡ 10 'I am the Lord your God,
who brought you up from the ' land of ' Egypt; ♦
open your mouth ' wide and ' I shall ' fill it.'

11 But my people would not ' hear my ' voice ♦
and ' Israel would ' not o ' bey me.

12 So I sent them away in the stubbornness ' of their ' hearts, ♦
and let them walk ' after their ' own ' counsels.

13 O that my people would ' listen to ' me, ♦
that ' Israel would ' walk • in my ' ways!

14 Then I should soon put ' down their ' enemies ♦
and turn my ' hand a ' gainst their ' adversaries.

15 Those who hate the Lord would be ' humbled be ' fore him, ♦
and their ' punishment would ' last for ' ever.

16 But Israel would I feed with the ' finest ' wheat ♦
and with honey ' from the ' rock • would I ' satisfy them.

Psalm 82

George A Macfarren

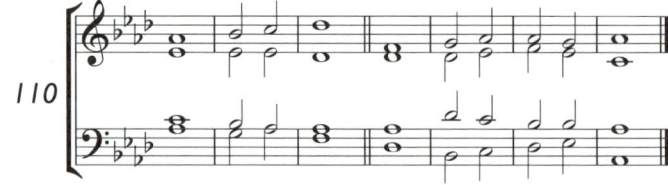

110

1 God has taken his stand in the ' council of ' heaven; ♦
in the midst of the ' gods ' he gives ' judgement:

2 'How long will you ' judge un ' justly ♦
and show such ' favour ' to the ' wicked?

3 'You were to judge the ' weak • and the ' orphan; ♦
defend the ' right • of the ' humble and ' needy;

4 'Rescue the ' weak • and the ' poor; ♦
deliver them ' from the ' hand of the ' wicked.

112 *Psalm 82*

5 'They have no knowledge or wisdom;
    they walk on ' still in ' darkness: ♦
  all the foun'dations • of the ' earth are ' shaken.

6 'Therefore I say that though ' you are ' gods ♦
  and all of you ' children • of the ' Most ' High,

7 'Nevertheless, you shall ' die like ' mortals ♦
  and ' fall like ' one of their ' princes.'

8 Arise, O God and ' judge the ' earth, ♦
  for it is you that shall take all ' nations ' for your pos'session.

Psalm 83
Noel Rawsthorne

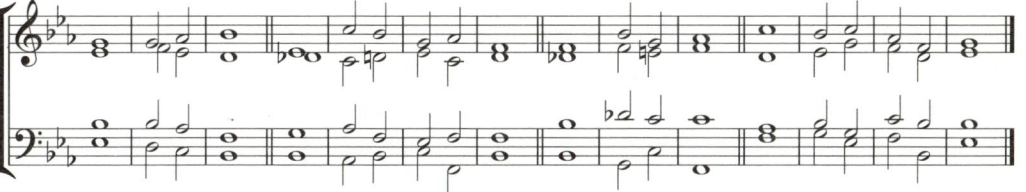

1 Hold not your peace, O God, do ' not keep ' silent; ♦
  be ' not un'moved, O ' God;

2 For your enemies ' are in ' tumult ♦
  and those who ' hate you ' lift up their ' heads.

3 They take secret counsel a'gainst your ' people ♦
  and plot against ' those ' whom you ' treasure.

4 They say, 'Come, let us destroy them ' as a ' nation, ♦
  that the name of Israel ' be re'membered no ' more.'

5 They have conspired together ' with one ' mind; ♦
  they ' are in ' league a'gainst you:

6,7 The tents of Edom and the Ishmaelites,
    ' Moab • and the ' Hagarenes, ♦
    Gebal and Ammon and Amalek,
    the Philistines and ' those who ' dwell in ' Tyre.

‡ 8 Ashur ' also has ' joined them ♦
  and has lent a strong ' arm • to the ' children of ' Lot.

9 Do to them as you ' did to ' Midian, ♦
  to Sisera and to Jabin ' at the ' river of ' Kishon,

10 Who ' perished at ' Endor ♦
   and be'came as ' dung • for the ' earth.

11 Make their commanders like ' Oreb and ' Zeëb, ♦
   and all their princes like ' Zebah ' and Zal'munna,

12 Who said, 'Let us ' take • for our'selves ♦
   the pastures of ' God as ' our pos'session.'

Noel Rawsthorne

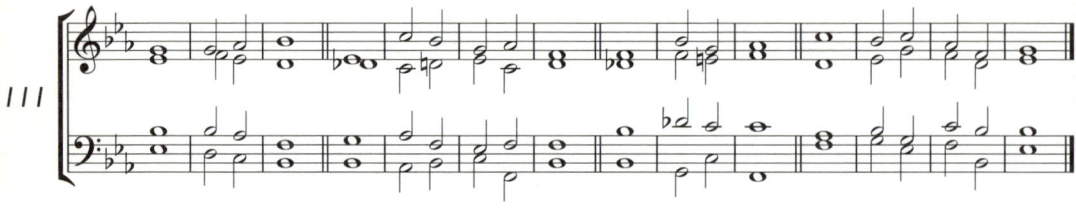

13 O my God, ' make them like ' thistledown, ♦
   like ' chaff be'fore the ' wind.

14 Like fire that con'sumes a ' forest, ♦
   like the ' flame • that sets ' mountains a'blaze,

15 So drive them ' with your ' tempest ♦
   and dis'may them ' with your ' storm.

16 Cover their faces with ' shame, O ' Lord, ♦
   that ' they may ' seek your ' name.

17 Let them be disgraced and dis'mayed for ' ever; ♦
   let them be ' put to con'fusion and ' perish;

18 And they shall know that you, whose ' name is the ' Lord, ♦
   are alone the Most High ' over ' all the ' earth.

Psalm 84

Raymond Lewis

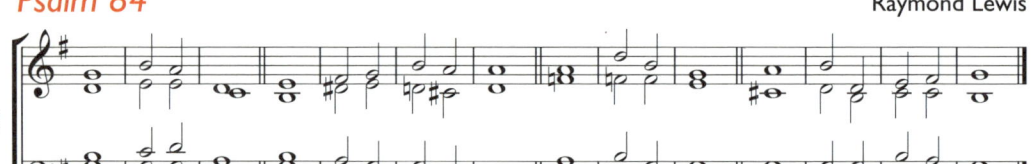

1 How lovely is your dwelling place, O ' Lord of ' hosts! ♦
   My soul has a desire and longing to enter the courts of the Lord;
   my heart and my flesh re'joice • in the ' living ' God.

2 The sparrow has found her a house
   and the swallow a nest where she may ' lay her ' young: ♦
   at your altars, O Lord of ' hosts, my ' King • and my ' God.

3 Blessed are they who ' dwell in your ' house: ♦
   they will ' always be ' praising ' you.

4 Blessed are those whose ' strength is in ' you, ♦
   in whose ' heart • are the ' highways to ' Zion,

5 Who going through the barren valley find ' there a ' spring, ♦
   and the early ' rains will ' clothe it with ' blessing.

6 They will go from ' strength to ' strength ♦
   and ap'pear before ' God in ' Zion.

7 O Lord God of hosts, ' hear my ' prayer; ♦
   listen, O ' God ' of ' Jacob.

8 Behold our de'fender, O ' God, ♦
   and look upon the ' face of ' your a'nointed.

9 For one day ' in your ' courts ♦
   is ' better ' than a ' thousand.

10 I would rather be a doorkeeper in the ' house of my ' God ♦
   than ' dwell • in the ' tents of un'godliness.

11 For the Lord God is both sun and shield;
   he will give ' grace and ' glory; ♦
   no good thing shall the Lord withhold
   from ' those who ' walk • with in'tegrity.

12 O Lord ' God of ' hosts, ♦
   blessed are those who ' put their ' trust in ' you.

Psalm 85

Noel Rawsthorne

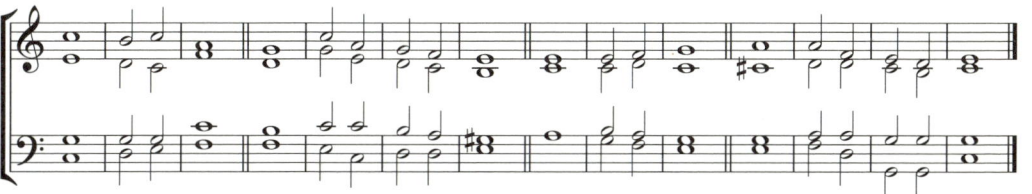

1 Lord, you were gracious ' to your ' land; ♦
   you re'stored the ' fortunes of ' Jacob.

2 You forgave the of'fence of your ' people ♦
   and ' covered ' all their ' sins.

‡ 3 You laid a'side • all your ' fury ♦
   and turned from your ' wrathful ' indig'nation.

4 Restore us again, O ' God our ' Saviour, ♦
   and ' let your ' anger ' cease from us.

5 Will you be displeased with ' us for ' ever? ♦
   Will you stretch out your wrath from one gene'ration ' to an'other?

6 Will you not give us ' life a'gain, ♦
   that your people ' may re'joice in ' you?

7 Show us your ' mercy, O ' Lord, ♦
   and ' grant us ' your sal'vation.

Noel Rawsthorne

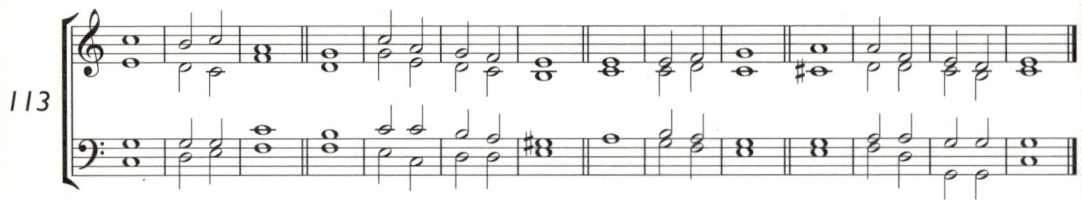

8 I will listen to what the Lord ' God will ' say, ♦
   for he shall speak peace to his people and to the faithful,
      that they ' turn not a'gain to ' folly.

9 Truly, his salvation is near to ' those who ' fear him, ♦
   that his ' glory may ' dwell • in our ' land.

10 Mercy and truth are ' met to'gether, ♦
    righteousness and ' peace have ' kissed each ' other;

11 Truth shall spring ' up • from the ' earth ♦
    and ' righteousness look ' down from ' heaven.

12 The Lord will indeed give ' all that is ' good, ♦
    and our ' land will ' yield its ' increase.

13 Righteousness shall ' go be'fore him ♦
    and di'rect his ' steps • in the ' way.

Psalm 86

John Stainer

1 Incline your ear, O ' Lord, and ' answer me, ♦
   for I am ' poor ' and in ' misery.

2 Preserve my soul, for ' I am ' faithful; ♦
   save your servant, for I ' put my ' trust in ' you.

3 Be merciful to me, O Lord, for ' you are my ' God; ♦
   I call up'on you ' all the day ' long.

4 Gladden the ' soul of your ' servant, ♦
   for to you, O ' Lord, I ' lift up my ' soul.

‡ 5 For you, Lord, are ' good and for'giving, ♦
     abounding in steadfast love to ' all who ' call up'on you.

6 Give ear, O ' Lord, • to my ' prayer ♦
   and listen to the ' voice of my ' suppli'cation.

7 In the day of my distress I will ' call up'on you, ♦
   for ' you will ' answer ' me.

8 Among the gods there is none like ' you, O ' Lord, ♦
   nor ' any ' works like ' yours.

9 All nations you have made shall come and ' worship • you, O ' Lord, ♦
   and shall ' glori'fy your ' name.

10 For you are great and do ' wonderful ' things; ♦
   you a'lone ' are ' God.

11 Teach me your way, O Lord, and I will ' walk in your ' truth; ♦
   knit my heart to you, that ' I may ' fear your ' name.

12 I will thank you, O Lord my God, with ' all my ' heart, ♦
   and glorify your ' name for ' ever'more;

13 For great is your steadfast ' love to'wards me, ♦
   for you have delivered my ' soul • from the ' depths of the ' grave.

14 O God, the proud rise up against me
       and a ruthless horde seek ' after my ' life; ♦
   they have not ' set you be'fore their ' eyes.

15 But you, Lord, are gracious and ' full of com'passion, ♦
   slow to anger and ' full of ' kindness and ' truth.

16 Turn to me and have ' mercy up'on me; ♦
   give your strength to your servant
       and ' save the ' child • of your ' handmaid.

17 Show me a token of your favour,
       that those who hate me may see it and ' be a'shamed; ♦
   because you, O ' Lord, have ' helped and ' comforted me.

Psalm 87

Jonathan Battishill

115

1 His foundation is on the ' holy ' mountains. ♦
   The Lord loves the gates of Zion
       more than ' all the ' dwellings of ' Jacob.

2 Glorious things are ' spoken of ' you, ♦
   Zion, ' city ' of our ' God.

3 I record Egypt and Babylon as ' those who ' know me; ♦
   behold Philistia, Tyre and Ethiopia:
       in ' Zion ' were they ' born.

4 And of Zion it shall be said, ' 'Each one was ' born in her, ♦
   and the Most ' High him'self • has es'tablished her.'

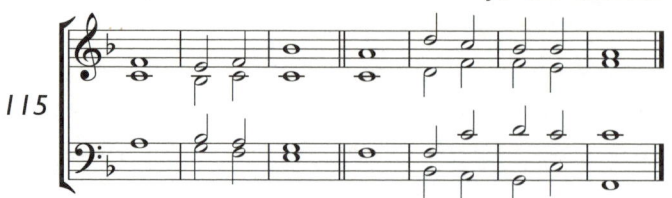

Jonathan Battishill

115

5 The Lord will record as he ' writes up the ' peoples, ♦
  'This one ' also was ' born ' there.'

6 And as they dance ' they shall ' sing, ♦
  'All my ' fresh ' springs are ' in you.'

Psalm 88

Joseph Barnby

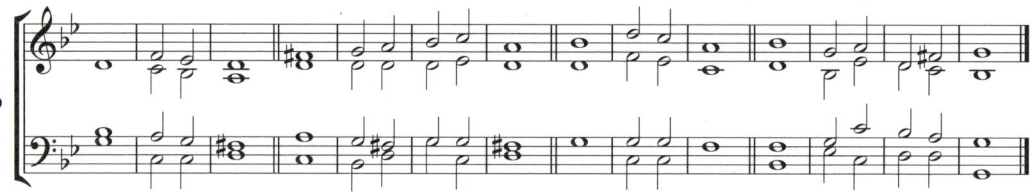

116

1 O Lord, God of ' my sal'vation, ♦
  I have cried ' day and ' night be'fore you.

2 Let my prayer come ' into your ' presence; ♦
  in'cline your ' ear • to my ' cry.

3 For my soul is ' full of ' troubles; ♦
  my life draws ' near • to the ' land of ' death.

4 I am counted as one gone ' down to the ' Pit; ♦
  I am like ' one that ' has no ' strength,

5 Lost a'mong the ' dead, ♦
  like the ' slain who ' lie in the ' grave,

6 Whom you re'member no ' more, ♦
  for ' they are cut ' off • from your ' hand.

7 You have laid me in the ' lowest ' pit, ♦
  in a place of ' darkness ' in the a'byss.

8 Your anger lies ' heavy up'on me, ♦
  and you have af'flicted me with ' all your ' waves.

9 You have put my ' friends ' far from me ♦
  and made me to ' be ab'horred ' by them.

10 I am so fast in prison that I ' cannot get ' free; ♦
   my eyes ' fail from ' all my ' trouble.

11 Lord, I have called ' daily up'on you; ♦
   I have stretched ' out my ' hands ' to you.

12 Do you work wonders ' for the ' dead? ♦
   Will the ' shades stand ' up and ' praise you?

13 Shall your loving-kindness be de'clared • in the ' grave, ♦
   your faithfulness ' in the ' land • of des'truction?

14 Shall your wonders be ' known • in the ' dark ♦
   or your righteous deeds in the ' land where ' all is for'gotten?

15 But as for me, O Lord, ' I will ' cry to you; ♦
   early in the morning my ' prayer shall ' come be'fore you.

16 Lord, why have you re'jected my ' soul? ♦
   Why have you ' hidden your ' face ' from me?

17 I have been wretched and at the point of death ' from my ' youth; ♦
   I suffer your terrors ' and am ' no more ' seen.

18 Your ' wrath sweeps ' over me; ♦
   your ' horrors are ' come • to des'troy me;

19 All day long they come a'bout me like ' water; ♦
   they close me ' in on ' every ' side.

20 Lover and friend have ' you put ' far from me ♦
   and hid my com'panions ' out of my ' sight.

Psalm 89

Gerald H. Knight

1 My song shall be always of the loving-kindness ' of the ' Lord: ♦
  with my mouth will I proclaim your faithfulness
      through'out all ' gene'rations.

2 I will declare that your love is es'tablished for ' ever; ♦
  you have set your faithfulness as ' firm ' as the ' heavens.

3 For you said: 'I have made a covenant ' with my ' chosen one; ♦
  I have sworn an ' oath to ' David my ' servant:

4 '"Your seed will I es'tablish for ' ever ♦
  and build up your throne for ' all ' gene'rations."'

5 The heavens praise your ' wonders, O ' Lord, ♦
  and your faithfulness in the as'sembly ' of the ' holy ones;

6 For who among the clouds can be com'pared to the ' Lord? ♦
  Who is like the Lord a'mong the ' host of ' heaven?

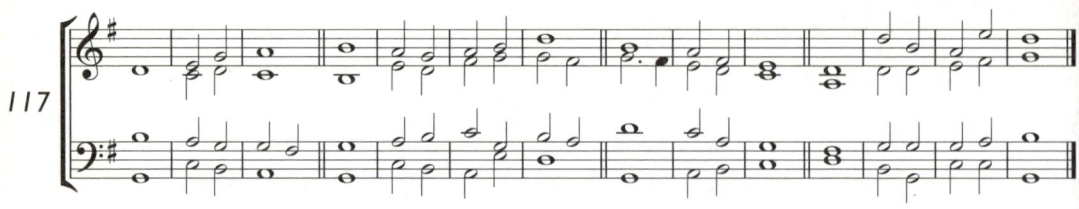

Gerald H. Knight

117

7 A God feared in the ' council • of the ' holy ones, ♦
great and terrible above ' all those ' round a'bout him.

8 Who is like you, Lord ' God of ' hosts? ♦
Mighty Lord, your ' faithfulness is ' all a'round you.

9 You rule the ' raging • of the ' sea; ♦
you still its ' waves when ' they a'rise.

10 You crushed Rahab with a ' deadly ' wound ♦
and scattered your enemies ' with your ' mighty ' arm.

11 Yours are the heavens; the earth ' also is ' yours; ♦
you established the ' world and ' all that ' fills it.

12 You created the ' north • and the ' south; ♦
Tabor and Hermon re'joice ' in your ' name.

13 You have a ' mighty ' arm; ♦
strong is your hand and ' high is ' your right ' hand.

14 Righteousness and justice are the foun'dation of your ' throne; ♦
steadfast love and faithfulness ' go be'fore your ' face.

15 Happy are the people who know the ' shout of ' triumph: ♦
they walk, O ' Lord, • in the ' light of your ' countenance.

16 In your name they rejoice ' all the day ' long ♦
and are ex'alted ' in your ' righteousness.

17 For you are the ' glory of their ' strength, ♦
and in your favour ' you lift ' up our ' heads.

18 Truly the ' Lord • is our ' shield; ♦
the Holy One of ' Israel ' is our ' king.

19 You spoke once in a vision and said to your ' faithful ' people: ♦
'I have set a youth above the mighty;
    I have raised a ' young man ' over the ' people.

20 'I have found ' David my ' servant; ♦
with my holy ' oil have ' I a'nointed him.

21 'My hand shall ' hold him ' fast ♦
and my ' arm shall ' strengthen ' him.

22 'No enemy ' shall de'ceive him, ♦
nor any ' wicked ' person af'flict him.

23 'I will strike down his foes be′fore his ′ face ♦
   and ′ beat down ′ those that ′ hate him.

24 'My truth also and my steadfast love ′ shall be ′ with him, ♦
   and in my ′ name • shall his ′ head be ex′alted.

25 'I will set his dominion up′on the ′ sea ♦
   and his ′ right hand up′on the ′ rivers.

26 'He shall call to me, ′ "You are my ′ Father, ♦
   my God, and the ′ rock of ′ my sal′vation;"

‡ 27 'And I will make ′ him my ′ firstborn, ♦
   the most high a′bove the ′ kings • of the ′ earth.

28 'The love I have pledged to him will I ′ keep for ′ ever, ♦
   and my covenant ′ will stand ′ fast with ′ him.

29 'His seed also will I make to en′dure for ′ ever ♦
   and his ′ throne • as the ′ days of ′ heaven.

30 'But if his children for′sake my ′ law ♦
   and ′ cease to ′ walk in my ′ judgements,

31,32 'If they break my statutes
      and do not ′ keep my com′mandments, ♦
   I will punish their offences with a rod
      ′ and their ′ sin with ′ scourges.

33 'But I will not take from him my ′ steadfast ′ love ♦
   nor ′ suffer my ′ truth to ′ fail.

34 'My covenant will ′ I not ′ break ♦
   nor alter ′ what has gone ′ out of my ′ lips.

35 'Once for all have I ′ sworn • by my ′ holiness ♦
   that I will ′ not prove ′ false to ′ David.

36 'His seed shall en′dure for ′ ever ♦
   and his ′ throne • as the ′ sun be′fore me;

‡ 37 'It shall stand fast for ever ′ as the ′ moon, ♦
   the enduring ′ witness ′ in the ′ heavens.'

John Stainer

38 But you have cast off and rejected ′ your a′nointed; ♦
   you have ′ shown fierce ′ anger a′gainst him.

39 You have broken the covenant ′ with your ′ servant, ♦
   and have ′ cast his ′ crown • to the ′ dust.

John Stainer

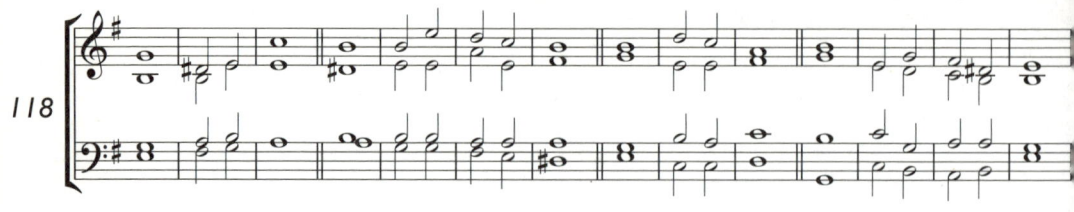

40 You have broken down ' all his ' walls ♦
 and ' laid his ' strongholds in ' ruins.

41 All who pass ' by de'spoil him, ♦
 and he has be'come the ' scorn • of his ' neighbours.

42 You have exalted the right hand ' of his ' foes ♦
 and made ' all his ' enemies re'joice.

43 You have turned back the ' edge of his ' sword ♦
 and have ' not up'held him in ' battle.

44 You have made an ' end of his ' radiance ♦
 and ' cast his ' throne • to the ' ground.

45 You have cut short the ' days of his ' youth ♦
 and have ' covered ' him with ' shame.

46 How long will you hide yourself so ' utterly, O ' Lord? ♦
 How long shall your ' anger ' burn like ' fire?

47 Remember how ' short my ' time is, ♦
 how frail you have ' made all ' mortal ' flesh.

48 Which of the living shall ' not see ' death, ♦
 and shall deliver their ' soul • from the ' power of ' darkness?

49 Where, O Lord, is your steadfast ' love of ' old, ♦
 which you swore to ' David ' in your ' faithfulness?

50 Remember, O Lord, how your ' servant is ' scorned, ♦
 how I bear in my bosom the ' taunts of ' many ' peoples,

51 While your enemies ' mock, O ' Lord, ♦
 while they mock the ' footsteps of ' your a'nointed.

‡ 52 Blessed be the Lord for ' ever'more. ♦
 A'men and 'A'men.

Psalm 90

Edmund Chipp

1 Lord, you have ' been our ' refuge ♦
    from one gene'ration ' to a'nother.

2 Before the mountains were brought forth,
       or the earth and the ' world were ' formed, ♦
    from everlasting to ever'lasting ' you are ' God.

3 You turn us back to ' dust and ' say: ♦
    'Turn ' back, O ' children of ' earth.'

4 For a thousand years in your sight are ' but as ' yesterday, ♦
    which passes ' like a ' watch • in the ' night.

5 You sweep them away ' like a ' dream; ♦
    they fade away ' suddenly ' like the ' grass.

6 In the morning it is ' green and ' flourishes; ♦
    in the evening it is ' dried ' up and ' withered.

7 For we consume away in ' your dis'pleasure; ♦
    we are afraid at your ' wrathful ' indig'nation.

8 You have set our mis'deeds be'fore you ♦
    and our secret ' sins • in the ' light of your ' countenance.

9 When you are angry, all our ' days are ' gone; ♦
    our years come to an ' end ' like a ' sigh.

10 The days of our life are three score years and ten,
       or if our strength endures, ' even ' four score; ♦
    yet the sum of them is but labour and sorrow,
       for they soon pass a'way and ' we are ' gone.

11 Who regards the ' power of your ' wrath ♦
    and your indig'nation like ' those who ' fear you?

12 So teach us to ' number our ' days ♦
    that we may ap'ply our ' hearts to ' wisdom.

13 Turn again, O Lord; how long will ' you de'lay? ♦
    Have com'passion ' on your ' servants.

14 Satisfy us with your loving-kindness ' in the ' morning, ♦
    that we may rejoice and be ' glad ' all our ' days.

15 Give us gladness for the days ' you have af'flicted us, ♦
    and for the years in which ' we have ' seen ad'versity.

16 Show your ' servants your ' works, ♦
    and let your ' glory be ' over their ' children.

‡ 17 May the gracious favour of the Lord our God ' be up'on us; ♦
    prosper our handiwork; O ' prosper the ' work • of our ' hands.

Psalm 90   123

Psalm 91   Raymond Lewi

120

1 Whoever dwells in the shelter of the ' Most ' High ♦
and abides under the ' shadow ' of the Al'mighty,

2 Shall say to the Lord, 'My refuge ' and my ' stronghold, ♦
my God, in ' whom I ' put my ' trust.'

3 For he shall deliver you from the ' snare of the ' fowler ♦
and ' from the ' deadly ' pestilence.

4 He shall cover you with his wings
  and you shall be safe ' under his ' feathers; ♦
his faithfulness shall ' be your ' shield and ' buckler.

5 You shall not be afraid of any ' terror by ' night, ♦
nor of the ' arrow that ' flies by ' day;

6 Of the pestilence that ' stalks in ' darkness, ♦
nor of the ' sickness • that des'troys at ' noonday.

7 Though a thousand fall at your side
  and ten thousand at ' your right ' hand, ♦
yet ' it shall ' not come ' near you.

8 Your eyes have ' only • to be'hold ♦
to ' see the re'ward • of the ' wicked.

9 Because you have made the ' Lord your ' refuge ♦
and the ' Most ' High your ' stronghold,

10 There shall no evil ' happen to ' you, ♦
neither shall any ' plague come ' near your ' tent.

11 For he shall give his angels ' charge ' over you, ♦
to ' keep you in ' all your ' ways.

12 They shall bear you ' in their ' hands, ♦
lest you dash your ' foot a'gainst a ' stone.

‡ 13 You shall tread upon the ' lion and ' adder; ♦
the young lion and the serpent you shall ' trample ' under'foot.

14 Because they have set their love upon me,
  therefore will ' I de'liver them; ♦
I will lift them up, be'cause they ' know my ' name.

15 They will call upon me and ' I will ' answer them; ♦
I am with them in trouble,
  I will de'liver them and ' bring them to ' honour.

‡ 16 With long life ' will I ' satisfy them ♦
and ' show them ' my sal'vation.

124   *Psalm 91*

Psalm 92

Henry T. Smart

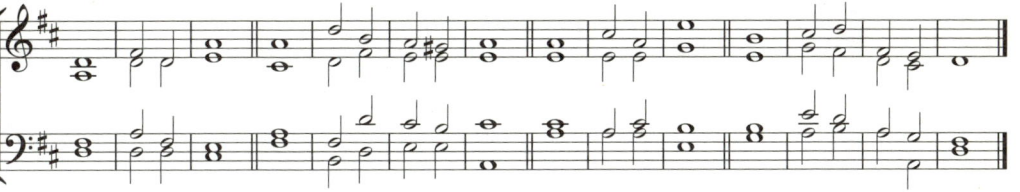

1 It is a good thing to give ' thanks • to the ' Lord ♦
   and to sing praises to your ' name, ' O Most ' High;

2 To tell of your love ' early • in the ' morning ♦
   and of your ' faithfulness ' in the ' night-time,

3 Upon the ten-stringed instrument, up'on the ' harp, ♦
   and to the ' melody ' of the ' lyre.

4 For you, Lord, have made me ' glad • by your ' acts, ♦
   and I sing a'loud • at the ' works of your ' hands.

‡ 5 O Lord, how glorious ' are your ' works! ♦
   Your ' thoughts are ' very ' deep.

6 The senseless ' do not ' know, ♦
   nor do ' fools ' under'stand,

7 That though the wicked ' sprout like ' grass ♦
   and all the ' workers • of in'iquity ' flourish,

8 It is only to be des'troyed for ' ever; ♦
   but you, O Lord, shall be ex'alted for ' ever'more.

9 For lo, your enemies, O Lord,
      lo, your ' enemies shall ' perish, ♦
   and all the workers of in'iquity ' shall be ' scattered.

10 But my horn you have exalted
      like the horns of ' wild ' oxen; ♦
   I am a'nointed with ' fresh ' oil.

11 My eyes will look ' down on my ' foes; ♦
   my ears shall hear the ruin of the evildoers
      ' who rise ' up a'gainst me.

12 The righteous shall ' flourish • like a ' palm tree, ♦
   and shall spread a'broad • like a ' cedar of ' Lebanon.

13 Such as are planted in the ' house of the ' Lord ♦
   shall ' flourish • in the ' courts of our ' God.

14 They shall still bear fruit in ' old ' age; ♦
   they shall be vigorous ' and in ' full ' leaf;

15 That they may show that the ' Lord is ' true; ♦
   he is my rock,
      and there is ' no un'righteousness ' in him.

Psalm 93

Jonathan Battishill

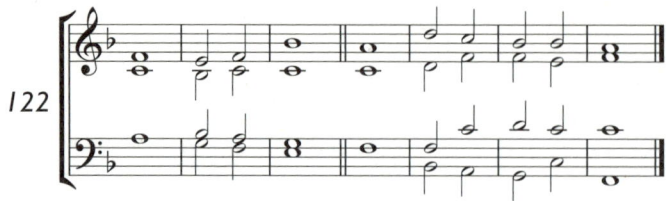

122

1 The Lord is king and has put on ' glorious ap'parel; ♦
    the Lord has put on his glory
        and ' girded him'self with ' strength.

2 He has made the whole ' world so ' sure ♦
    that ' it can'not be ' moved.

3 Your throne has been es'tablished • from of ' old; ♦
    you ' are from ' ever'lasting.

4 The floods have lifted up, O Lord,
        the floods have lifted ' up their ' voice; ♦
    the floods lift ' up their ' pounding ' waves.

5 Mightier than the thunder of many waters,
        mightier than the ' breakers • of the ' sea, ♦
    the ' Lord on ' high is ' mightier.

6 Your testimonies are ' very ' sure; ♦
    holiness adorns your ' house, O ' Lord, for ' ever.

Psalm 94

James Turle

123

1 Lord God to whom ' vengeance be'longs, ♦
    O God to whom vengeance be'longs, shine ' out in ' majesty.

2 Rise up, O ' Judge • of the ' earth; ♦
    give the ' arrogant their ' just de'serts.

3 Lord, how ' long • shall the ' wicked, ♦
    how ' long • shall the ' wicked ' triumph?

4 How long shall the evil'doers ' boast ♦
    and pour ' out such ' impudent ' words?

5,6 They crush your people, O Lord, and af'flict your ' heritage. ♦
    They murder the widow and the stranger;
        the ' orphans they ' put to ' death.

7 And yet they say, 'The ' Lord • will not ' see, ♦
    neither shall the ' God of ' Jacob re'gard it.'

8 Consider, most ' stupid of ' people; ♦
  you fools, ' when will you ' under'stand?

9 He that planted the ear, shall ' he not ' hear? ♦
  He that formed the ' eye, shall ' he not ' see?

10 He who corrects the nations, shall ' he not ' punish? ♦
  He who teaches the ' peoples, does ' he lack ' knowledge?

11 The Lord knows every ' human ' thought, ♦
  that ' they are ' but a ' breath.

12 Blessed are those whom you ' chasten, O ' Lord, ♦
  whom ' you in'struct • from your ' law;

13 That you may give them rest in ' days of ad'versity, ♦
  until a ' pit is ' dug • for the ' wicked.

14 For the Lord will not ' fail his ' people, ♦
  neither will ' he for'sake • his in'heritance.

15 For justice shall re'turn • to the ' righteous, ♦
  and all that are ' true of ' heart shall ' follow it.

16 Who will rise up for me a'gainst the ' wicked? ♦
  Who will take my part a'gainst the ' evil'doers?

17 If the Lord ' had not ' helped me, ♦
  my soul would ' soon • have been ' put to ' silence.

18 And when I said, 'My ' foot has ' slipped', ♦
  your loving ' mercy, O ' Lord, up'held me.

19 In the multitude of cares that ' troubled my ' heart, ♦
  your comforts ' have re'freshed my ' soul.

20 Will you have anything to do with the ' throne of ' wickedness, ♦
  which fashions ' evil ' through its ' law?

21 They gather together against the ' life • of the ' righteous ♦
  and con'demn the ' innocent to ' death.

22 But the Lord has be'come my ' stronghold ♦
  and my ' God the ' rock of my ' trust.

23 He will turn against them their own wickedness
      and silence them through their ' own ' malice; ♦
  the Lord our ' God will ' put them to ' silence.

Psalm 95

Edward J. Hopkins

1 O come, let us ' sing • to the ' Lord; ♦
   let us heartily rejoice in the ' rock of ' our sal'vation.

2 Let us come into his ' presence with ' thanksgiving ♦
   and be ' glad in ' him with ' psalms.

3 For the Lord is a ' great ' God ♦
   and a great ' king a'bove all ' gods.

4 In his hand are the ' depths • of the ' earth ♦
   and the heights of the ' mountains are ' his ' also.

‡ 5 The sea is his, ' for he ' made it, ♦
   and his hands have ' moulded the ' dry ' land.

6 Come, let us worship and ' bow ' down ♦
   and kneel be'fore the ' Lord our ' Maker.

7 For ' he is our ' God; ♦
   we are the people of his ' pasture • and the ' sheep of his ' hand.

8 O that today you would ' listen • to his ' voice: ♦
   'Harden not your hearts as at Meribah,
      on that day at ' Massah ' in the ' wilderness,

9 'When your forebears tested me, and ' put me • to the ' proof, ♦
   though ' they had ' seen my ' works.

10 'Forty years long I detested that gene'ration and ' said, ♦
   "This people are wayward in their hearts;
      they ' do not ' know my ' ways."

11 'So I ' swore • in my ' wrath, ♦
   "They shall not ' enter ' into my ' rest."'

Psalm 96

George M. Garrett

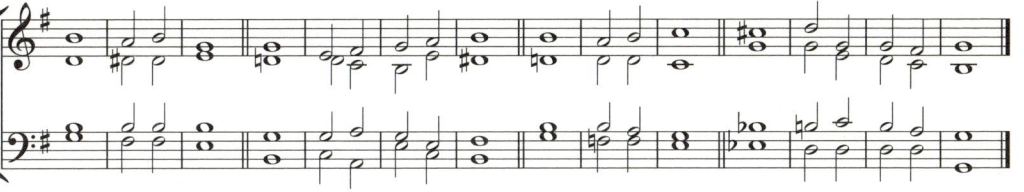

1 Sing to the Lord a ' new ' song; ♦
  sing to the ' Lord, ' all the ' earth.

2 Sing to the Lord and ' bless his ' name; ♦
  tell out his sal'vation from ' day to ' day.

3 Declare his glory a'mong the ' nations ♦
  and his ' wonders a'mong all ' peoples.

4 For great is the Lord and ' greatly • to be ' praised; ♦
  he is more to be ' feared than ' all ' gods.

5 For all the gods of the nations ' are but ' idols; ♦
  it is the ' Lord who ' made the ' heavens.

6 Honour and majesty ' are be'fore him; ♦
  power and ' splendour are ' in his ' sanctuary.

7 Ascribe to the Lord, you families ' of the ' peoples; ♦
  ascribe to the ' Lord ' honour and ' strength.

8 Ascribe to the Lord the honour ' due to his ' name; ♦
  bring offerings and ' come in'to his ' courts.

9 O worship the Lord in the ' beauty of ' holiness; ♦
  let the ' whole earth ' tremble be'fore him.

10 Tell it out among the nations that the ' Lord is ' king. ♦
   He has made the world so firm that it cannot be moved;
     he will ' judge the ' peoples with ' equity.

11 Let the heavens rejoice and let the ' earth be ' glad; ♦
   let the sea ' thunder and ' all • that is ' in it;

12 Let the fields be joyful and ' all • that is ' in them; ♦
   let all the trees of the wood shout for ' joy be'fore the ' Lord.

‡ 13 For he comes, he comes to ' judge the ' earth; ♦
   with righteousness he will judge the world
     and the ' peoples ' with his ' truth.

Psalm 97

Charles F. South

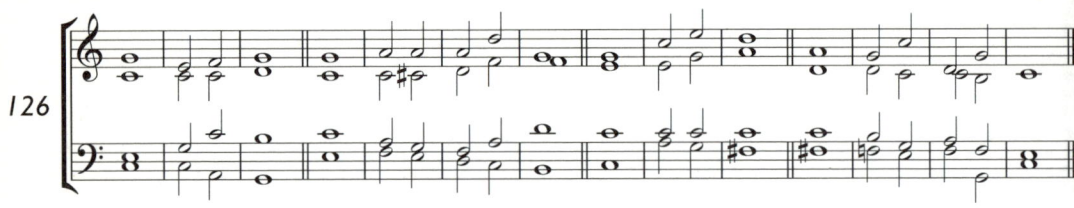

126

1 The Lord is king: let the ' earth re'joice; ♦
  let the multitude ' of the ' isles be ' glad.

2 Clouds and darkness are ' round a'bout him; ♦
  righteousness and justice are the foun'dation ' of his ' throne.

3 Fire ' goes be'fore him ♦
  and burns up his ' enemies on ' every ' side.

4 His lightnings ' lit up the ' world; ♦
  the ' earth ' saw it and ' trembled.

5 The mountains melted like wax at the ' presence • of the ' Lord, ♦
  at the presence of the ' Lord • of the ' whole ' earth.

6 The heavens de'clared his ' righteousness, ♦
  and all the ' peoples have ' seen his ' glory.

7 Confounded be all who worship carved images
    and delight in ' mere ' idols. ♦
  Bow down be'fore him, ' all you ' gods.

8 Zion heard and was glad, and the daughters of ' Judah re'joiced, ♦
  be'cause of your ' judgements, O ' Lord.

9 For you, Lord, are most high over ' all the ' earth; ♦
  you are exalted ' far a'bove all ' gods.

10 The Lord loves ' those who hate ' evil; ♦
   he preserves the lives of his faithful
     and delivers them ' from the ' hand • of the ' wicked.

11 Light has sprung ' up • for the ' righteous ♦
   and ' joy • for the ' true of ' heart.

12 Rejoice in the ' Lord, you ' righteous, ♦
   and give ' thanks • to his ' holy ' name.

Psalm 98

George J. Elvey

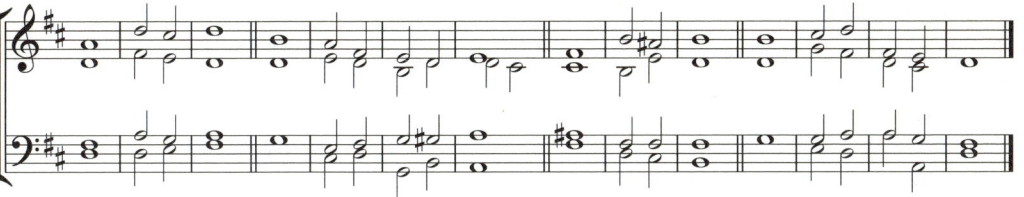

1. Sing to the Lord a ' new ' song, ♦
   for ' he • has done ' marvellous ' things.

2. His own right hand and his ' holy ' arm ♦
   have ' won for ' him the ' victory.

3. The Lord has made ' known • his sal'vation; ♦
   his deliverance has he openly ' shown • in the ' sight of the ' nations.

4. He has remembered his mercy and faithfulness
       towards the ' house of ' Israel, ♦
   and all the ends of the earth have seen the sal'vation ' of our ' God.

5. Sound praises to the Lord, ' all the ' earth; ♦
   break into ' singing ' and make ' music.

6. Make music to the ' Lord • with the ' lyre, ♦
   with the ' lyre • and the ' voice of ' melody.

7. With trumpets and the ' sound of the ' horn ♦
   sound praises be'fore the ' Lord, the ' King.

8. Let the sea thunder and ' all that ' fills it, ♦
   the world and ' all that ' dwell up'on it.

9. Let the rivers ' clap their ' hands ♦
   and let the hills ring out together before the Lord,
       for he ' comes to ' judge the ' earth.

10. In righteousness shall he ' judge the ' world ♦
    and the ' peoples ' with ' equity.

Psalm 99

James Turle

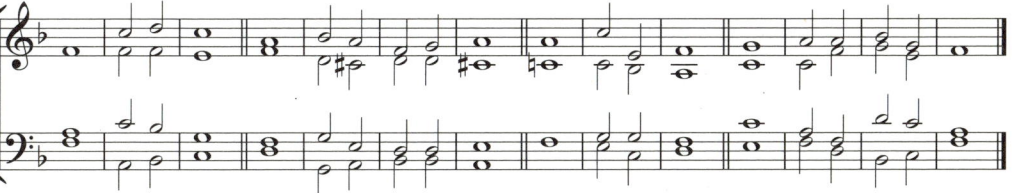

1. The Lord is king: let the ' peoples ' tremble; ♦
   he is enthroned above the cherubim: ' let the ' earth ' shake.

2. The Lord is ' great in ' Zion ♦
   and ' high a'bove all ' peoples.

James Turle

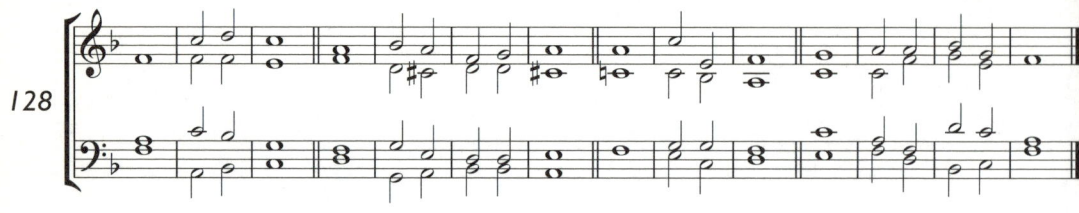

3 Let them praise your name, which is ' great and ' awesome; ♦
  the ' Lord our ' God is ' holy.

4 Mighty king, who loves justice, you have es'tablished ' equity; ♦
  you have executed ' justice and ' righteousness in ' Jacob.

‡ 5 *Exalt the ' Lord our ' God; ♦*
  bow down before his ' footstool, for ' he is ' holy.

6 Moses and Aaron among his priests
    and Samuel among those who ' call upon his ' name; ♦
  they called upon the ' Lord ' and he ' answered them.

7 He spoke to them out of the ' pillar of ' cloud; ♦
  they kept his testimonies ' and the ' law • that he ' gave them.

8 You answered them, O ' Lord our ' God; ♦
  you were a God who forgave them
    and ' pardoned • them for ' their of'fences.

9 *Exalt the Lord our God*
    and worship him upon his ' holy ' hill, ♦
  for the ' Lord our ' God is ' holy.

Psalm 100

Jonathan Battishill

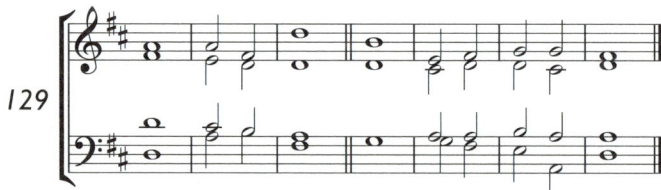

1 O be joyful in the Lord, ' all the ' earth; ♦
  serve the Lord with gladness
    and come before his ' presence ' with a ' song.

2 Know that the ' Lord is ' God; ♦
  it is he that has made us and we are his;
    we are his ' people • and the ' sheep of his ' pasture.

3 Enter his gates with thanksgiving
    and his ' courts with ' praise; ♦
  give thanks to ' him and ' bless his ' name.

4 For the Lord is gracious; his steadfast love is ' ever'lasting, ♦
  and his faithfulness endures from gene'ration to ' gene'ration.

Psalm 101
First setting

Raymond Lewis

1 I will sing of ' faithfulness and ' justice; ♦
 to you, O ' Lord, ' will I ' sing.

2 Let me be wise in the ' way that is ' perfect: ♦
 when ' will you ' come to ' me?

3 I will walk with ' purity of ' heart ♦
 with'in the ' walls • of my ' house.

4 I will not set be'fore my ' eyes ♦
 a ' counsel ' that is ' evil.

5 I abhor the ' deeds • of un'faithfulness; ♦
 they ' shall not ' cling to ' me.

6 A crooked heart ' shall de'part from me; ♦
 I will not ' know a ' wicked ' person.

7 One who slanders a ' neighbour in ' secret ♦
 I will ' quickly ' put to ' silence.

8 Haughty eyes and an ' arrogant ' heart ♦
 I ' will ' not en'dure.

9 My eyes are upon the ' faithful • in the ' land, ♦
 that ' they may ' dwell with ' me.

10 One who walks in the ' way • that is ' pure ♦
 shall ' be ' my ' servant.

11 There shall not ' dwell in my ' house ♦
 one that ' practis'es de'ceit.

12 One who ' utters ' falsehood ♦
 shall not con'tinue ' in my ' sight.

13 Morning by morning will I ' put to ' silence ♦
 all the ' wicked ' in the ' land,

14 To cut off from the ' city • of the ' Lord ♦
 all ' those who ' practise ' evil.

Psalm 101
Second setting

Raymond Lewis

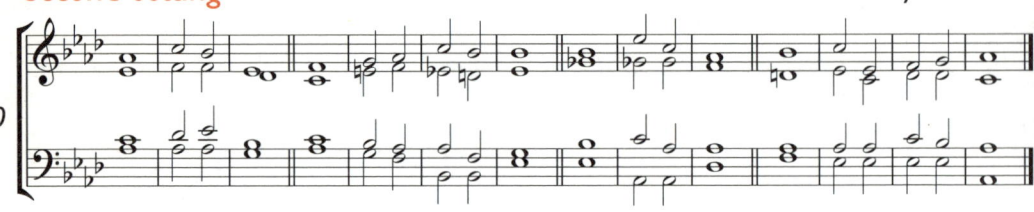

130

1,2 I will sing of faithfulness and justice;
    to you, O Lord, ' will I ' sing. ♦
  Let me be wise in the way that is perfect:
    ' when will you ' come to ' me?

3,4 I will walk with purity of heart
    within the ' walls • of my ' house. ♦
  I will not set before my eyes
    a ' counsel ' that is ' evil.

5,6 I abhor the deeds of unfaithfulness;
    they ' shall not ' cling to me. ♦
  A crooked heart shall depart from me;
    I will not ' know a ' wicked ' person.

7,8 One who slanders a neighbour in secret
    I will quickly ' put to ' silence. ♦
  Haughty eyes and an arrogant heart
    ' I will ' not en'dure.

9,10 My eyes are upon the faithful in the land,
    that ' they may ' dwell with me. ♦
  One who walks in the way that is ' pure
    shall ' be my ' servant.

11,12 There shall not dwell in my house
    one that ' practises de'ceit. ♦
  One who utters falsehood
    shall not con'tinue ' in my ' sight.

‡13,14 Morning by morning will I put to silence
    all the ' wicked • in the ' land, ♦
  To cut off from the city of the Lord
    all ' those who ' practise ' evil.

Psalm 102 — Matthew Camidge

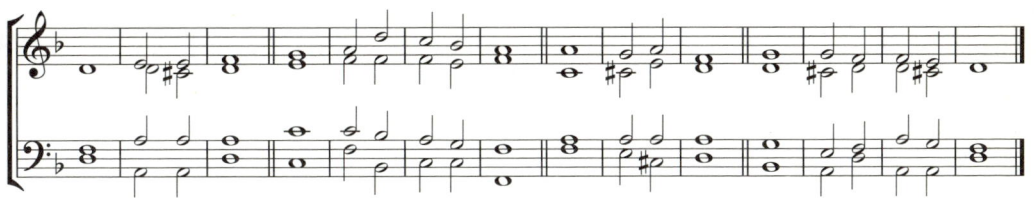

1 O Lord, ' hear my ' prayer ♦
   and let my ' crying ' come be'fore you.

2 Hide not your ' face ' from me ♦
   in the ' day of ' my dis'tress.

3 Incline your ' ear to ' me; ♦
   when I ' call, make ' haste to ' answer me,

4 For my days are con'sumed in ' smoke ♦
   and my bones burn a'way as ' in a ' furnace.

5 My heart is smitten down and ' withered like ' grass, ♦
   so that I for'get to ' eat my ' bread.

6 From the ' sound of my ' groaning ♦
   my ' bones cleave ' fast to my ' skin.

7 I am become like a ' vulture • in the ' wilderness, ♦
   like an ' owl that ' haunts the ' ruins.

8 I ' keep ' watch ♦
   and am become like a sparrow
      ' solitary up'on the ' housetop.

9 My enemies revile me ' all the day ' long, ♦
   and those who rage at me have ' sworn to'gether a'gainst me.

10 I have eaten ' ashes for ' bread ♦
   and ' mingled my ' drink with ' weeping,

11 Because of your indig'nation and ' wrath, ♦
   for you have taken me ' up and ' cast me ' down.

12 My days fade a'way • like a ' shadow, ♦
   and ' I am ' withered like ' grass.

Matthew Camidge

13 But you, O Lord, shall en'dure for ' ever ♦
   and your ' name through ' all • gene'rations.

14 You will arise and have ' pity on ' Zion; ♦
   it is time to have mercy upon her;
      ' surely the ' time has ' come.

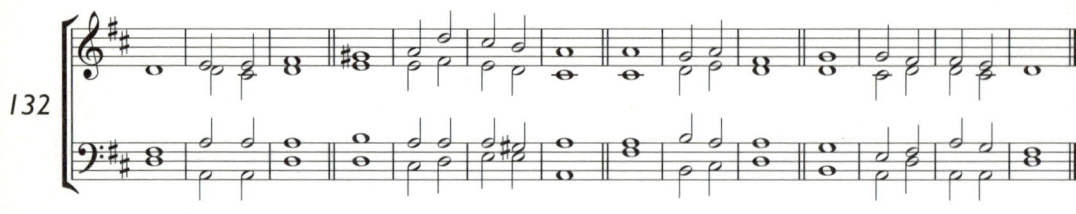

Matthew Camidge

132

‡ 15 For your servants love her ' very ' stones ♦
and feel com'passion ' for her ' dust.

16 Then shall the nations fear your ' name, O ' Lord, ♦
and all the ' kings • of the ' earth your ' glory,

17 When the Lord has ' built up ' Zion ♦
and ' shown him'self in ' glory;

18 When he has turned to the ' prayer • of the ' destitute ♦
and has ' not des'pised their ' plea.

19 This shall be written for ' those • that come ' after, ♦
and a people yet un'born shall ' praise the ' Lord.

20 For he has looked down from his ' holy ' height; ♦
from the heavens ' he be'held the ' earth,

21 That he might hear the ' sighings • of the ' prisoner ♦
and set free ' those con'demned to ' die;

22 That the name of the Lord may be pro'claimed in ' Zion ♦
and his ' praises ' in Je'rusalem,

23 When peoples are ' gathered to'gether ♦
and kingdoms ' also, to ' serve the ' Lord.

24 He has brought down my ' strength • in my ' journey ♦
and has ' shortened ' my ' days.

25 I pray, 'O my God, do not take me in the ' midst of my ' days; ♦
your years endure through'out all ' gene'rations.

26 'In the beginning you laid the foun'dations • of the ' earth, ♦
and the ' heavens • are the ' work of your ' hands;

27 'They shall perish, but ' you • will en'dure; ♦
they all shall ' wear out ' like a ' garment.

28 'You change them like clothing, and ' they • shall be ' changed; ♦
but you are the same, ' and your ' years • will not ' fail.

29 'The children of your servants ' shall con'tinue, ♦
and their descendants shall be es'tablished ' in your ' sight.'

Psalm 103

Charles F. South

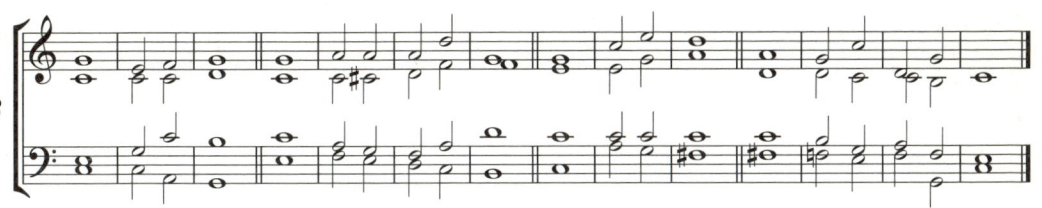

1 Bless the Lord,ˈ O myˈ soul, ♦
  and all that is within meˈ bless hisˈ holyˈ name.

2 Bless the Lord,ˈ O myˈ soul, ♦
  and forˈget notˈ all hisˈ benefits;

3 Who forgivesˈ all yourˈ sins ♦
  andˈ heals allˈ your inˈfirmities;

4 Who redeems yourˈ life • from theˈ Pit ♦
  and crowns you withˈ faithfulˈ love • and comˈpassion;

‡ 5 Who satisfiesˈ you withˈ good things, ♦
  so that yourˈ youth is reˈnewed • like anˈ eagle's.

6 The Lordˈ executesˈ righteousness ♦
  and judgement forˈ all whoˈ are opˈpressed.

7 He made his waysˈ known toˈ Moses ♦
  and hisˈ works • to theˈ children ofˈ Israel.

8 The Lord is full of comˈpassion andˈ mercy, ♦
  slow to angerˈ and ofˈ greatˈ kindness.

9 He will notˈ always acˈcuse us, ♦
  neither will heˈ keep hisˈ anger forˈ ever.

‡ 10 He has not dealt with us acˈcording • to ourˈ sins, ♦
  nor rewarded us acˈcordingˈ to ourˈ wickedness.

11 For as the heavens are high aˈbove theˈ earth, ♦
  so great is hisˈ mercy • uponˈ those whoˈ fear him.

12 As far as the east isˈ from theˈ west, ♦
  so far has heˈ set ourˈ sinsˈ from us.

13 As a father has comˈpassion • on hisˈ children, ♦
  so is the Lord merciful toˈwardsˈ those whoˈ fear him.

14 For he knows of whatˈ we areˈ made; ♦
  he reˈmembers • that weˈ are butˈ dust.

15 Our days areˈ but asˈ grass; ♦
  weˈ flourish • as aˈ flower of theˈ field;

16 For as soon as the wind goes over it,ˈ it isˈ gone, ♦
  and itsˈ place shallˈ know it noˈ more.

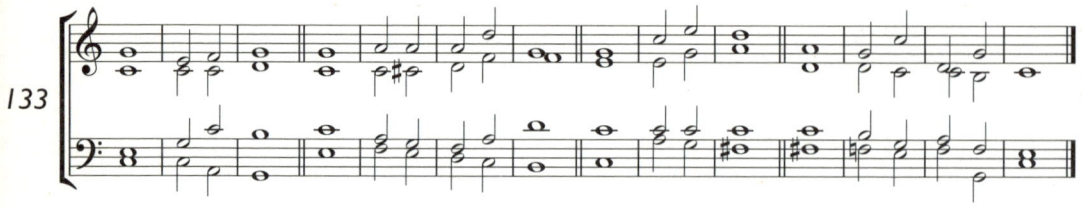

Charles F. South

17 But the merciful goodness of the Lord is from of old
    and endures for ever on ' those who ' fear him, ♦
    and his ' righteousness on ' children's ' children;

18 On those who ' keep his ' covenant ♦
    and re'member • his com'mandments to ' do them.

19 The Lord has established his ' throne in ' heaven, ♦
    and his kingdom has do'minion ' over ' all.

20 Bless the Lord, you ' angels of ' his, ♦
    you mighty ones who do his bidding
    and ' hearken • to the ' voice of his ' word.

21 Bless the Lord, all ' you his ' hosts, ♦
    you ministers of ' his who ' do his ' will.

22 Bless the Lord, all you works of his,
    in all places of ' his do'minion; ♦
    bless the ' Lord, ' O my ' soul.

Psalm 104

John Harper

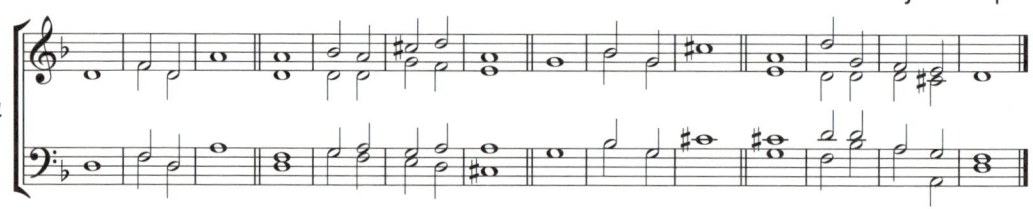

1 Bless the Lord, ' O my ' soul. ♦
  O Lord my God, how ' excellent ' is your ' greatness!

2 You are clothed with ' majesty and ' honour, ♦
  wrapped in ' light as ' in a ' garment.

3 You spread out the heavens ' like a ' curtain ♦
  and lay the beams of your dwelling place ' in the ' waters a'bove.

4 You make the ' clouds your ' chariot ♦
  and ' ride on the ' wings • of the ' wind.

5 You make the ' winds your ' messengers ♦
  and ' flames of ' fire your ' servants.

6 You laid the foun'dations • of the ' earth, ♦
  that it never should ' move at ' any ' time.

7 You covered it with the ' deep • like a ' garment; ♦
   the waters stood ' high a'bove the ' hills.

8 At your re'buke they ' fled; ♦
   at the voice of your ' thunder they ' hastened a'way.

9 They rose up to the hills and flowed down to the ' valleys be'neath, ♦
   to the place which ' you • had ap'pointed ' for them.

10 You have set them their bounds that they ' should not ' pass, ♦
   nor turn a'gain to ' cover the ' earth.

John Harper

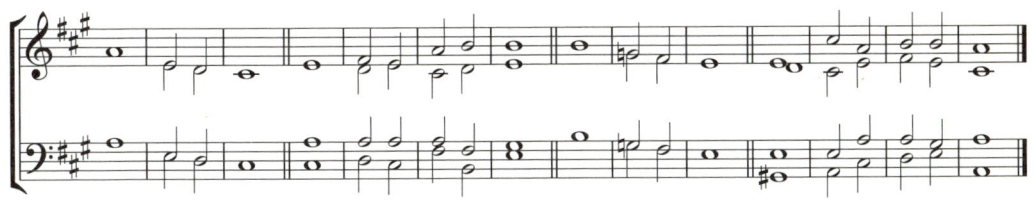

11 You send the springs ' into the ' brooks, ♦
   which ' run a'mong the ' hills.

12 They give drink to every ' beast • of the ' field, ♦
   and the wild ' asses ' quench their ' thirst.

13 Beside them the birds of the air ' make their ' nests ♦
   and ' sing a'mong the ' branches.

14 You water the hills from your ' dwelling on ' high; ♦
   the earth is ' filled • with the ' fruit of your ' works.

15 You make grass to ' grow • for the ' cattle ♦
   and ' plants to ' meet our ' needs,

16 Bringing forth ' food • from the ' earth ♦
   and ' wine to ' gladden our ' hearts,

‡ 17 Oil to give us a ' cheerful ' countenance ♦
   and ' bread to ' strengthen our ' hearts.

18 The trees of the Lord are ' full of ' sap, ♦
   the cedars of ' Lebanon ' which he ' planted,

19 In which the birds ' build their ' nests, ♦
   while the fir trees are a ' dwelling ' for the ' stork.

‡ 20 The mountains are a refuge for the ' wild ' goats ♦
   and the ' stony ' cliffs • for the ' conies.

Psalm 104

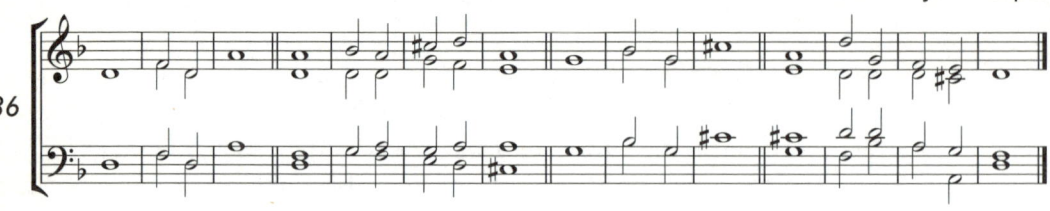

John Harper

136

21 You appointed the moon to ' mark the ' seasons, ♦
and the sun ' knows the ' time • for its ' setting.

22 You make darkness that it ' may be ' night, ♦
in which all the beasts of the ' forest ' creep ' forth.

23 The lions ' roar • for their ' prey ♦
and ' seek their ' food from ' God.

24 The sun rises and ' they are ' gone ♦
to lay themselves ' down ' in their ' dens.

25 People go ' forth • to their ' work ♦
and to their ' labour un'til the ' evening.

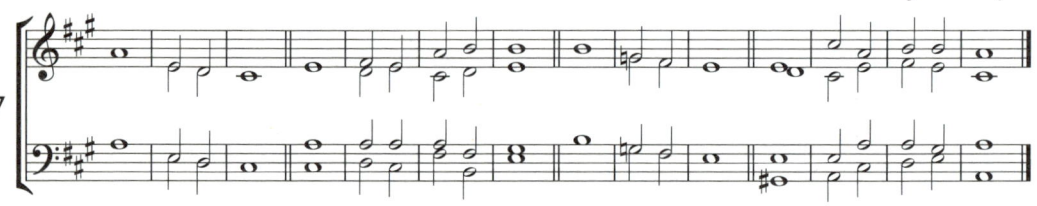

John Harper

137

26 O Lord, how manifold ' are your ' works! ♦
In wisdom you have made them all;
   the ' earth is ' full • of your ' creatures.

27 There is the sea, spread ' far and ' wide, ♦
and there move creatures beyond ' number, both ' small and ' great.

28 There go the ships, and there is ' that Le'viathan ♦
which you have ' made to ' play • in the ' deep.

29 All of these ' look to ' you ♦
to give them their ' food in ' due ' season.

30 When you give it ' them, they ' gather it; ♦
you open your hand and ' they are ' filled with ' good.

31 When you hide your face ' they are ' troubled; ♦
when you take away their breath,
   they die and re'turn a'gain • to the ' dust.

‡ 32 When you send forth your spirit, they ' are cre'ated, ♦
and you re'new the ' face • of the ' earth.

33 May the glory of the Lord en'dure for ' ever; ♦
may the ' Lord re'joice • in his ' works;

140 *Psalm 104*

34 He looks on the ' earth • and it ' trembles; ♦
    he touches the ' mountains ' and they ' smoke.

35 I will sing to the Lord as ' long as I ' live; ♦
    I will make music to my God ' while I ' have my ' being.

36 So shall my ' song ' please him ♦
    while I re'joice ' in the ' Lord.

37 Let sinners be consumed ' out of the ' earth ♦
    and the ' wicked ' be no ' more.

37a Bless the Lord, ' O my ' soul. ♦
    Alle'luia, ' Alle'luia.   [*or* Praise the ' Lord, ' praise the ' Lord.]

Psalm 105

John Soaper

1   O give thanks to the Lord and ' call up•on his ' name; ♦
    make known his ' deeds a'mong the ' peoples.

2   Sing to ' him, sing ' praises, ♦
    and tell of ' all his ' marvellous ' works.

3   Rejoice in the praise of his ' holy ' name; ♦
    let the hearts of them re'joice who ' seek the ' Lord.

4,5 Seek the Lord and his strength;
        seek his ' face con'tinually. ♦
    Remember the marvels he has done,
        his wonders and the ' judgements ' of his ' mouth,

6   O seed of ' Abraham his ' servant, ♦
    O ' children of ' Jacob his ' chosen.

7   He is the ' Lord our ' God; ♦
    his ' judgements • are in ' all the ' earth.

8   He has always been ' mindful • of his ' covenant, ♦
    the promise that he made for a ' thousand ' gene'rations:

9   The covenant he ' made with ' Abraham, ♦
    the ' oath • that he ' swore to ' Isaac,

10 Which he established as a ' statute for ' Jacob, ♦
    an everlasting ' coven'ant for ' Israel,

11 Saying, 'To you will I give the ' land of ' Canaan ♦
    to be the ' portion of ' your in'heritance.'

12 When they were but ' few in ' number, ♦
    of little account, and ' sojourners ' in the ' land,

John Soaper

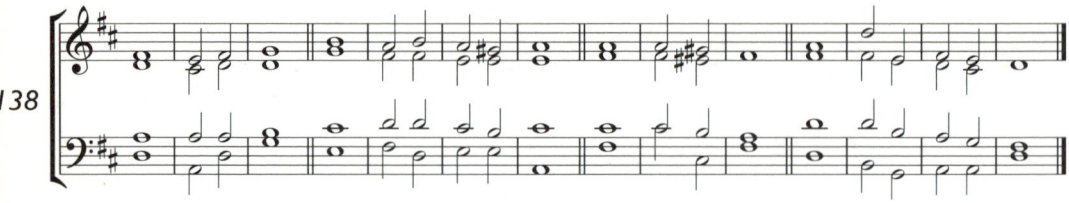

138

13 Wandering from ' nation to ' nation, ♦
from one ' kingdom • to an'other ' people,

14 He suffered no one to ' do them ' wrong ♦
and rebuked even ' kings ' for their ' sake,

15 Saying, 'Touch not ' my a'nointed ♦
and ' do my ' prophets no ' harm.'

James Turle

139

16 Then he called down famine ' over the ' land ♦
and broke ' every ' staff of ' bread.

17 But he had sent a ' man be'fore them, ♦
Joseph, ' who was ' sold • as a ' slave.

18 They shackled his ' feet with ' fetters; ♦
his ' neck was ' ringed with ' iron.

19 Until all he foretold ' came to ' pass, ♦
the ' word • of the ' Lord ' tested him.

20 The king sent ' and re'leased him; ♦
the ruler of ' peoples ' set him ' free.

21 He appointed him ' lord • of his ' household ♦
and ' ruler of ' all • he pos'sessed,

‡ 22 To instruct his princes ' as he ' willed ♦
and to ' teach his ' counsellors ' wisdom.

23 Then Israel ' came • into ' Egypt; ♦
Jacob ' sojourned • in the ' land of ' Ham.

24 And the Lord made his people ex'ceedingly ' fruitful; ♦
he made them too ' many ' for their ' adversaries,

‡ 25 Whose heart he turned, so that they ' hated his ' people ♦
and dealt ' craftily ' with his ' servants.

26 Then sent he ' Moses his ' servant ♦
and ' Aaron whom ' he had ' chosen.

27 He showed his signs ' through their ' word ♦
and his wonders ' in the ' land of ' Ham.

28 He sent darkness and ' it grew ' dark; ♦
yet they ' did not ' heed his ' words.

29 He turned their waters ' into ' blood ♦
and ' slew ' all their ' fish.

30 Their land ' swarmed with ' frogs, ♦
even ' in their ' kings' ' chambers.

31 He spoke the word, and there came ' clouds of ' flies, ♦
swarms of ' gnats within ' all their ' borders.

32 He gave them ' hailstones for ' rain ♦
and flames of ' lightning ' in their ' land.

33 He blasted their vines ' and their ' fig trees ♦
and shattered ' trees a'cross their ' country.

34 He spoke the word, and the ' grasshoppers ' came ♦
and young ' locusts ' without ' number;

35 They ate every ' plant in their ' land ♦
and de'voured the ' fruit of their ' soil.

‡ 36 He smote all the firstborn ' in their ' land, ♦
the ' first fruits of ' all their ' strength.

John Soaper

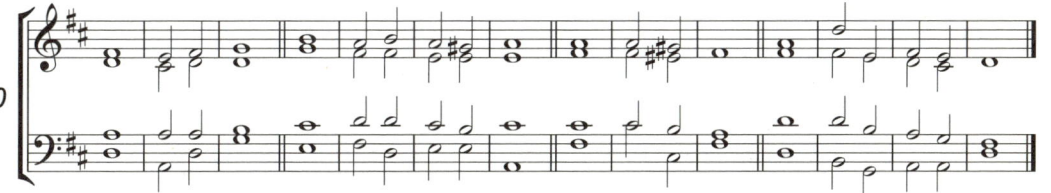

37 Then he brought them out with ' silver and ' gold; ♦
there was not one a'mong their ' tribes that ' stumbled.

38 Egypt was glad at ' their de'parting, ♦
for a ' dread of them had ' fallen up'on them.

39 He spread out a ' cloud • for a ' covering ♦
and a ' fire to ' light up the ' night.

40 They asked and he ' brought them ' quails; ♦
he satisfied them ' with the ' bread of ' heaven.

41 He opened the rock, and the waters ' gushed ' out ♦
and ran in the dry ' places ' like a ' river.

42 For he remembered his ' holy ' word ♦
and ' Abra'ham, his ' servant.

43 So he brought forth his ' people with ' joy, ♦
his ' chosen ' ones with ' singing.

44 He gave them the ' lands • of the ' nations ♦
and they took pos'session • of the ' fruit of their ' toil,

‡ 45 That they might ' keep his ' statutes ♦
and faithfully observe his ' laws.
' Alle'luia. [or ' Praise the ' Lord.]

Psalm 106

James Turle

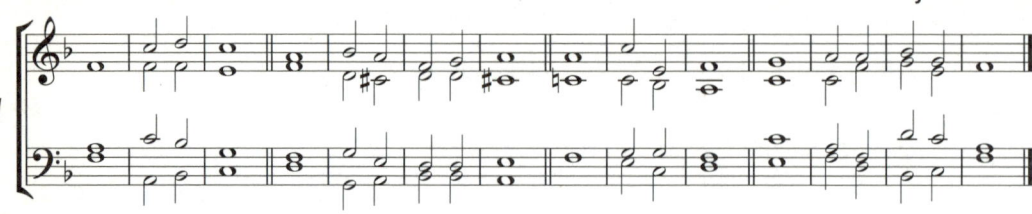
141

1 Alleluia.   [*or* Praise the Lord.]
    Give thanks to the Lord, for ' he is ' gracious, ♦
for his ' faithfulness en'dures for ' ever.

2 Who can express the mighty ' acts • of the ' Lord ♦
or ' show forth ' all his ' praise?

3 Blessed are those who ob'serve • what is ' right ♦
and ' always ' do • what is ' just.

4 Remember me, O Lord, in the favour you ' bear • for your ' people; ♦
visit me in the ' day of ' your sal'vation;

‡ 5 That I may see the prosperity of your chosen
    and rejoice in the ' gladness • of your ' people, ♦
and ex'ult with ' your in'heritance.

6 We have ' sinned • like our ' forebears; ♦
we have done ' wrong and ' dealt ' wickedly.

7 In Egypt they did not consider your wonders,
    nor remember the abundance of your ' faithful ' love; ♦
they rebelled against the Most ' High • at the ' Red ' Sea.

8 But he saved them for his ' name's ' sake, ♦
that he might ' make his ' power • to be ' known.

9 He rebuked the Red Sea and it was ' dried ' up; ♦
so he led them through the ' deep as ' through the ' wilderness.

10 He saved them from the ' adversary's ' hand ♦
and redeemed them ' from the ' hand • of the ' enemy.

11 As for those that troubled them, the waters ' over'whelmed them; ♦
there ' was not ' one of them ' left.

‡ 12 Then they be'lieved his ' words ♦
and ' sang a'loud his ' praise.

Norman Warren

142

13 But soon they for'got his ' deeds ♦
and ' would not ' wait • for his ' counsel.

14 A craving ' seized them • in the ' wilderness, ♦
   and they put ' God • to the ' test • in the ' desert.

15 He gave them ' their de'sire, ♦
   but sent a ' wasting ' sickness a'mong them.

16 They grew jealous of ' Moses • in the ' camp ♦
   and of Aaron, the ' holy one ' of the ' Lord.

17 So the earth opened and ' swallowed up ' Dathan ♦
   and covered the ' company ' of A'biram.

18 A fire was ' kindled • in their ' company; ♦
   the ' flame burnt ' up the ' wicked.

19 They made a ' calf at ' Horeb ♦
   and ' worshipped the ' molten ' image;

20 Thus they ex'changed their ' glory ♦
   for the image of an ' ox that ' feeds on ' hay.

21 They forgot ' God their ' saviour, ♦
   who had done such ' great ' things in ' Egypt,

22 Wonderful deeds in the ' land of ' Ham ♦
   and fearful things ' at the ' Red ' Sea.

‡ 23 So he would have destroyed them,
      had not Moses his chosen stood before him ' in the ' breach, ♦
   to turn a'way his ' wrath • from con'suming them.

24 Then they scorned the ' Promised ' Land ♦
   and ' would not be'lieve his ' word,

25 But ' murmured • in their ' tents ♦
   and would not ' heed the ' voice • of the ' Lord.

26 So he lifted his ' hand a'gainst them ♦
   and swore to over'throw them ' in the ' wilderness,

27 To disperse their descendants a'mong the ' nations, ♦
   and to ' scatter them through'out the ' lands.

28 They joined themselves to the ' Baal of ' Peor ♦
   and ate sacrifices ' offered ' to the ' dead.

29 They provoked him to anger with their ' evil ' deeds ♦
   and a ' plague broke ' out a'mong them.

30 Then Phinehas stood up and ' inter'ceded ♦
   and ' so the ' plague was ' stayed.

31 This was counted to ' him for ' righteousness ♦
   throughout all ' gene'rations for ' ever.

32 They angered him also at the ' waters of ' Meribah, ♦
   so that Moses ' suffered ' for their ' sake;

33 For they so em'bittered his ' spirit ♦
   that he spoke ' rash words ' with his ' lips.

Psalm 106

Norman Warren

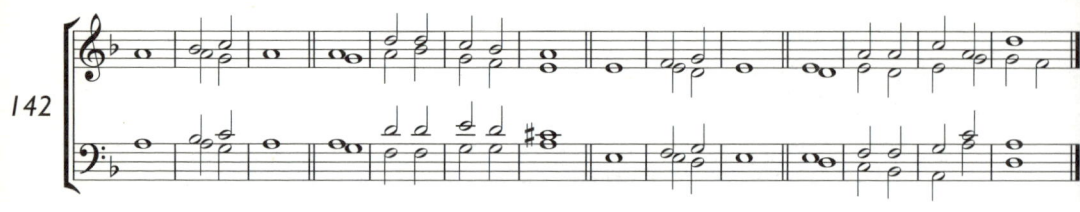

142

34 They did not des'troy the ' peoples ♦
   as the ' Lord ' had com'manded them.

35 They ' mingled • with the ' nations ♦
   and ' learned to ' follow their ' ways,

36 So that they ' worshipped their ' idols, ♦
   which be'came to ' them a ' snare.

37 Their own ' sons and ' daughters ♦
   they ' sacrificed to ' evil ' spirits.

38 They shed ' innocent ' blood, ♦
   the ' blood • of their ' sons and ' daughters,

39 Which they offered to the ' idols of ' Canaan, ♦
   and the ' land • was de'filed with ' blood.

40 Thus were they ' polluted • by their ' actions, ♦
   and in their wanton deeds went ' whoring • after ' other ' gods.

41 Therefore was the wrath of the Lord
      kindled a'gainst his ' people, ♦
   and he ab'horred ' his in'heritance.

42 He gave them over to the ' hand • of the ' nations, ♦
   and those who ' hated ' them ruled ' over them.

43 So their ' enemies op'pressed them ♦
   and put them in sub'jection ' under their ' hand.

44 Many a time did he deliver them,
      but they rebelled through their ' own de'vices ♦
   and were ' brought down ' through their ' wickedness.

45 Nevertheless, he ' saw • their ad'versity, ♦
   when he ' heard their ' lamen'tation.

46 He remembered his ' covenant ' with them ♦
   and relented according to the ' greatness • of his ' faithful ' love.

47 He made them ' also • to be ' pitied ♦
   by ' all • who had ' taken them ' captive.

James Turle

143

48 Save us, O ' Lord our ' God,
       and gather us ' from a'mong the ' nations, ♦

48a that we may give thanks to your ' holy ' name
       and ' glory ' in your ' praise.

49 Blessed be the Lord, the ' God of ' Israel,
       from everlasting ' and to ' ever'lasting; ♦

49a and let all the ' people ' say, ♦
       A'men. ' Alle'luia.   [*or* ' Praise the ' Lord.]

Psalm 107

Charles V. Stanford

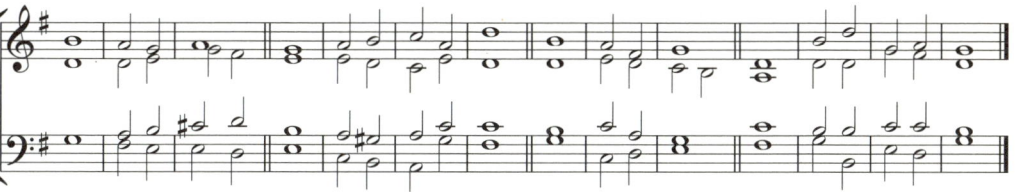

1 O give thanks to the Lord, for ' he is ' gracious, ♦
     for his steadfast ' love en'dures for ' ever.

2 Let the redeemed of the ' Lord ' say this, ♦
     those he re'deemed • from the ' hand of the ' enemy,

‡ 3 And gathered out of the lands
         from the east and ' from the ' west, ♦
       from the ' north and ' from the ' south.

4 Some went astray in ' desert ' wastes ♦
     and found no ' path • to a ' city to ' dwell in.

5 Hungry ' and ' thirsty, ♦
     their ' soul was ' fainting with'in them.

6 So they cried to the Lord ' in their ' trouble
     and he de'livered them from ' their dis'tress.

7 He set their feet on the ' right ' way ♦
     till they ' came • to a ' city to ' dwell in.

8 Let them give thanks to the ' Lord • for his ' goodness ♦
     and the ' wonders he ' does • for his ' children.

9 *For he satisfies the ' longing ' soul ♦
     and fills the ' hungry ' soul with ' good.*

10 Some sat in darkness and in the ' shadow of ' death, ♦
      bound ' fast in ' misery and ' iron,

11 For they had rebelled against the ' words of ' God ♦
      and despised the ' counsel • of the ' Most ' High.

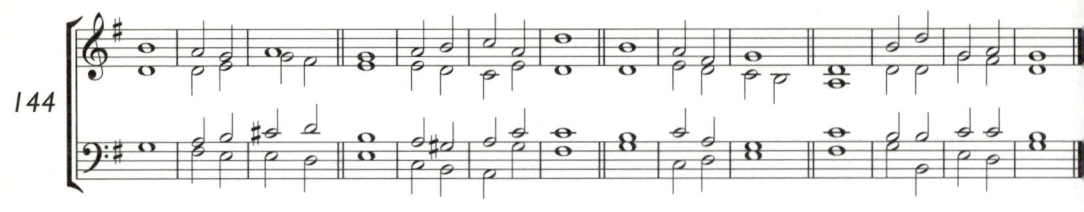

Charles V. Stanford

144

12 So he bowed down their ' heart with ' heaviness; ♦
   they stumbled and ' there was ' none to ' help them.

13 Then they cried to the ' Lord • in their ' trouble, ♦
   and he de'livered them from ' their dis'tress.

‡ 14 He brought them out of darkness and out of the ' shadow of ' death, ♦
   and ' broke their ' bonds a'sunder.

15 Let them give thanks to the ' Lord • for his ' goodness ♦
   and the ' wonders he ' does • for his ' children.

16 For he has broken the ' doors of ' bronze ♦
   and breaks the ' bars of ' iron in ' pieces.

17 Some were foolish and took a re'bellious ' way, ♦
   and were ' plagued be'cause of their ' wrongdoing.

18 Their soul abhorred all ' manner of ' food ♦
   and drew ' near • to the ' gates of ' death.

19 Then they cried to the ' Lord • in their ' trouble, ♦
   and he de'livered them from ' their dis'tress.

20 He sent forth his ' word and ' healed them, ♦
   and ' saved them ' from des'truction.

21 Let them give thanks to the ' Lord • for his ' goodness ♦
   and the ' wonders he ' does • for his ' children.

22 Let them offer him ' sacrifices of ' thanksgiving ♦
   and tell of his ' acts with ' shouts of ' joy.

23 Those who go down to the ' sea in ' ships ♦
   and ply their ' trade in ' great ' waters,

24 These have seen the ' works • of the ' Lord ♦
   and his ' wonders ' in the ' deep.

25 For at his word the stormy ' wind a'rose ♦
   and lifted ' up the ' waves of the ' sea.

26 They were carried up to the heavens
      and down a'gain • to the ' deep; ♦
   their soul ' melted a'way • in their ' peril.

27 They reeled and ' staggered • like a ' drunkard ♦
   and were ' at their ' wits' ' end.

148 Psalm 107

28 Then they cried to the ' Lord • in their ' trouble, ♦
and he brought them ' out of ' their dis'tress.

29 He made the ' storm be ' still ♦
and the ' waves of the ' sea were ' calmed.

30 Then were they glad because they ' were at ' rest, ♦
and he brought them to the ' haven ' they de'sired.

31 Let them give thanks to the ' Lord • for his ' goodness ♦
and the ' wonders he ' does • for his ' children.

32 Let them exalt him in the congre'gation • of the ' people ♦
and praise him in the ' council ' of the ' elders.

Charles V. Stanford

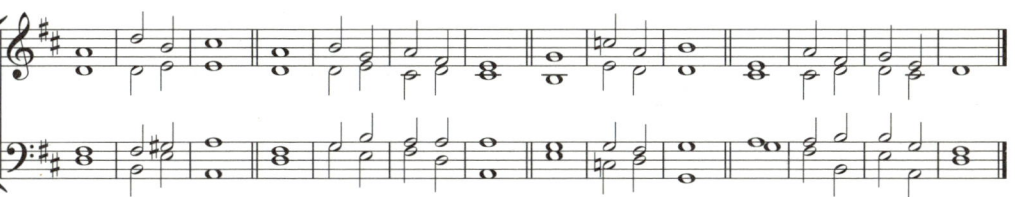

33 The Lord turns rivers ' into ' wilderness ♦
and water springs ' into ' thirsty ' ground;

34 A fruitful land he makes a ' salty ' waste, ♦
because of the ' wickedness of ' those who ' dwell there.

35 He makes the wilderness a ' pool of ' water ♦
and water springs ' out • of a ' thirsty ' land.

36 There he ' settles the ' hungry ♦
and they ' build a ' city to ' dwell in.

37 They sow fields and ' plant ' vineyards ♦
and bring ' in a ' fruitful ' harvest.

38 He blesses them, so that they ' multiply ' greatly; ♦
he does not let their ' herds of ' cattle de'crease.

39 He pours con'tempt on ' princes ♦
and makes them ' wander in ' trackless ' wastes.

40 They are diminished and ' brought ' low, ♦
through ' stress • of mis'fortune and ' sorrow,

‡ 41 But he raises the ' poor • from their ' misery ♦
and multiplies their ' families like ' flocks of ' sheep.

42 The upright will see this ' and re'joice, ♦
but all ' wickedness will ' shut its ' mouth.

43 Whoever is wise will ' ponder these ' things ♦
and consider the loving'kindness ' of the ' Lord.

Psalm 107

Psalm 108 — Noel Rawsthorne

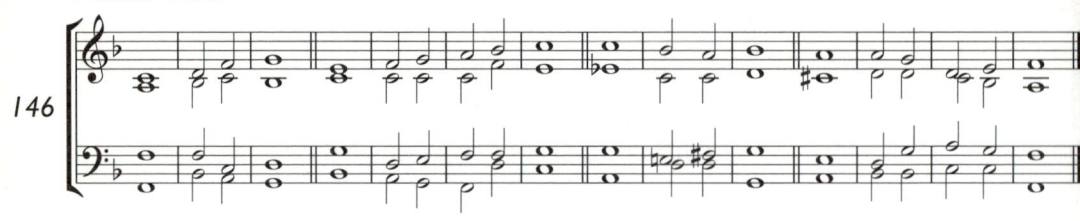

1 My heart is ready, O God, my ' heart is ' ready; ♦
  I will ' sing and ' give you ' praise.

2 Awake, my soul; awake, ' harp and ' lyre, ♦
  that I ' may a'waken the ' dawn.

3 I will give you thanks, O Lord, a'mong the ' peoples; ♦
  I will sing praise to ' you a'mong the ' nations.

4 For your loving-kindness is as ' high as the ' heavens ♦
  and your faithfulness ' reaches ' to the ' clouds.

5 Be exalted, O God, a'bove the ' heavens ♦
  and your glory ' over ' all the ' earth.

6 That your beloved may ' be de'livered, ♦
  save us by ' your right ' hand and ' answer me.

7 God has spoken ' in his ' holiness: ♦
  'I will triumph and divide Shechem
      and share ' out the ' valley of ' Succoth.

8 'Gilead is mine and Ma'nasseh is ' mine; ♦
  Ephraim is my ' helmet and ' Judah my ' sceptre.

‡ 9 'Moab shall be my wash pot,
      over Edom will I ' cast my ' sandal, ♦
      across Philistia ' will I ' shout in ' triumph.'

10 Who will lead me into the ' strong ' city? ♦
   Who will ' bring me ' into ' Edom?

11 Have you not cast us ' off, O ' God? ♦
   Will you no longer go ' forth ' with our ' troops?

12 O grant us your help a'gainst the ' enemy, ♦
   for ' earthly ' help • is in ' vain.

13 Through God will we ' do great ' acts, ♦
   for it is he that ' shall tread ' down our ' enemies.

Psalm 109

James Turle from H. Purcell

1 Keep silent no longer, O ' God of my ' praise, ♦
   for the mouth of wickedness and ' treachery
      is ' opened a'gainst me.

2 They have spoken against me with a ' lying ' tongue; ♦
   they encompassed me with words of hatred
      and fought a'gainst me with'out a ' cause.

3 In return for my love, they set them'selves a'gainst me, ♦
   even though ' I had ' prayed ' for them.

4 Thus have they repaid me with ' evil for ' good, ♦
   and ' hatred for ' my good ' will.

5 They say, 'Appoint a ' wicked man ' over him, ♦
   and let an accuser ' stand at his ' right ' hand.

6 'When he is judged, let ' him be found ' guilty, ♦
   and let his ' prayer be ' counted as ' sin.

7 'Let his ' days be ' few ♦
   and let an'other ' take his ' office.

8 'Let his ' children be ' fatherless ♦
   and his ' wife be'come a ' widow.

9 'Let his children wander to ' beg their ' bread; ♦
   let them ' seek it in ' desolate ' places.

10 'Let the creditor seize ' all • that he ' has; ♦
    let strangers ' plunder the ' fruit • of his ' toil.

11 'Let there be no one to keep ' faith ' with him, ♦
    or have compassion ' on his ' fatherless ' children.

12 'Let his line soon ' come • to an ' end ♦
    and his name be blotted ' out • in the ' next • gene'ration.

13 'Let the wickedness of his fathers
      be remembered be'fore the ' Lord, ♦
    and no sin of his ' mother be ' blotted ' out;

14 'Let their sin be always be'fore the ' Lord, ♦
    that he may ' root out their ' name • from the ' earth;

15 'Because he was not minded to ' keep ' faith, ♦
    but persecuted the poor and needy
      and sought to ' kill the ' broken'hearted.

16 'He loved cursing ' and it ' came to him; ♦
    he took no delight in ' blessing ' and it was ' far from him.

James Turle from H. Purcell

147

17 'He clothed himself with cursing | as • with a | garment: ♦
it seeped into his body like water
    and | into his | bones like | oil;

18 'Let it be to him like the cloak
    which he | wraps a|round him ♦
    and like the | belt • that he | wears con|tinually.'

‡ 19 Thus may the Lord re|pay • my ac|cusers ♦
    and | those • who speak | evil a|gainst me.

20 But deal with me, O Lord my God, ac|cording • to your | name; ♦
    O de|liver me, for | sweet • is your | faithfulness.

21 For I am | helpless and | poor ♦
    and my | heart • is dis|quieted with|in me.

22 I fade like a | shadow that | lengthens; ♦
    I am | shaken | off • like a | locust.

23 My knees are | weak through | fasting ♦
    and my | flesh is dried | up and | wasted.

‡ 24 I have become a re|proach to | them; ♦
    those who see me | shake their | heads in | scorn.

25 Help me, O | Lord my | God; ♦
    save me for your | loving | mercy's | sake,

26 And they shall know that | this is your | hand, ♦
    that | you, O | Lord, have | done it.

27 Though they curse, | may you | bless; ♦
    let those who rise up against me be confounded,
    but | let your | servant re|joice.

28 Let my accusers be | clothed • with dis|grace ♦
    and wrap themselves in their | shame as | in a | cloak.

29 I will give great thanks to the | Lord • with my | mouth; ♦
    in the midst of the | multitude | will I | praise him;

30 Because he has stood at the right hand | of the | needy, ♦
    to save them from | those who | would con|demn them.

Psalm 110
Joseph Barnby

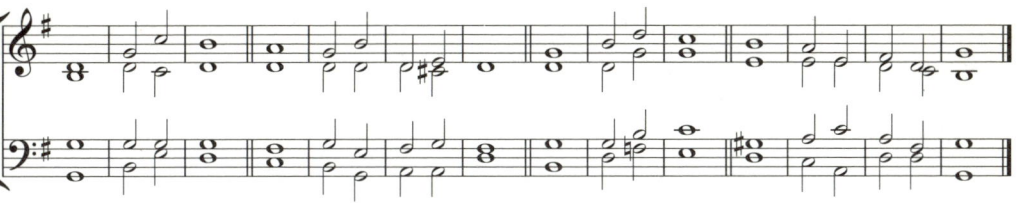

1. The Lord said to my lord, ˈ 'Sit at my ˈ right hand, ♦
   until I ˈ make your ˈ enemies your ˈ footstool.'

2. May the Lord stretch forth the ˈ sceptre • of your ˈ power; ♦
   rule from Zion ˈ in the ˈ midst • of your ˈ enemies.

3. 'Noble are you on this ˈ day of your ˈ birth; ♦
   on the holy mountain, from the womb of the dawn
      the dew of your ˈ new birth ˈ is upˈon you.'

4. The Lord has sworn and ˈ will not reˈtract: ♦
   'You are a priest for ever after the ˈ order ˈ of Melˈchizedek.'

5. The king at your ˈ right hand, O ˈ Lord, ♦
   shall smite down ˈ kings • in the ˈ day of his ˈ wrath.

6. In all his majesty, he shall judge aˈmong the ˈ nations, ♦
   smiting heads over ˈ all the ˈ wide ˈ earth.

‡ 7. He shall drink from the brook beˈside the ˈ way; ♦
   therefore ˈ shall he lift ˈ high his ˈ head.

Psalm 111
Henry T. Smart

1. Alleluia.   [*or* Praise the Lord.]
     I will give thanks to the Lord with my ˈ whole ˈ heart, ♦
   in the company of the faithful and ˈ in the ˈ congreˈgation.

2. The works of the ˈ Lord are ˈ great, ♦
   sought ˈ out by ˈ all • who deˈlight in them.

3. His work is full of ˈ majesty and ˈ honour ♦
   and his ˈ righteousness enˈdures for ˈ ever.

4. He appointed a memorial for his ˈ marvellous ˈ deeds; ♦
   the Lord is ˈ gracious and ˈ full of comˈpassion.

5. He gave food to ˈ those who ˈ feared him; ♦
   he is ever ˈ mindful ˈ of his ˈ covenant.

6. He showed his people the ˈ power • of his ˈ works ♦
   in giving them the ˈ heritage ˈ of the ˈ nations.

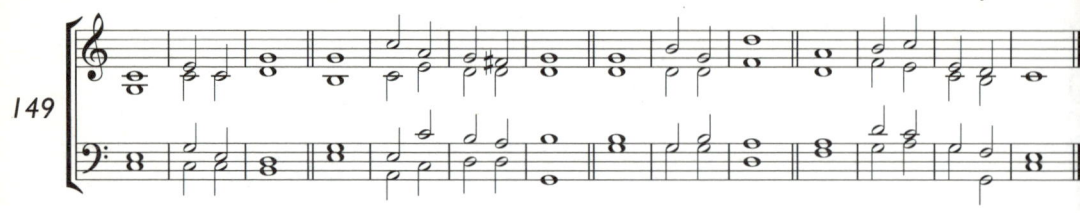

Henry T. Smart

7 The works of his hands are ' truth and ' justice; ♦
   all ' his com'mandments are ' sure.

8 They stand fast for ' ever and ' ever; ♦
   they are ' done in ' truth and ' equity.

9 He sent redemption to his people;
      he commanded his ' covenant for ' ever; ♦
   holy and ' awesome ' is his ' name.

10 The fear of the Lord is the beginning of wisdom;
      a good understanding have ' those who ' live by it; ♦
   his ' praise en'dures for ' ever.

Psalm 112

Edward J. Hopkins

1 Alleluia.   [*or* Praise the Lord.]
      Blessed are those who ' fear the ' Lord ♦
   and have great de'light in ' his com'mandments.

2 Their descendants will be ' mighty • in the ' land, ♦
   a generation of the ' faithful that ' will be ' blest.

3 Wealth and riches will be ' in their ' house, ♦
   and their ' righteousness en'dures for ' ever.

4 Light shines in the darkness ' for the ' upright; ♦
   gracious and full of com'passion ' are the ' righteous.

5 It goes well with those who are ' generous in ' lending ♦
   and order ' their af'fairs with ' justice,

6 For they will ' never be ' shaken; ♦
   the righteous will be held in ' ever'lasting re'membrance.

7 They will not be afraid of any ' evil ' tidings; ♦
   their heart is steadfast, ' trusting ' in the ' Lord.

8 Their heart is sustained and ' will not ' fear, ♦
   until they see the ' downfall ' of their ' foes.

9 They have given freely to the poor;
   their righteousness stands ' fast for ' ever; ♦
  their head will ' be ex'alted with ' honour.

10 The wicked shall see it and be angry;
   they shall gnash their ' teeth • in des'pair; ♦
  the de'sire • of the ' wicked shall ' perish.

Psalm 113

Barry Ferguson

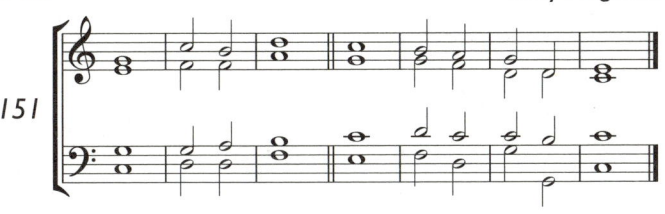

151

1 Alleluia.   [*or* Praise the Lord.]
   Give praise, you ' servants • of the ' Lord, ♦
  O ' praise the ' name • of the ' Lord.

2 Blessed be the ' name • of the ' Lord, ♦
  from this time ' forth • and for ' ever'more.

3 From the rising of the ' sun • to its ' setting ♦
  let the ' name • of the ' Lord be ' praised.

4 The Lord is high a'bove all ' nations ♦
  and his ' glory a'bove the ' heavens.

5 Who is like the ' Lord our ' God, ♦
  that ' has his ' throne so ' high,

5a Yet humbles him'self • to be'hold ♦
  the ' things of ' heaven and ' earth?

6 He raises the ' poor • from the ' dust ♦
  and lifts the ' needy ' from the ' ashes,

7 To ' set them with ' princes, ♦
  with the ' princes ' of his ' people.

8 He gives the barren woman a ' place in the ' house ♦
  and makes her a joyful mother of ' children.
     ' Alle'luia.   [*or* ' Praise the ' Lord.]

Psalm 114

Tonus Peregrinus

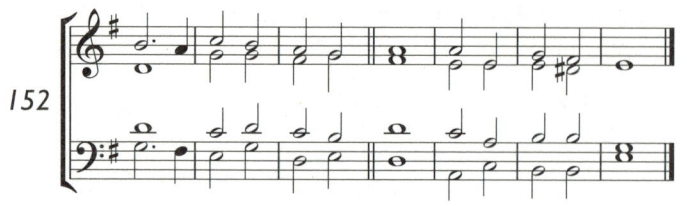

152

or

John Harper

153

1, 2 When Israel came out of Egypt,
the house of Jacob from a people of a ' strange ' tongue, ♦
Judah became his sanctuary,
' Israel ' his do'minion.

3, 4 The sea saw that, and fled;
Jordan was ' driven ' back. ♦
The mountains skipped like rams,
the little ' hills like ' young ' sheep.

5 What ailed you, O ' sea, • that you ' fled? ♦
O Jordan, that ' you were ' driven ' back?

6 You mountains, that you ' skipped like ' rams, ♦
you little ' hills like ' young ' sheep?

7 Tremble, O earth, at the ' presence • of the ' Lord, ♦
at the ' presence • of the ' God of ' Jacob,

8 Who turns the hard rock into a ' pool of ' water, ♦
the flint-stone ' into a ' springing ' well.

Psalm 115

Edward J. Hopkins

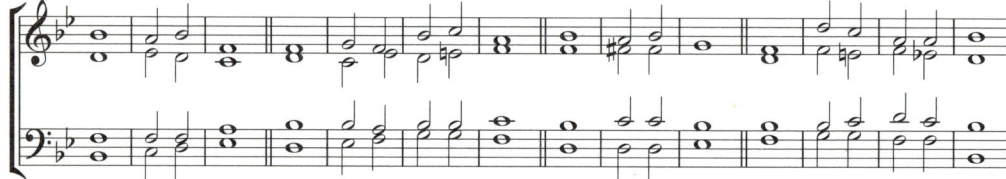

154

1 Not to us, Lord, not to us,
but to your name ' give the ' glory, ♦
for the sake of your ' loving ' mercy and ' truth.

2 Why should the ' nations ' say, ♦
'Where is ' now ' their ' God?'

3 As for our God, ' he is in ' heaven; ♦
he ' does what'ever he ' pleases.

4 Their idols are ' silver and ' gold, ♦
the ' work of ' human ' hands.

5 They have mouths, but ' cannot ' speak; ♦
eyes have ' they, but ' cannot ' see;

6 They have ears, but ' cannot ' hear; ♦
noses have ' they, but ' cannot ' smell;

7 They have hands, but cannot feel;
feet have they, but ' cannot ' walk; ♦
not a whisper ' do they ' make • from their ' throats.

8 Those who make them ' shall be'come like them ♦
and so will ' all who ' put their ' trust in them.

9 But you, Israel, put your ' trust • in the ' Lord; ♦
he is their ' help ' and their ' shield.

10 House of Aaron, ' trust • in the ' Lord; ♦
he is their ' help ' and their ' shield.

11 You that fear the Lord, ' trust • in the ' Lord; ♦
he is their ' help ' and their ' shield.

12 The Lord has been mindful of us and ' he will ' bless us; ♦
may he bless the house of Israel;
may he ' bless the ' house of ' Aaron;

13 May he bless those who ' fear the ' Lord, ♦
both ' small and ' great to'gether.

14 May the Lord increase you ' more and ' more, ♦
you ' and your ' children ' after you.

15 May you be ' blest • by the ' Lord, ♦
the ' maker of ' heaven and ' earth.

16 The heavens are the ' heavens • of the ' Lord, ♦
but the earth he has en'trusted ' to his ' children.

17 The dead do not ' praise the ' Lord, ♦
nor ' those gone ' down into ' silence;

18 But we will ' bless the ' Lord, ♦
from this time forth for ever'more.
' Alle'luia.   [or ' Praise the ' Lord.]

Psalm 116   John Robinson

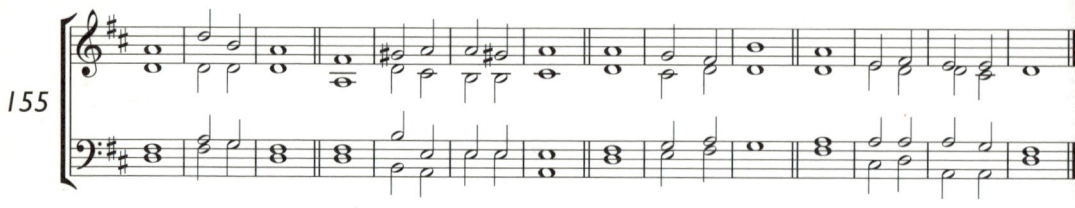

1 I love the Lord,
    for he has heard the voice of my ' suppli'cation; ♦
because he inclined his ear to me
    on the ' day I ' called to ' him.

2 The snares of death encompassed me;
    the pains of ' hell took ' hold of me; ♦
by grief and ' sorrow ' was I ' held.

3 Then I called upon the ' name • of the ' Lord: ♦
'O Lord, I ' beg you, de'liver my ' soul.'

4 Gracious is the ' Lord and ' righteous; ♦
our ' God is ' full of com'passion.

5 The Lord watches ' over the ' simple; ♦
I was brought very ' low ' and he ' saved me.

6 Turn again to your rest, ' O my ' soul, ♦
for the ' Lord • has been ' gracious to ' you.

7 For you have delivered my ' soul from ' death, ♦
my eyes from ' tears • and my ' feet from ' falling.

8 I will walk be'fore the ' Lord ♦
in the ' land ' of the ' living.

9 I believed that I should perish
    for I was ' sorely ' troubled; ♦
and I said in my alarm, ' 'Everyone ' is a ' liar.'

10 How shall I re'pay the ' Lord ♦
for all the benefits ' he has ' given to ' me?

11 I will lift up the ' cup of sal'vation ♦
and ' call upon the ' name • of the ' Lord.

12 I will fulfil my ' vows • to the ' Lord ♦
in the ' presence of ' all his ' people.

13 Precious in the ' sight • of the ' Lord ♦
is the ' death • of his ' faithful 'servants.

14 O Lord, ' I am your ' servant, ♦
your servant, the child of your handmaid;
    you have ' freed me ' from my ' bonds.

15 I will offer to you a ' sacrifice of ' thanksgiving ♦
and ' call upon the ' name • of the ' Lord.

16 I will fulfil my ' vows • to the ' Lord ♦
in the ' presence of ' all his ' people,

‡ 17 In the courts of the ' house • of the ' Lord, ♦
in the midst of you, O Je'rusalem.
' Alle'luia.   [*or* ' Praise the ' Lord.]

Psalm 117

James Nares

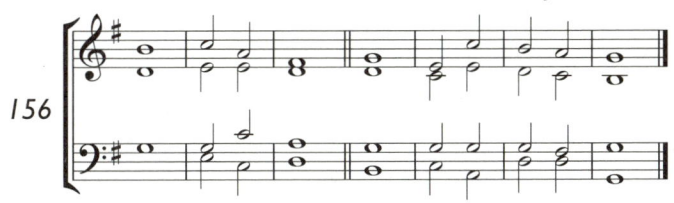

156

1 O praise the Lord, ' all you ' nations; ♦
praise ' him, ' all you ' peoples.

2 For great is his steadfast ' love to'wards us, ♦
and the faithfulness of the Lord endures for ' ever.
' Alle'luia.   [*or* ' Praise the ' Lord.]

Psalm 118

John Camidge, jun.

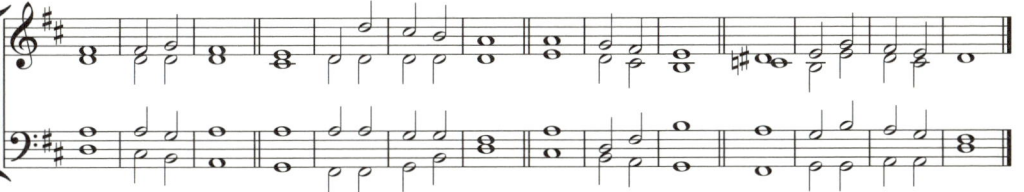

1 O give thanks to the Lord, for ' he is ' good; ♦
his ' mercy en'dures for ' ever.

2 Let Israel ' now pro'claim, ♦
'His ' mercy en'dures for ' ever.'

3 Let the house of Aaron ' now pro'claim, ♦
'His ' mercy en'dures for ' ever.'

4 Let those who fear the ' Lord pro'claim, ♦
'His ' mercy en'dures for ' ever.'

5 In my constraint I ' called • to the ' Lord; ♦
the Lord ' answered and ' set me ' free.

6 The Lord is at my side; I ' will not ' fear; ♦
what can ' flesh ' do to ' me?

John Camidge, jun.

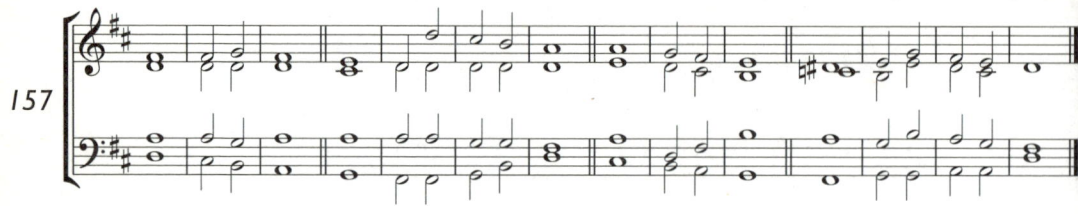

7 With the Lord at my ' side • as my ' saviour, ♦
   I shall see the ' downfall ' of my ' enemies.

8 It is better to take ' refuge • in the ' Lord ♦
   than to put ' any ' confidence in ' flesh.

9 It is better to take ' refuge • in the ' Lord ♦
   than to put ' any ' confidence in ' princes.

10 All the ' nations en'compassed me, ♦
   but by the name of the ' Lord I ' drove them ' back.

11 They hemmed me in, they hemmed me in on ' every ' side, ♦
   but by the name of the ' Lord I ' drove them ' back.

12 They swarmed about me like bees;
       they blazed like ' fire among ' thorns, ♦
   but by the name of the ' Lord I ' drove them ' back.

‡ 13 Surely, I was ' thrust • to the ' brink, ♦
   but the ' Lord ' came • to my ' help.

John Goss

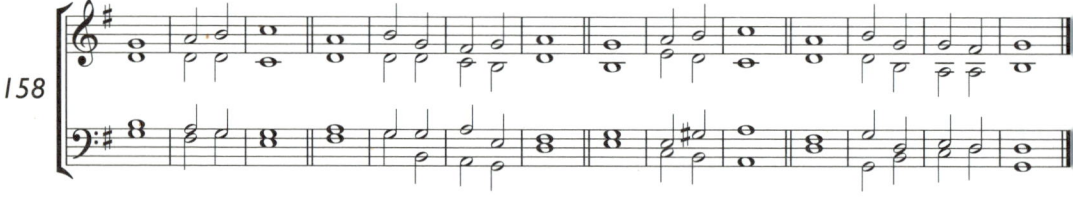

14 The Lord is my ' strength • and my ' song, ♦
   and he has be'come ' my sal'vation.

15 Joyful ' shouts • of sal'vation ♦
   sound ' from the ' tents • of the ' righteous:

‡ 16 'The right hand of the Lord does mighty deeds;
       the right hand of the Lord ' raises ' up; ♦
   the right hand of the ' Lord does ' mighty ' deeds.'

17 I shall not ' die, but ' live ♦
   and de'clare the ' works • of the ' Lord.

18 The Lord has ' punished me ' sorely, ♦
   but he has not ' given me ' over to ' death.

19 Open to me the ' gates of ' righteousness, ♦
that I may ' enter • and give ' thanks • to the ' Lord.

20 This is the ' gate • of the ' Lord; ♦
the ' righteous shall ' enter ' through it.

21 I will give thanks to you, for ' you have ' answered me ♦
and have be'come ' my sal'vation.

22 The stone which the ' builders re'jected ♦
has be'come the ' chief ' cornerstone.

‡ 23 This is the ' Lord's ' doing, ♦
and it is ' marvellous ' in our ' eyes.

24 This is the day that the ' Lord has ' made; ♦
we will re'joice ' and be ' glad in it.

25 Come, O Lord, and ' save us we ' pray. ♦
Come, Lord, ' send us ' now pros'perity.

26 Blessed is he who comes in the ' name • of the ' Lord; ♦
we ' bless you • from the ' house • of the ' Lord.

27 The Lord is God; he has ' given us ' light; ♦
link the pilgrims with cords
   ' right • to the ' horns • of the ' altar.

28 You are my God and ' I will ' thank you; ♦
you are my ' God and ' I • will ex'alt you.

29 O give thanks to the Lord, for ' he is ' good; ♦
his ' mercy en'dures for ' ever.

Psalm 118 161

Psalm 119

Noel Rawsthorne

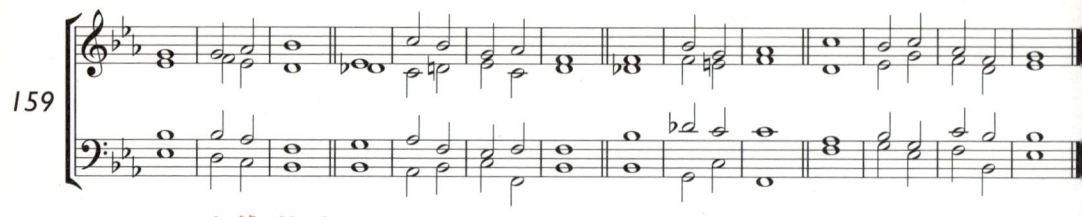

159

1 א Aleph

1 Blessed are those whose ' way is ' pure, ♦
  who ' walk • in the ' law of the ' Lord.

2 Blessed are those who ' keep his ' testimonies ♦
  and ' seek him • with their ' whole ' heart,

3 Those who ' do no ' wickedness, ♦
  but ' walk in ' his ' ways.

4 You, O ' Lord, have ' charged ♦
  that we should ' diligently ' keep • your com'mandments.

5 O that my ways were made ' so di'rect ♦
  that ' I might ' keep your ' statutes.

6 Then should I not be ' put to ' shame, ♦
  because I have re'gard for ' all • your com'mandments.

7 I will thank you with an ' unfeigned ' heart, ♦
  when I have ' learned your ' righteous ' judgements.

8 I will ' keep your ' statutes; ♦
  O for'sake me ' not ' utterly.

2 ב Beth

9 How shall young people ' cleanse their ' way ♦
  to keep themselves ac'cording ' to your ' word?

10 With my whole heart ' have I ' sought you; ♦
   O let me not go a'stray from ' your com'mandments.

11 Your words have I hidden with'in my ' heart, ♦
   that I ' should not ' sin a'gainst you.

12 Blessed are ' you, O ' Lord; ♦
   O ' teach ' me your ' statutes.

13 With my lips have ' I been ' telling ♦
   of all the ' judgements ' of your ' mouth.

14 I have taken greater delight in the ' way of your ' testimonies ♦
   than ' in all ' manner of ' riches.

15 I will meditate on ' your com'mandments ♦
   and ' contem'plate your ' ways.

16 My delight shall be ' in your ' statutes ♦
   and I will ' not for'get your ' word.

John Foster

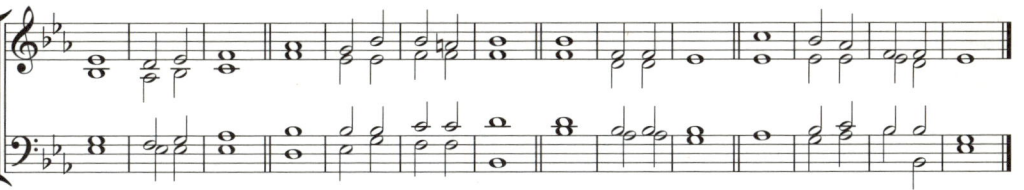

3 ג Gimel

17 O do good to your servant that ' I may ' live, ♦
and ' so • shall I ' keep your ' word.

18 Open my eyes, that ' I may ' see ♦
the ' wonders ' of your ' law.

19 I am a ' stranger • upon ' earth; ♦
hide not ' your com'mandments ' from me.

20 My soul is con'sumed at ' all times ♦
with fervent ' longing ' for your ' judgements.

21 You have re'buked the ' arrogant; ♦
cursed are those who ' stray from ' your com'mandments.

22 Turn from me ' shame • and re'buke, ♦
for ' I have ' kept your ' testimonies.

23 Rulers also sit and ' speak a'gainst me, ♦
but your servant ' meditates ' on your ' statutes.

24 For your testimonies are ' my de'light; ♦
they ' are my ' faithful ' counsellors.

4 ד Daleth

25 My soul ' cleaves • to the ' dust; ♦
O give me life ac'cording ' to your ' word.

26 I have acknowledged my ways and ' you have ' answered me; ♦
O ' teach ' me your ' statutes.

27 Make me understand the way of ' your com'mandments, ♦
and so shall I meditate ' on your ' wondrous ' works.

28 My soul melts away in ' tears of ' sorrow; ♦
raise me up ac'cording ' to your ' word.

29 Take from me the ' way of ' falsehood; ♦
be ' gracious to ' me • through your ' law.

30 I have chosen the ' way of ' truth ♦
and your judgements ' have I ' laid be'fore me.

31 I hold ' fast • to your ' testimonies; ♦
O Lord, let me ' not be ' put to ' shame.

32 I will run the way of ' your com'mandments, ♦
when you have ' set my ' heart at ' liberty.

Psalm 119

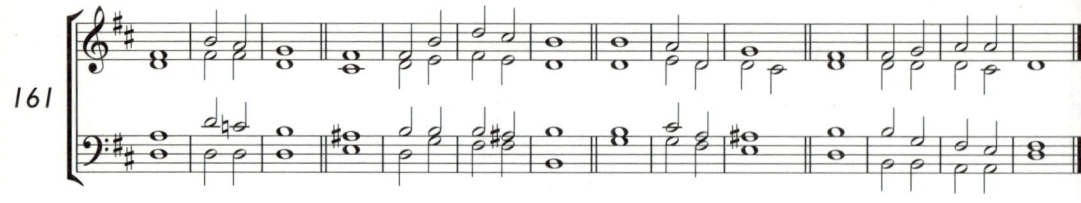

Haydn Keeton

5 ה He

33 Teach me, O Lord, the | way of your | statutes ♦
and I shall | keep it | to the | end.

34 Give me understanding and I shall | keep your | law; ♦
I shall | keep it • with my | whole | heart.

35 Lead me in the path of | your com|mandments, ♦
for there|in is | my de|light.

36 Incline my | heart • to your | testimonies ♦
and | not to | unjust | gain.

37 Turn away my eyes lest they | gaze on | vanities; ♦
O | give me | life • in your | ways.

38 Confirm to your | servant your | promise, ♦
which | stands for | all who | fear you.

39 Turn away the reproach | which I | dread, ♦
be|cause your | judgements are | good.

40 Behold, I long for | your com|mandments; ♦
in your | righteousness | give me | life.

6 ו Waw

41 Let your faithful love come unto | me, O | Lord, ♦
even your salvation, ac|cording | to your | promise.

42 Then shall I answer | those who | taunt me, ♦
for my | trust is | in your | word.

43 O take not the word of truth utterly | out of my | mouth, ♦
for my | hope is | in your | judgements.

44 So shall I always | keep your | law; ♦
I shall | keep it for | ever and | ever.

45 I will | walk at | liberty, ♦
because I | study | your com|mandments.

46 I will tell of your testimonies, | even before | kings, ♦
and | will not | be a|shamed.

47 My delight shall | be in • your com|mandments, ♦
which | I have | greatly | loved.

48 My hands will I lift up to your commandments, | which I | love, ♦
and I will | meditate | on your | statutes.

Robert Cooke

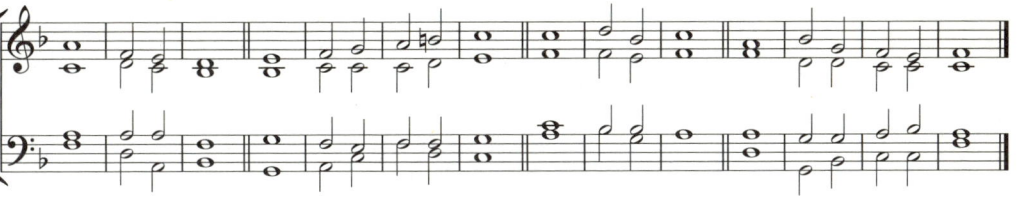

7 ז Zayin

49 Remember your ' word • to your ' servant, ♦
   on which ' you have ' built my ' hope.

50 This is my comfort ' in my ' trouble, ♦
   that your ' promise ' gives me ' life.

51 The proud have de'rided me ' cruelly, ♦
   but I have not ' turned a'side from your ' law.

52 I have remembered your everlasting ' judgements, O ' Lord, ♦
   and ' have ' been ' comforted.

53 I am seized with indig'nation • at the ' wicked, ♦
   for ' they • have for'saken your ' law.

54 Your statutes have ' been like ' songs to me ♦
   in the ' house ' of my ' pilgrimage.

55 I have thought on your name in the ' night, O ' Lord, ♦
   and ' so • have I ' kept your ' law.

56 These blessings ' have been ' mine, ♦
   for ' I have ' kept • your com'mandments.

8 ח Heth

57 You only are my ' portion, O ' Lord; ♦
   I have ' promised to ' keep your ' words.

58 I entreat you with ' all my ' heart, ♦
   be merciful to me ac'cording ' to your ' promise.

59 I have con'sidered my ' ways ♦
   and turned my ' feet ' back • to your ' testimonies.

60 I made haste and ' did not de'lay ♦
   to ' keep ' your com'mandments.

61 Though the cords of the ' wicked en'tangle me, ♦
   I do ' not for'get your ' law.

62 At midnight I will rise to ' give you ' thanks, ♦
   be'cause of your ' righteous ' judgements.

63 I am a companion of all ' those who ' fear you, ♦
   those who ' keep ' your com'mandments.

64 The earth, O Lord, is full of your ' faithful ' love; ♦
   in'struct me ' in your ' statutes.

Psalm 119

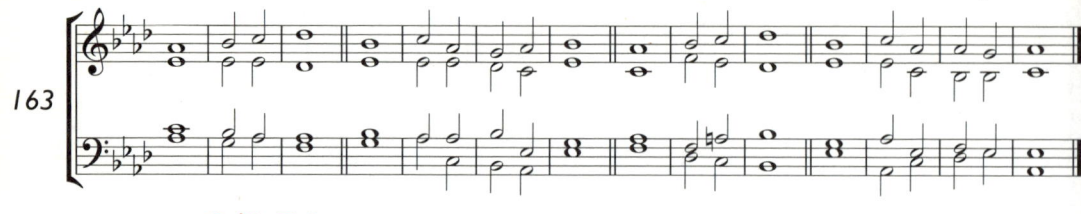

John Goss

163

9 ט Teth

65 You have dealt graciously ' with your ' servant, ♦
ac'cording • to your ' word, O ' Lord.

66 O teach me true under'standing and ' knowledge, ♦
for I have ' trusted in ' your com'mandments.

67 Before I was afflicted I ' went a'stray, ♦
but ' now I ' keep your ' word.

68 You are gracious ' and do ' good; ♦
O ' Lord, ' teach me your ' statutes.

69 The proud have ' smeared me with ' lies, ♦
but I will keep your com'mandments • with my ' whole ' heart.

70 Their heart has become ' gross with ' fat, ♦
but my de'light is ' in your ' law.

71 It is good for me that I have ' been af'flicted, ♦
that ' I may ' learn your ' statutes.

72 The law of your mouth is ' dearer to ' me ♦
than a ' hoard of ' gold and ' silver.

10 י Yodh

73 Your hands have ' made me and ' fashioned me; ♦
give me understanding, that ' I may ' learn • your com'mandments.

74 Those who fear you will be glad ' when they ' see me, ♦
because ' I have ' hoped • in your ' word.

75 I know, O Lord, that your ' judgements are ' right, ♦
and that in very faithfulness you ' caused me ' to be ' troubled.

76 Let your faithful love ' be my ' comfort, ♦
according to your ' promise ' to your ' servant.

77 Let your tender mercies come to me, that ' I may ' live, ♦
for your ' law is ' my de'light.

78 Let the proud be put to shame, for they ' wrong me with ' lies; ♦
but I will ' meditate on ' your com'mandments.

79 Let those who fear you ' turn to ' me, ♦
even ' those who ' know your ' testimonies.

80 Let my heart be ' sound • in your ' statutes, ♦
that I may ' not be ' put to ' shame.

Psalm 119

Kellow J. Pye

11 כ Kaph

81 My soul is pining for ' your sal'vation; ♦
I have ' hoped ' in your ' word.

82 My eyes fail with ' watching • for your ' word, ♦
while I ' say, 'O ' when will you ' comfort me?'

83 I have become like a wineskin ' in the ' smoke, ♦
yet I do ' not for'get your ' statutes.

84 How many are the ' days of your ' servant? ♦
When will you bring ' judgement on ' those who ' persecute me?

85 The proud ' have dug ' pits for me ♦
in de'fiance ' of your ' law.

86 All your com'mandments are ' true; ♦
help me, for they ' persecute ' me with ' falsehood.

87 They had almost made an ' end of me on ' earth, ♦
but I have not for'saken ' your com'mandments.

88 Give me life according to your ' loving'kindness; ♦
so shall I keep the ' testi•monies ' of your ' mouth.

12 ל Lamedh

89 O Lord, your word is ' ever'lasting; ♦
it ever stands ' firm ' in the ' heavens.

90 Your faithfulness also remains from one gene'ration • to an'other; ♦
you have established the ' earth and ' it a'bides.

91 So also your judgements stand ' firm this ' day, ♦
for ' all things ' are your ' servants.

92 If your law had not been ' my de'light, ♦
I should have ' perished ' in my ' trouble.

93 I will never for'get • your com'mandments, ♦
for by ' them • you have ' given me ' life.

94 I am ' yours, O ' save me! ♦
For ' I have ' sought • your com'mandments.

95 The wicked have waited for me ' to des'troy me, ♦
but I will ' meditate ' on your ' testimonies.

96 I have seen an end of ' all per'fection, ♦
but your com'mandment ' knows no ' bounds.

Psalm 119

William Havergal

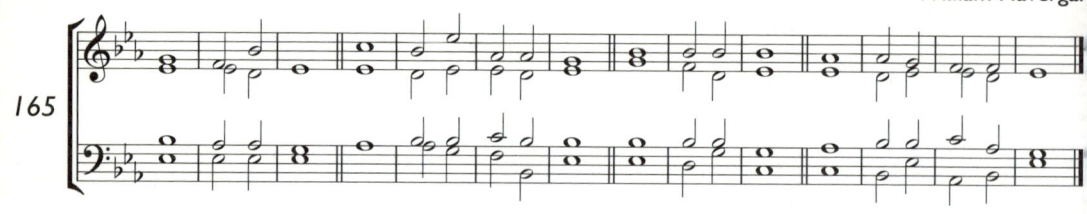

165

13 מ Mem

97 Lord, how I ' love your ' law! ♦
All the day ' long it ' is my ' study.

98 Your commandments have made me ' wiser • than my ' enemies, ♦
for ' they are ' ever ' with me.

99 I have more understanding than ' all my ' teachers, ♦
for your testimonies ' are my ' medi'tation.

100 I am ' wiser • than the ' aged, ♦
be'cause I ' keep • your com'mandments.

101 I restrain my feet from every ' evil ' way, ♦
that ' I may ' keep your ' word.

102 I have not turned a'side • from your ' judgements, ♦
for ' you have ' been my ' teacher.

103 How sweet are your ' words • on my ' tongue! ♦
They are sweeter than ' honey ' to my ' mouth.

104 Through your commandments I get ' under'standing; ♦
therefore I ' hate all ' lying ' ways.

14 נ Nun

105 Your word is a ' lantern • to my ' feet ♦
and a ' light up'on my ' path.

106 I have sworn and ' will ful'fil it, ♦
to ' keep your ' righteous ' judgements.

107 I am ' troubled • above ' measure; ♦
give me life, O Lord, ac'cording ' to your ' word.

108 Accept the freewill offering of my ' mouth, O ' Lord, ♦
and ' teach ' me your ' judgements.

109 My soul is ' ever • in my ' hand, ♦
yet I do ' not for'get your ' law.

110 The wicked have ' laid a ' snare for me, ♦
but I have not ' strayed from ' your com'mandments.

111 Your testimonies have I claimed as my ' heritage for ' ever; ♦
for they are the ' very ' joy • of my ' heart.

112 I have applied my heart to ful'fil your ' statutes: ♦
always, ' even ' to the ' end.

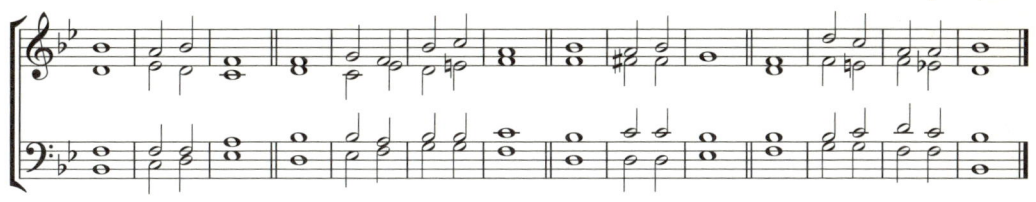

Edward J. Hopkins

15 ס Samekh

113 I hate those who are ' double ' minded, ♦
 but your ' law ' do I ' love.

114 You are my hiding place ' and my ' shield ♦
 and my ' hope is ' in your ' word.

115 Away from ' me, you ' wicked! ♦
 I will keep the com ' mandments ' of my ' God.

116 Sustain me according to your promise, that ' I may ' live, ♦
 and let me not be disap ' pointed ' in my ' hope.

117 Hold me up and ' I shall be ' saved, ♦
 and my delight shall be ' ever ' in your ' statutes.

118 You set at nought those who de ' part • from your ' statutes, ♦
 for their de ' ceiving ' is in ' vain.

119 You consider all the ' wicked as ' dross; ♦
 there ' fore I ' love your ' testimonies.

120 My flesh ' trembles for ' fear of you ♦
 and ' I am a ' fraid • of your ' judgements.

16 ע Ayin

121 I have done what is ' just and ' right; ♦
 O give me not ' over to ' my op ' pressors.

122 Stand surety for your ' servant's ' good; ♦
 let ' not the ' proud op ' press me.

123 My eyes fail with watching for ' your sal ' vation ♦
 and ' for your ' righteous ' promise.

124 O deal with your servant according to your ' faithful ' love ♦
 and ' teach ' me your ' statutes.

125 I am your servant; O grant me ' under ' standing, ♦
 that ' I may ' know your ' testimonies.

126 It is time for you to ' act, O ' Lord, ♦
 for ' they frus ' trate your ' law.

127 Therefore I ' love • your com ' mandments ♦
 above gold, ' even ' much fine ' gold.

128 Therefore I direct my steps by ' all your ' precepts, ♦
 and all false ' ways I ' utterly ab ' hor.

Psalm 119

John Jones

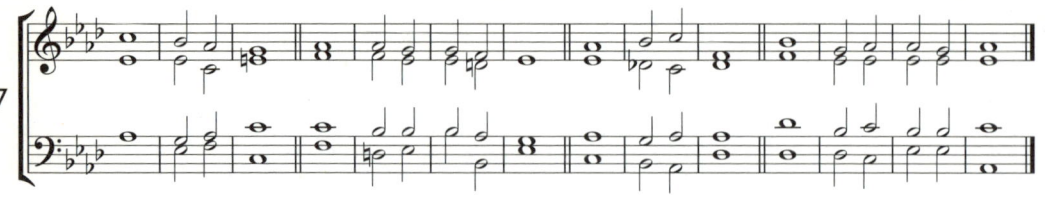

167

17 פ Pe

129 Your ' testimonies are ' wonderful; ♦
    there'fore my ' soul ' keeps them.

130 The opening of your ' word gives ' light; ♦
    it gives under'standing ' to the ' simple.

131 I open my mouth and ' draw in my ' breath, ♦
    as I ' long for ' your com'mandments.

132 Turn to me and be ' gracious ' to me, ♦
    as is your way with ' those who ' love your ' name.

133 Order my ' steps • by your ' word, ♦
    and let no wickedness ' have do'minion ' over me.

134 Redeem me from ' earthly op'pressors ♦
    so that ' I may ' keep • your com'mandments.

135 Show the light of your countenance up'on your ' servant ♦
    and ' teach ' me your ' statutes.

136 My eyes run down with ' streams of ' water, ♦
    because the wicked ' do not ' keep your ' law.

18 צ Tsadhe

137 Righteous are ' you, O ' Lord, ♦
    and ' true ' are your ' judgements.

138 You have ' ordered • your de'crees ♦
    in ' righteousness and ' in great ' faithfulness.

139 My indig'nation des'troys me, ♦
    because my ' adversaries for'get your ' word.

140 Your word has been ' tried • to the ' uttermost ♦
    and ' so your ' servant ' loves it.

141 I am small and of ' no • repu'tation, ♦
    yet do I ' not for'get • your com'mandments.

142 Your righteousness is an ever'lasting ' righteousness ♦
    and your ' law ' is the ' truth.

143 Trouble and heaviness have taken ' hold up'on me, ♦
    yet my de'light • is in ' your com'mandments.

144 The righteousness of your testimonies is ' ever'lasting; ♦
    O grant me under'standing and ' I shall ' live.

Joseph Barnby

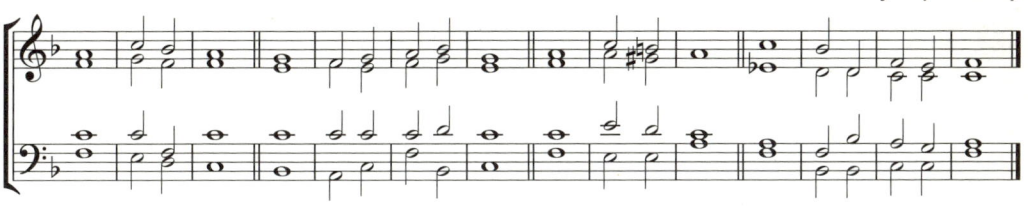

19 ק Qoph

145 I call with my ' whole ' heart; ♦
answer me, O Lord, that ' I may ' keep your ' statutes.

146 To you I ' call, O ' save me! ♦
And ' I shall ' keep your ' testimonies.

147 Early in the morning I ' cry to ' you, ♦
for ' in your ' word • is my ' trust.

148 My eyes are open before the ' night ' watches, ♦
that I may ' meditate ' on your ' word.

149 Hear my voice, O Lord, according to your ' faithful ' love; ♦
according to your ' judgement, ' give me ' life.

150 They draw near that in ' malice ' persecute me, ♦
who are ' far ' from your ' law.

151 You, O Lord, are ' near at ' hand, ♦
and ' all • your com'mandments are ' true.

152 Long have I ' known • of your ' testimonies, ♦
that you have ' founded ' them for ' ever.

20 ר Resh

153 O consider my af'fliction • and de'liver me, ♦
for I do ' not for'get your ' law.

154 Plead my ' cause • and re'deem me; ♦
according to your ' promise, ' give me ' life.

155 Salvation is ' far • from the ' wicked, ♦
for they ' do not ' seek your ' statutes.

156 Great is your com'passion, O ' Lord; ♦
give me life, ac'cording ' to your ' judgements.

157 Many there are that persecute ' and op'press me, ♦
yet do I not ' swerve ' from your ' testimonies.

158 It grieves me when I ' see the ' treacherous, ♦
for they ' do not ' keep your ' word.

159 Consider, O Lord, how I ' love • your com'mandments; ♦
give me life ac'cording • to your ' loving'kindness.

160 The sum of your ' word is ' truth, ♦
and all your righteous judgements en'dure for ' ever'more.

Psalm 119

J. L. Rogers

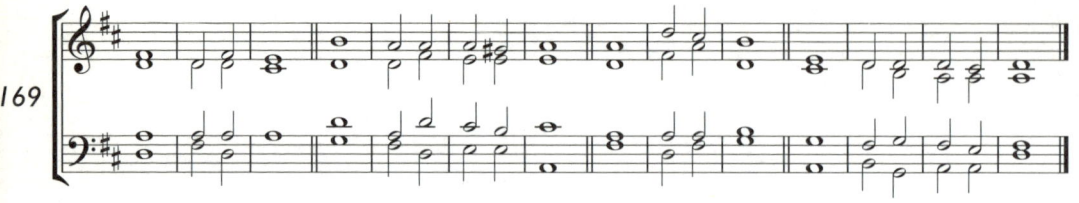

169

21 ש Shin

161 Princes have persecuted me with'out a ' cause, ♦
    but my heart ' stands in ' awe of your ' word.

162 I am as ' glad of your ' word ♦
    as ' one who ' finds great ' spoils.

163 As for lies, I ' hate • and ab'hor them, ♦
    but your ' law ' do I ' love.

164 Seven times a day ' do I ' praise you, ♦
    be'cause of your ' righteous ' judgements.

165 Great peace have they who ' love your ' law; ♦
    nothing ' shall ' make them ' stumble.

166 Lord, I have looked for ' your sal'vation ♦
    and ' I have ful'filled • your com'mandments.

167 My soul has ' kept your ' testimonies ♦
    and ' greatly ' have I ' loved them.

168 I have kept your com'mandments and ' testimonies, ♦
    for ' all my ' ways • are be'fore you.

22 ת Taw

169 Let my cry come be'fore you, O ' Lord; ♦
    give me understanding, ac'cording ' to your ' word.

170 Let my supplication ' come be'fore you; ♦
    deliver me, ac'cording ' to your ' promise.

171 My lips shall pour ' forth your ' praise, ♦
    when ' you have ' taught me your ' statutes.

172 My tongue shall ' sing of your ' word, ♦
    for ' all • your com'mandments are ' righteous.

173 Let your hand reach ' out to ' help me, ♦
    for I have ' chosen ' your com'mandments.

174 I have longed for your sal'vation, O ' Lord, ♦
    and your ' law is ' my de'light.

175 Let my soul live and ' it shall ' praise you, ♦
    and let your ' judgements ' be my ' help.

176 I have gone astray like a ' sheep • that is ' lost; ♦
    O seek your servant, for I do ' not for'get • your com'mandments.

Psalm 120

Joseph Barnby

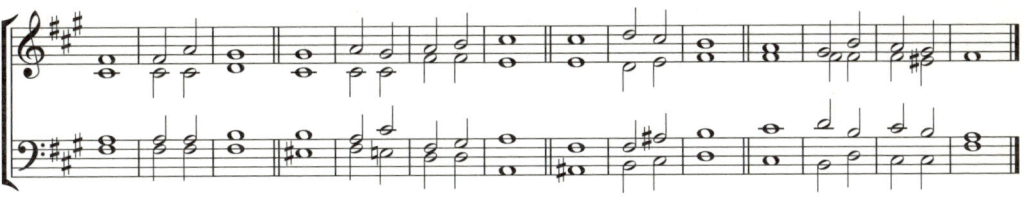

1 When I was in trouble I ' called • to the ' Lord; ♦
   I ' called • to the ' Lord ' and he ' answered me.

2 Deliver me, O Lord, from ' lying ' lips ♦
   and ' from a de'ceitful ' tongue.

3 What shall be ' given ' to you? ♦
   What more shall be done to ' you, de'ceitful ' tongue?

4 The ' sharp ' arrows ♦
   of a warrior, ' tempered in ' burning ' coals!

5 Woe is me, that I must ' lodge in ' Meshech ♦
   and ' dwell a•mong the ' tents of ' Kedar.

6,7 My soul has dwelt too long with ' enemies of ' peace. ♦
     I am for making peace,
     but when I speak of it, ' they make ' ready for ' war.

Psalm 121

H. Walford Davies

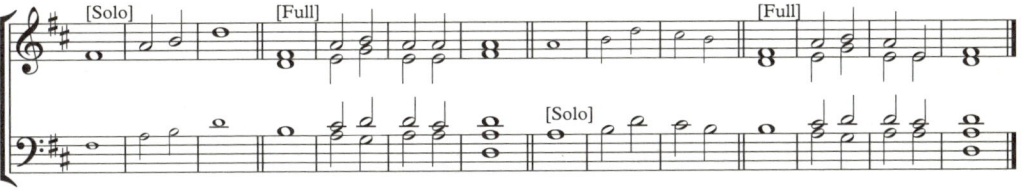

or

Stanley Vann

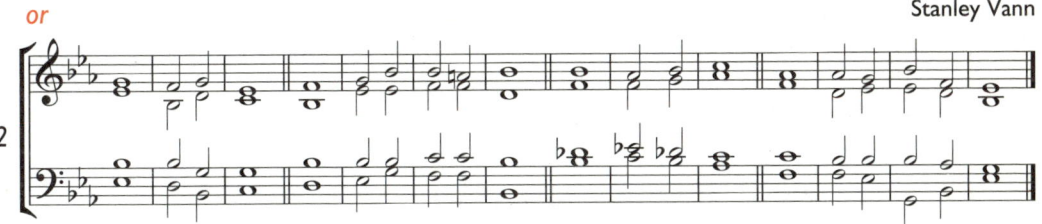

1 I lift up my ' eyes • to the ' hills; ♦
   from ' where • is my ' help to ' come?

2 My help ' comes • from the ' Lord, ♦
   the ' maker of ' heaven and ' earth.

3 He will not suffer your ' foot to ' stumble; ♦
   he who watches ' over you ' will not ' sleep.

4 Behold, he who keeps ' watch • over ' Israel ♦
   shall ' neither ' slumber nor ' sleep.

H. Walford Davies

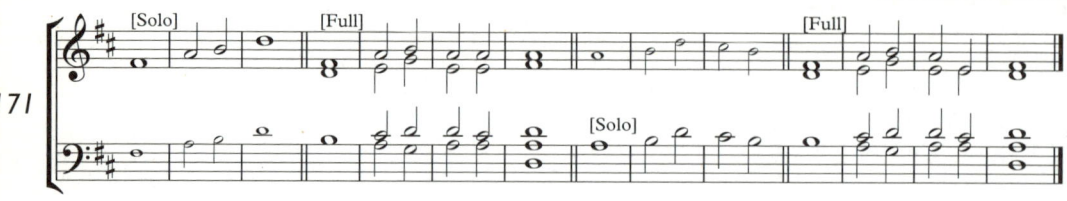

or

Stanley Vann

5 The Lord himself ' watches ' over you; ♦
   the Lord is your ' shade at ' your right ' hand,

6 So that the sun shall not ' strike you by ' day, ♦
   nei'ther the ' moon by ' night.

7 The Lord shall keep you ' from all ' evil; ♦
   it is ' he • who shall ' keep your ' soul.

8 The Lord shall keep watch over your going out
         and your ' coming ' in, ♦
   from this time ' forth for ' ever'more.

Psalm 122

Joseph Barnby

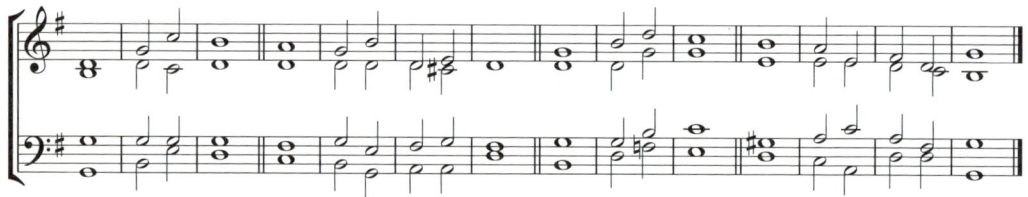

1 I was glad when they ' said to ' me, ♦
   'Let us ' go • to the ' house of the ' Lord.'

2 And now our ' feet are ' standing ♦
   within your ' gates, ' O Je'rusalem;

3 Jerusalem, ' built • as a ' city ♦
   that is at ' unity ' in it'self.

4 Thither the tribes go up, the ' tribes • of the ' Lord, ♦
   as is decreed for Israel,
         to give ' thanks • to the ' name of the ' Lord.

‡ 5 For there are set the ' thrones of ' judgement, ♦
   the ' thrones • of the ' house of ' David.

6 O pray for the ' peace • of Je'rusalem: ♦
   'May they ' prosper who ' love ' you.

7 'Peace be with'in your ' walls ♦
   and tran'quillity with'in your ' palaces.'

8 For my kindred and com'panions' ' sake, ♦
   I will ' pray that ' peace be ' with you.

9 For the sake of the house of the ' Lord our ' God, ♦
   I will ' seek to ' do you ' good.

Psalm 123

Jonathan Battishill

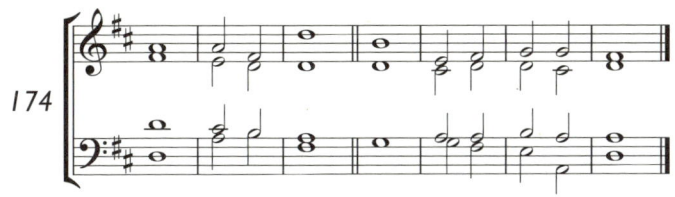

1 To you I lift ' up my ' eyes, ♦
   to you that ' are en'throned • in the ' heavens.

2 As the eyes of servants look to the ' hand of their ' master, ♦
   or the eyes of a ' maid • to the ' hand of her ' mistress,

3 So our eyes wait upon the ' Lord our ' God, ♦
   until ' he have ' mercy up'on us.

4 Have mercy upon us, O Lord, have ' mercy up'on us, ♦
   for we have had ' more than e'nough • of con'tempt.

‡ 5 Our soul has had more than enough of the ' scorn • of the ' arrogant, ♦
   and ' of the con'tempt • of the ' proud.

Psalm 124

J. Harrison

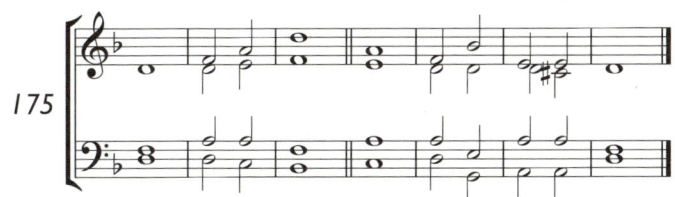

1,2 If the Lord himself had not been on our side,
      now may ' Israel ' say; ♦
    If the Lord had not been on our side,
      when ' enemies rose ' up a'gainst us;

3 Then would they have ' swallowed • us a'live ♦
   when their ' anger ' burned a'gainst us;

4 Then would the waters have overwhelmed us
      and the torrent gone ' over our ' soul; ♦
   over our soul would have ' swept the ' raging ' waters.

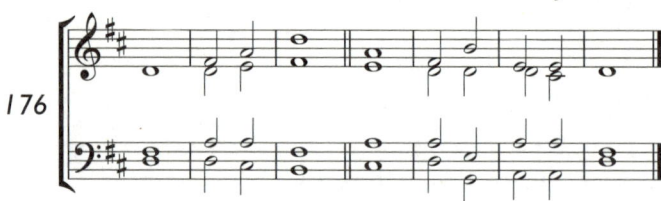

176

5 But blessed ' be the ' Lord ♦
   who has not given us over to ' be a ' prey • for their ' teeth.

6 Our soul has escaped
      as a bird from the ' snare • of the ' fowler; ♦
   the snare is ' broken and ' we are de'livered.

7 Our help is in the ' name • of the ' Lord, ♦
   who ' has made ' heaven and ' earth.

Psalm 125

Barry Ferguson

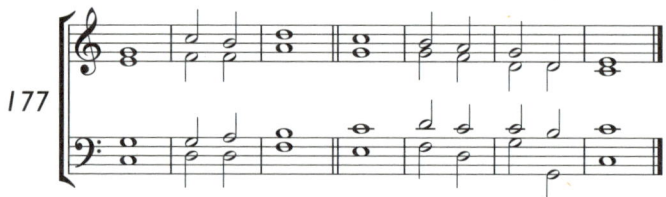

177

1 Those who trust in the Lord are ' like Mount ' Zion, ♦
   which cannot be moved, ' but stands ' fast for ' ever.

2 As the hills stand a'bout Je'rusalem, ♦
   so the Lord stands round about his people,
      from this time ' forth for ' ever'more.

3 The sceptre of wickedness shall not hold sway
      over the land al'lotted • to the ' righteous, ♦
   lest the righteous ' turn their ' hands to ' evil.

4 Do good, O Lord, to ' those • who are ' good, ♦
   and to ' those • who are ' true of ' heart.

‡ 5 Those who turn aside to crooked ways
      the Lord shall take away with the ' evil'doers; ♦
   but let there be ' peace ' upon ' Israel.

Psalm 126

George M. Garrett

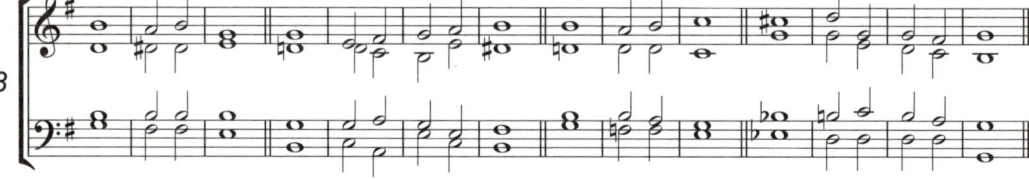

178

1 When the Lord restored the ' fortunes of ' Zion, ♦
   then were ' we like ' those who ' dream.

2 Then was our mouth ' filled with ' laughter ♦
   and our ' tongue with ' songs of ' joy.

3 Then said they a'mong the ' nations, ♦
   'The ' Lord • has done ' great things ' for them.'

4 The Lord has indeed done ' great things ' for us, ♦
   and ' therefore ' we re'joiced.

5 Restore again our ' fortunes, O ' Lord, ♦
   as the ' river beds ' of the ' desert.

6 Those who ' sow in ' tears ♦
   shall ' reap with ' songs of ' joy.

‡ 7 Those who go out weeping, ' bearing the ' seed, ♦
   will come back with shouts of joy,
      ' bearing their ' sheaves ' with them.

Psalm 127

Barry Ferguson

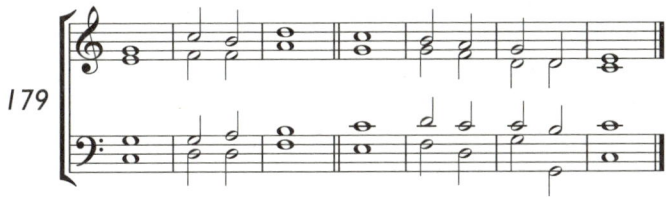

179

1 Unless the Lord ' builds the ' house, ♦
   those who ' build it ' labour in ' vain.

2 Unless the Lord ' keeps the ' city, ♦
   the ' guard keeps ' watch in ' vain.

3 It is in vain that you hasten to rise up early
      and go so late to rest, eating the ' bread of ' toil, ♦
   for he ' gives • his be'loved ' sleep.

4 Children are a heritage ' from the ' Lord ♦
   and the fruit of the ' womb ' is his ' gift.

5 Like arrows in the ' hand • of a ' warrior, ♦
   so are the ' children ' of one's ' youth.

6 Happy are those who have their ' quiver ' full of them: ♦
   they shall not be put to shame
      when they dispute with their ' enemies ' in the ' gate.

Psalm 128

John Goss

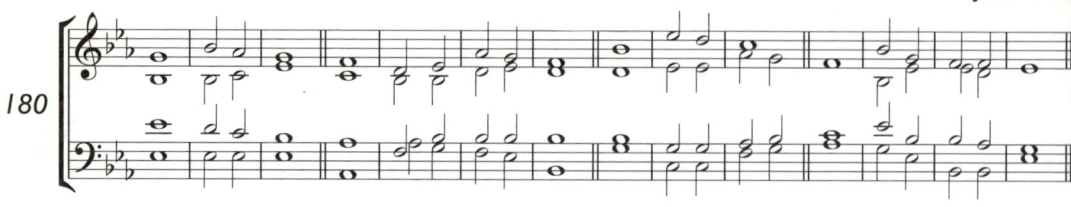

1 Blessed are all those who ' fear the ' Lord, ♦
 and ' walk ' in his ' ways.

2 You shall eat the fruit of the ' toil • of your ' hands; ♦
 it shall go well with you, and ' happy ' shall you ' be.

3 Your wife within your house
  shall be like a ' fruitful ' vine; ♦
 your children round your table,
  like ' fresh ' olive ' branches.

4 Thus shall the ' one be ' blest ♦
 who ' fears ' – the ' Lord.

5 The Lord from out of ' Zion ' bless you, ♦
 that you may see Jerusalem in prosperity
  ' all the ' days of your ' life.

6 May you see your ' children's ' children, ♦
 and may there be ' peace ' upon ' Israel.

Psalm 129

James Turle from H. Purcell

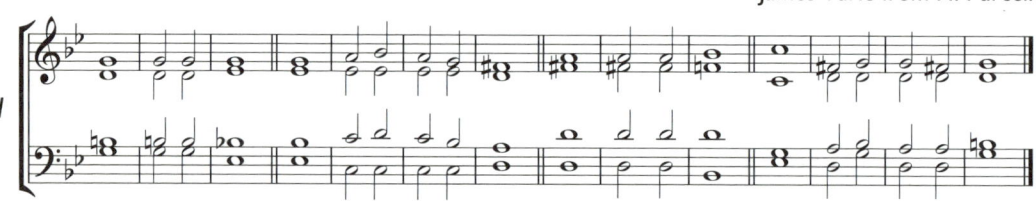

1 'Many a time have they fought against me ' from my ' youth,' ♦
 may ' Israel ' now ' say;

2 'Many a time have they fought against me ' from my ' youth, ♦
 but they have ' not pre'vailed a'gainst me.'

3 The ploughers ' ploughed upon my ' back ♦
 and ' made their ' furrows ' long.

4 But the ' righteous ' Lord ♦
 has cut the ' cords • of the ' wicked in ' pieces.

5 Let them be put to shame and ' turned ' backwards, ♦
 as many ' as are ' enemies of ' Zion.

6 Let them be like grass up'on the ' housetops, ♦
 which ' withers be'fore it can ' grow,

7 So that no reaper can ' fill his ' hand, ♦
    nor a ' binder of ' sheaves his ' bosom;

8 And none who go by may say,
    'The blessing of the Lord ' be up'on you. ♦
    We ' bless you • in the ' name of the ' Lord.'

Psalm 130
John Goss

1 Out of the depths have I cried to you, O Lord;
    Lord, ' hear my ' voice; ♦
    let your ears consider well the ' voice • of my ' suppli'cation.

2 If you, Lord, were to mark what is ' done a'miss, ♦
    O ' Lord, ' who could ' stand?

‡ 3 But there is for'giveness with ' you, ♦
    so ' that you ' shall be ' feared.

4 I wait for the Lord; my ' soul ' waits for him; ♦
    in his ' word ' is my ' hope.

5 My soul waits for the Lord,
    more than the night watch ' for the ' morning, ♦
    more than the ' night watch ' for the ' morning.

6 O Israel, ' wait • for the ' Lord, ♦
    for with the ' Lord ' there is ' mercy;

7 With him is ' plenteous re'demption ♦
    and he shall redeem ' Israel from ' all their ' sins.

Psalm 131
William Croft

183

1 O Lord, my ' heart • is not ' proud; ♦
    my eyes are not ' raised in ' haughty ' looks.

2 I do not occupy myself with ' great ' matters, ♦
    with ' things that ' are too ' high for me.

William Croft

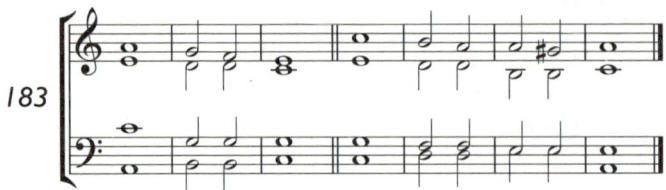

183

3 But I have quieted and stilled my soul,
  like a weaned child on its ' mother's ' breast; ♦
  so my ' soul is ' quieted with'in me.

4 O Israel,' trust • in the ' Lord, ♦
  from this time ' forth for ' ever'more.

Psalm 132

Richard Langdon

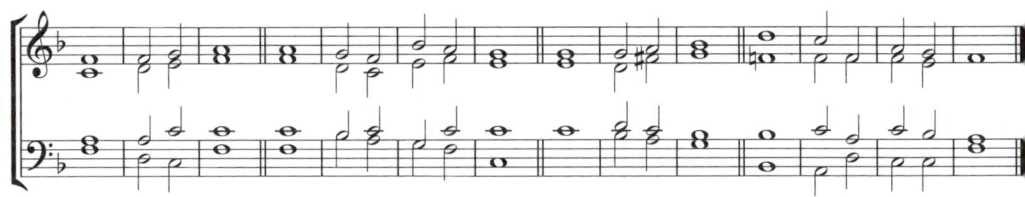

184

1 Lord, re'member for ' David ♦
  all the ' hardships ' he en'dured;

2 How he swore an ' oath • to the ' Lord ♦
  and vowed a vow to the ' Mighty ' One of ' Jacob:

3 'I will not come within the ' shelter • of my ' house, ♦
  nor ' climb up ' into my ' bed;

4 'I will not allow my ' eyes to ' sleep, ♦
  nor ' let my ' eyelids ' slumber,

‡ 5 'Until I find a ' place • for the ' Lord, ♦
  a dwelling for the ' Mighty ' One of ' Jacob.'

6 Now, we heard of the ' ark in ' Ephrathah ♦
  and found it ' in the ' fields of ' Ja-ar.

7 Let us ' enter his ' dwelling place ♦
  and fall ' low be'fore his ' footstool.

8 Arise, O Lord,' into your ' resting place, ♦
  you ' and the ' ark • of your ' strength.

9 Let your priests be ' clothed with ' righteousness ♦
  and your ' faithful ones ' sing with ' joy.

‡ 10 For your servant ' David's ' sake, ♦
  turn not away the ' face of ' your a'nointed.

11 The Lord has sworn an ' oath to ' David, ♦
a promise from ' which he ' will not ' shrink:

12 'Of the ' fruit • of your ' body ♦
shall I ' set up'on your ' throne.

13 'If your children keep my covenant
   and my testimonies that ' I shall ' teach them, ♦
their children also shall sit upon your ' throne for ' ever'more.'

14 For the Lord has chosen ' Zion • for him'self; ♦
he has desired her ' for his ' habi'tation:

15 'This shall be my ' resting place for ' ever; ♦
here will I dwell, for ' I have ' longed ' for her.

16 'I will abundantly ' bless • her pro'vision; ♦
her ' poor • will I ' satisfy with ' bread.

17 'I will clothe her ' priests • with sal'vation, ♦
and her faithful ones ' shall re'joice and ' sing.

18 'There will I make a horn to spring ' up for ' David; ♦
I will keep a lantern ' burning for ' my a'nointed.

‡ 19 'As for his enemies, I will ' clothe them with ' shame; ♦
but on ' him • shall his ' crown be ' bright.'

Psalm 133

George A. Macfarren

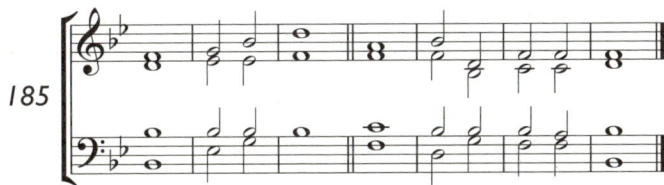

185

1 Behold how good and ' pleasant it ' is ♦
to ' dwell to'gether in ' unity.

2 It is like the precious oil up'on the ' head, ♦
running ' down up'on the ' beard,

‡ 3 Even on ' Aaron's ' beard, ♦
running down upon the ' collar ' of his ' clothing.

4 It is like the ' dew of ' Hermon ♦
running ' down up•on the ' hills of ' Zion.

5 For there the Lord has ' promised his ' blessing: ♦
even ' life for ' ever'more.

Psalm 134

George A. Macfarren

186

1 Come, bless the Lord, all you ʹservants • of the ʹLord, ♦
    you that by night ʹ stand • in the ʹ house of the ʹ Lord.

2,3 Lift up your hands towards the sanctuary
        and ʹ bless the ʹ Lord. ♦
    The Lord who made heaven and earth
        give you ʹ blessing ʹ out of ʹ Zion.

Psalm 135

Henry Lawe

187

1 Alleluia.   [*or* Praise the Lord.]
    Praise the ʹ name of the ʹ Lord; ♦
    give praise, you ʹ servants ʹ of the ʹ Lord,

2 You that stand in the ʹ house of the ʹ Lord, ♦
    in the ʹ courts • of the ʹ house of our ʹ God.

3 Praise the Lord, for the ʹ Lord is ʹ good; ♦
    make music to his ʹ name, for ʹ it is ʹ lovely.

4 For the Lord has chosen Jacob ʹ for himʹself ♦
    and Israel ʹ for his ʹ own posʹsession.

5 For I know that the ʹ Lord is ʹ great ♦
    and that our Lord ʹ is aʹbove all ʹ gods.

6 The Lord does whatever he pleases in heaven ʹ and on ʹ earth, ♦
    in the seas ʹ and in ʹ all the ʹ deeps.

7 He brings up the clouds from the ʹ ends of the ʹ earth; ♦
    he makes lightning with the rain
        and brings the ʹ winds ʹ out of his ʹ treasuries.

8 He smote the ʹ firstborn of ʹ Egypt, ♦
    the ʹ firstborn of ʹ man and ʹ beast.

9 He sent signs and wonders into your ʹ midst, O ʹ Egypt, ♦
    upon ʹ Pharaoh and ʹ all his ʹ servants.

10 He smote ʹ many ʹ nations ♦
    and ʹ slew ʹ mighty ʹ kings:

11 Sihon, king of the Amorites, and Og, the ' king of ' Bashan, ♦
and ' all the ' kingdoms of ' Canaan.

12 He gave their land ' as a ' heritage, ♦
a ' heritage for ' Israel his ' people.

13 Your name, O Lord, en'dures for ' ever ♦
and shall be remembered through ' all ' gene'rations.

14 For the Lord will ' vindicate his ' people ♦
and have com'passion ' on his ' servants.

15 The idols of the nations are but ' silver and ' gold, ♦
the ' work of ' human ' hands.

16 They have mouths, but ' cannot ' speak; ♦
eyes ' have they, but ' cannot ' see;

17 They have ears, but ' cannot ' hear; ♦
neither is there ' any ' breath • in their ' mouths.

18 Those who make them ' shall become ' like them, ♦
and so will ' all who ' put their ' trust in them.

19 Bless the Lord, O ' house of ' Israel; ♦
O house of ' Aaron, ' bless the ' Lord.

20 Bless the Lord, O ' house of ' Levi; ♦
you who fear the ' Lord, ' bless the ' Lord.

‡ 21 Blessed be the ' Lord from ' Zion, ♦
who dwells in Je'rusalem.
    ' Alle'luia.   [_or_ ' Praise the ' Lord.]

Psalm 136

James Turle

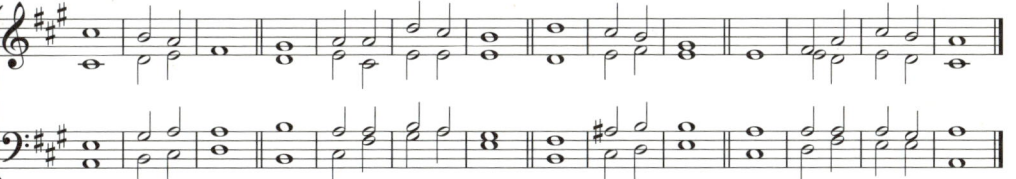

1 Give thanks to the Lord, for ' he is ' gracious, ♦
for his ' mercy en'dures for ' ever.

2 Give thanks to the ' God of ' gods, ♦
for his ' mercy en'dures for ' ever.

3 Give thanks to the ' Lord of ' lords, ♦
for his ' mercy en'dures for ' ever;

4 Who alone ' does great ' wonders, ♦
for his ' mercy en'dures for ' ever;

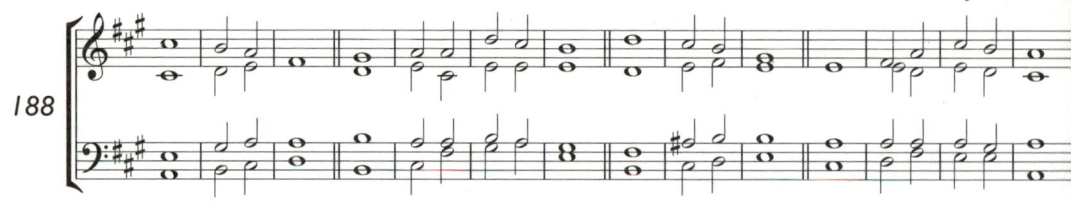

5 Who by wisdom ' made the ' heavens, ♦
   for his ' mercy en'dures for ' ever;

6 Who laid out the earth up'on the ' waters, ♦
   for his ' mercy en'dures for ' ever;

7 Who made the ' great ' lights, ♦
   for his ' mercy en'dures for ' ever;

8 The sun to ' rule the ' day, ♦
   for his ' mercy en'dures for ' ever;

‡ 9 The moon and the stars to ' govern the ' night, ♦
   for his ' mercy en'dures for ' ever;

10 Who smote the ' firstborn of ' Egypt, ♦
   for his ' mercy en'dures for ' ever;

11 And brought out Israel ' from a'mong them, ♦
   for his ' mercy en'dures for ' ever;

12 With a mighty hand and ' outstretched ' arm, ♦
   for his ' mercy en'dures for ' ever;

13 Who divided the Red ' Sea in ' two, ♦
   for his ' mercy en'dures for ' ever;

14 And made Israel to ' pass • through the ' midst of it, ♦
   for his ' mercy en'dures for ' ever;

15 But Pharaoh and his host he overthrew in the ' Red ' Sea, ♦
   for his ' mercy en'dures for ' ever;

16 Who led his people ' through the ' wilderness, ♦
   for his ' mercy en'dures for ' ever;

17 Who ' smote great ' kings, ♦
   for his ' mercy en'dures for ' ever;

18 And slew ' mighty ' kings, ♦
   for his ' mercy en'dures for ' ever;

19 Sihon, ' king of the ' Amorites, ♦
   for his ' mercy en'dures for ' ever;

20 And Og, the ' king of ' Bashan, ♦
   for his ' mercy en'dures for ' ever;

21 And gave away their land ' for a ' heritage, ♦
   for his ' mercy en'dures for ' ever;

‡ 22 A heritage for ' Israel his ' servant, ♦
for his ' mercy en'dures for ' ever;

23 Who remembered us when we ' were in ' trouble, ♦
for his ' mercy en'dures for ' ever;

24 And delivered us ' from our ' enemies, ♦
for his ' mercy en'dures for ' ever;

25 Who gives food to ' all ' creatures, ♦
for his ' mercy en'dures for ' ever.

26 Give thanks to the ' God of ' heaven, ♦
for his ' mercy en'dures for ' ever.

Psalm 137

Samuel Wesley

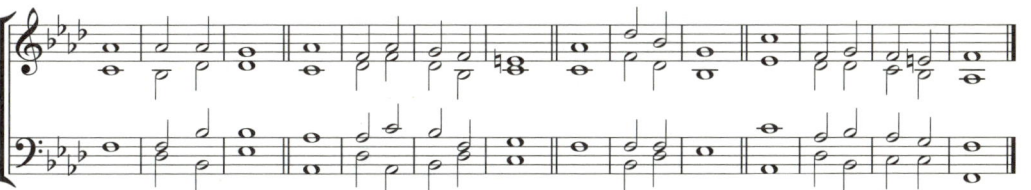

1 By the waters of Babylon we sat ' down and ' wept, ♦
when ' we re'membered ' Zion.

2 As for our lyres, we ' hung them ' up ♦
on the ' willows that ' grow • in that ' land.

3 For there our captors asked for a song,
our tormentors ' called for ' mirth: ♦
'Sing us ' one of the ' songs of ' Zion.'

4 How shall we sing the 'Lord's 'song ♦
in a ' strange ' – ' land?

5 If I forget you, ' O Je'rusalem, ♦
let my right ' hand for'get its ' skill.

6 Let my tongue cleave to the roof of my mouth
if I do ' not re'member you, ♦
If I set not Jerusalem a'bove my ' highest ' joy.

7 Remember, O Lord, against the people of Edom
the ' day of Je'rusalem, ♦
how they said, 'Down with it, down with it,
' even ' to the ' ground.'

8 O daughter of Babylon, ' doomed • to des'truction, ♦
happy the one who repays you
for ' all • you have ' done to ' us;

‡ 9 Who ' takes your ' little ones, ♦
and ' dashes them a'gainst the ' rock.

Psalm 138

Thomas Attwood

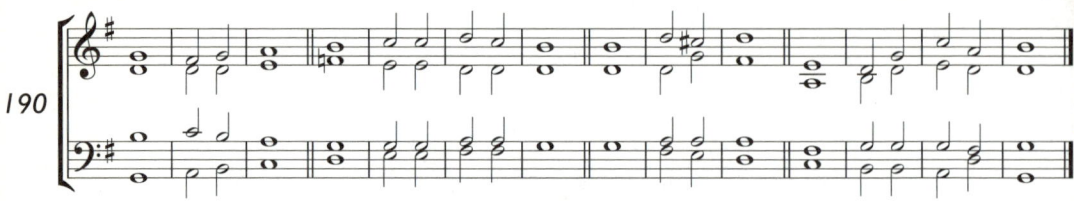

190

1 I will give thanks to you, O Lord, with my ' whole ' heart; ♦
    before the gods will ' I sing ' praise to ' you.

2 I will bow down towards your holy temple and praise your name,
    because of your ' love and ' faithfulness; ♦
  for you have glorified your name
    ' and your ' word above ' all things.

3 In the day that I called to you, you ' answered ' me; ♦
  you ' put new ' strength in my ' soul.

4 All the kings of the earth shall ' praise you, O ' Lord, ♦
  for they have ' heard the ' words of your ' mouth.

5 They shall sing of the ' ways of the ' Lord, ♦
  that great is the ' glory ' of the ' Lord.

6 Though the Lord be high, he watches ' over the ' lowly; ♦
  as for the proud, he re'gards them ' from a'far.

7 Though I walk in the midst of trouble,
    ' you • will pre'serve me; ♦
  you will stretch forth your hand against the fury of my enemies;
    ' your right ' hand will ' save me.

8 The Lord shall make good his ' purpose ' for me; ♦
  your loving-kindness, O Lord, endures for ever;
    for'sake • not the ' work of your ' hands.

Psalm 139

Thomas A. Walmisley

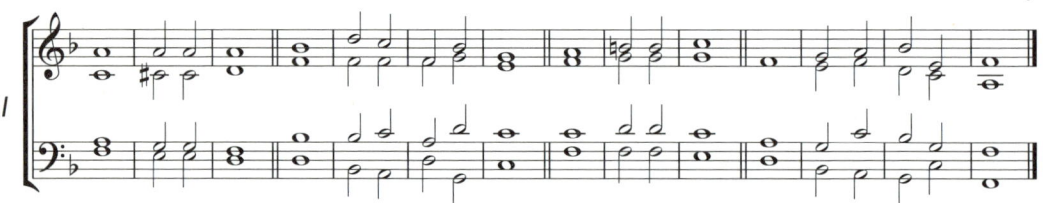

191

1 O Lord, you have searched me ' out and ' known me; ♦
  you know my sitting down and my rising up;
    you dis'cern my ' thoughts • from a'far.

2 You mark out my journeys ' and my ' resting place ♦
  and are ac'quainted with ' all my ' ways.

3 For there is not a word ' on my ' tongue, ♦
  but you, O Lord, ' know it ' alto'gether.

4 You encompass me behind ' and be'fore ♦
   and ' lay your ' hand up'on me.

☩ 5 Such knowledge is too ' wonderful ' for me, ♦
   so high ' that I ' cannot at'tain it.

6 Where can I go then ' from your ' spirit? ♦
   Or where can I ' flee ' from your ' presence?

7 If I climb up to heaven, ' you are ' there; ♦
   if I make the grave my bed, ' you are ' there ' also.

8 If I take the ' wings of the ' morning ♦
   and dwell in the ' uttermost ' parts • of the ' sea,

9 Even there your ' hand shall ' lead me, ♦
   your ' right hand ' hold me ' fast.

10 If I say, 'Surely the ' darkness will ' cover me ♦
   and the light a'round me ' turn to ' night,'

11 Even darkness is no darkness with you;
      the night is as ' clear as the ' day; ♦
   darkness and light to ' you are ' both a'like.

12 For you yourself created my ' inmost ' parts; ♦
   you knit me together ' in my ' mother's ' womb.

13 I thank you, for I am fearfully and ' wonderfully ' made; ♦
   marvellous are your ' works, my ' soul knows ' well.

14 My frame was not ' hidden ' from you, ♦
   when I was made in secret
      and woven in the ' depths ' of the ' earth.

15 Your eyes beheld my form, as ' yet un'finished; ♦
   already in your book were ' all my ' members ' written,

☩ 16 As day by day ' they were ' fashioned ♦
   when as ' yet ' there was ' none of them.

17 How deep are your counsels to ' me, O ' God! ♦
   How ' great ' is the ' sum of them!

18 If I count them, they are more in number ' than the ' sand, ♦
   and at the end, I am ' still ' in your ' presence.

19 O that you would slay the ' wicked, O ' God, ♦
   that the ' bloodthirsty ' might de'part from me!

20 They speak against you with ' wicked in'tent; ♦
   your enemies take 'up your ' name for ' evil.

21 Do I not oppose those, O Lord, ' who op'pose you? ♦
   Do I not abhor ' those who rise ' up a'gainst you?

22 I hate them with a ' perfect ' hatred; ♦
   they have become my ' own ' enemies ' also.

Thomas A. Walmisley

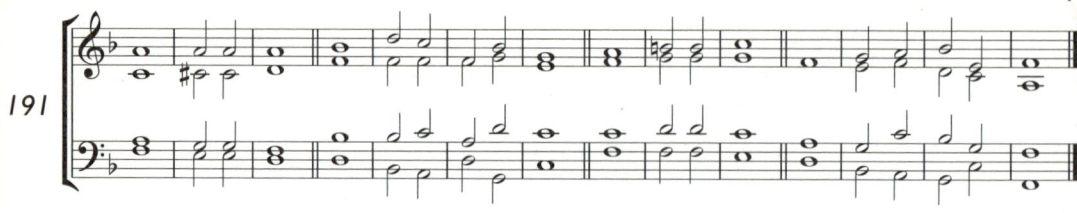

23 Search me out, O God, and ' know my ' heart; ♦
   try me ' and ex'amine my ' thoughts.

24 See if there is any way of ' wickedness ' in me ♦
   and lead me in the ' way ' ever'lasting.

Psalm 140

Henry Smart

1 Deliver me, O Lord, from ' evil'doers ♦
  and pro'tect me ' from the ' violent,

2 Who devise evil ' in their ' hearts ♦
  and stir up ' strife ' all the day ' long.

‡ 3 They have sharpened their tongues ' like a ' serpent; ♦
  adder's ' poison is ' under their ' lips.

4 Keep me, O Lord, from the ' hands of the ' wicked; ♦
  protect me from the violent
     who ' seek to ' make me ' stumble.

5 The proud have laid a snare for me
     and spread out a ' net of ' cords; ♦
  they have set ' traps a'long my ' path.

6 I have said to the Lord, ' 'You are my ' God; ♦
  listen, O Lord, to the ' voice of my ' suppli'cation.

7 'O Lord God, the strength of ' my sal'vation, ♦
  you have covered my ' head • in the ' day of ' battle.

8 'Do not grant the desires of the ' wicked, O ' Lord, ♦
  do not ' prosper their ' wicked ' plans.

9 'Let not those who surround me lift ' up their ' heads; ♦
  let the evil of their own ' lips ' fall up'on them.

10 'Let hot burning coals ' rain up'on them; ♦
   let them be cast into the depths, ' that they ' rise not a'gain.'

11 No slanderer shall prosper ' on the ' earth, ♦
and evil shall hunt down the ' violent to ' over'throw them.

12 I know that the Lord will bring justice ' for the op'pressed ♦
and main'tain the ' cause of the ' needy.

13 Surely, the righteous will give ' thanks • to your ' name, ♦
and the upright shall ' dwell ' in your ' presence.

Psalm 141

Kellow J. Pye

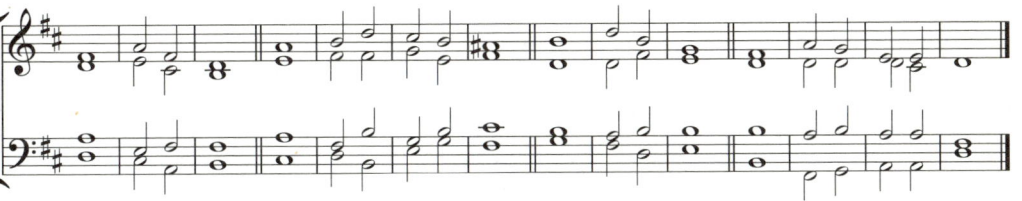

1 O Lord, I call to you; ' come to me ' quickly; ♦
hear my voice ' when I ' cry to ' you.

2 Let my prayer rise be'fore you as ' incense, ♦
the lifting up of my hands ' as the ' evening ' sacrifice.

3 Set a watch before my ' mouth, O ' Lord, ♦
and ' guard the ' door of my ' lips;

4 Let not my heart incline to any ' evil ' thing; ♦
let me not be occupied in wickedness with evildoers,
    nor taste the ' pleasures ' of their ' table.

5 Let the righteous smite me in friendly rebuke;
    but let not the oil of the unrighteous a'noint my ' head; ♦
for my prayer is continually a'gainst their ' wicked ' deeds.

6 Let their rulers be overthrown in ' stony ' places; ♦
then they may ' know • that my ' words are ' sweet.

7 As when a plough turns over the ' earth in ' furrows, ♦
let their bones be ' scattered • at the ' mouth of the ' Pit.

8 But my eyes are turned to ' you, Lord ' God; ♦
in you I take refuge; ' do not ' leave me de'fenceless.

9 Protect me from the snare which ' they have ' laid for me ♦
and from the ' traps of the ' evil'doers.

10 Let the wicked fall into their ' own ' nets, ♦
while ' I pass ' by in ' safety.

Psalm 142

Joseph Barnby

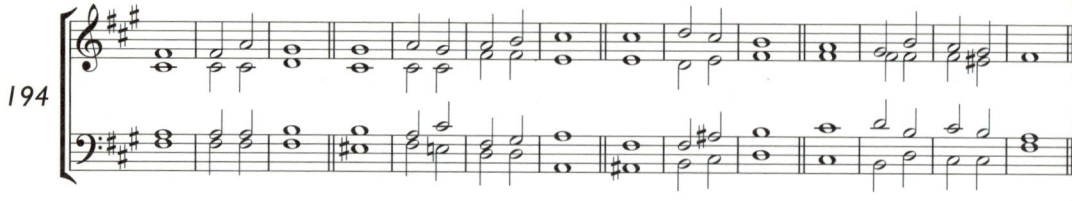

1 I cry a'loud • to the ' Lord; ♦
    to the Lord I ' make my ' suppli'cation.

2 I pour out my com'plaint be'fore him ♦
    and ' tell him ' of my ' trouble.

3 When my spirit faints within me, you ' know my ' path; ♦
    in the way wherein I walk ' have they ' laid a ' snare for me.

4 I look to my right hand, and find ' no one who ' knows me; ♦
    I have no place to flee to, and ' no one ' cares for my ' soul.

5 I cry out to you, O ' Lord, and ' say: ♦
    'You are my refuge, my ' portion • in the ' land of the ' living.

6 'Listen to my cry, for I am brought ' very ' low; ♦
    save me from my persecutors, for they ' are too ' strong ' for me.

7 'Bring my ' soul • out of ' prison, ♦
    that I may give ' thanks ' to your ' name;

7a When you have dealt ' bountifully ' with me, ♦
    then shall the ' righteous ' gather a'round me.'

Psalm 143

John Stainer
from Beethoven

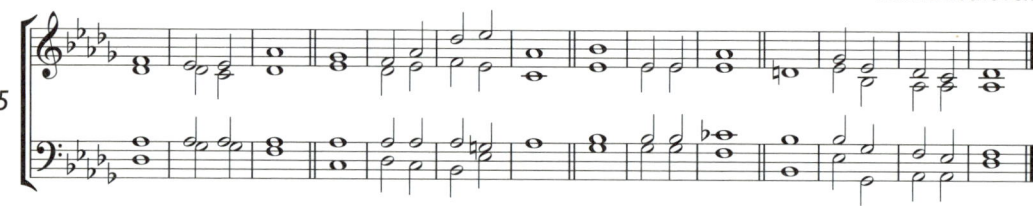

1 Hear my ' prayer, O ' Lord, ♦
    and in your faithfulness give ear to my supplications;
        ' answer me ' in your ' righteousness.

2 Enter not into judgement ' with your ' servant, ♦
    for in your sight shall ' no one ' living be ' justified.

3 For the enemy has pursued me,
        crushing my ' life • to the ' ground, ♦
    making me sit in ' darkness like ' those long ' dead.

4 My spirit ' faints with'in me; ♦
    my ' heart with'in me is ' desolate.

5 I remember the time past; I muse upon ' all your ' deeds; ♦
   I con'sider the ' works of your ' hands.

6 I stretch ' out my ' hands to you; ♦
   my soul gasps for you ' like a ' thirsty ' land.

7 O Lord, make haste to answer me; my ' spirit ' fails me; ♦
   hide not your face from me
      lest I be like ' those who go ' down • to the ' Pit.

8 Let me hear of your loving-kindness in the morning,
      for in you I ' put my ' trust; ♦
   show me the way I should walk in,
      for I ' lift up my ' soul to ' you.

9 Deliver me, O Lord, ' from my ' enemies, ♦
   for I ' flee to ' you for ' refuge.

10 Teach me to do what pleases you, for ' you are my ' God; ♦
    let your kindly spirit lead me ' on a ' level ' path.

11 Revive me, O Lord, ' for your ' name's sake; ♦
    for your righteousness' sake, ' bring me ' out of ' trouble.

12 In your faithfulness, slay my enemies,
       and destroy all the adversaries ' of my ' soul, ♦
    for ' truly ' I am your ' servant.

Psalm 144

Charles F. South

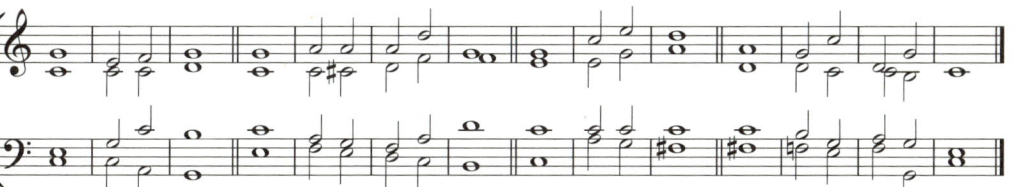

1 Blessed be the ' Lord my ' rock, ♦
  who teaches my hands for war ' and my ' fingers for ' battle;

2 My steadfast help and my fortress,
     my stronghold and my deliverer,
     my shield in ' whom I ' trust, ♦
  who sub'dues the ' peoples ' under me.

3 O Lord, what are mortals that ' you should con'sider them; ♦
  mere human beings, that ' you should take ' thought for ' them?

4 They are like a ' breath of ' wind; ♦
  their days pass a'way ' like a ' shadow.

5 Bow your heavens, O Lord, ' and come ' down; ♦
  touch the ' mountains and ' they shall ' smoke.

6 Cast down your ' lightnings and ' scatter them; ♦
  shoot out your arrows ' and let ' thunder ' roar.

Charles F. South

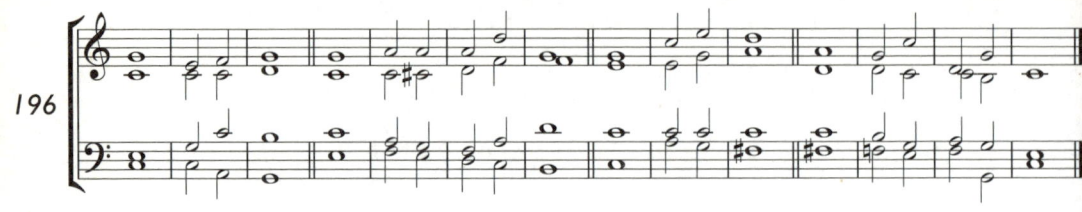

7 Reach down your ' hand from on ' high; ♦
  deliver me and take me out of the great waters,
    from the ' hand of ' foreign ' enemies,

8 Whose ' mouth speaks ' wickedness ♦
  and their right hand ' is the ' hand of ' falsehood.

9 O God, I will sing to you a ' new ' song; ♦
  I will play to you ' on a ' ten-stringed ' harp,

10 You that give sal'vation to ' kings ♦
   and have de'livered ' David your ' servant.

11 Save me from the ' peril • of the ' sword ♦
   and deliver me from the ' hand of ' foreign ' enemies,

12 Whose ' mouth speaks ' wickedness ♦
   and whose right hand ' is the ' hand of ' falsehood;

13 So that our sons in their youth
     may be like well'nurtured ' plants, ♦
   and our daughters like pillars
     carved for the ' corners ' of the ' temple;

14 Our barns be filled with all ' manner of ' store; ♦
   our flocks bearing thousands,
     and ten ' thousands ' in our ' fields;

15 Our cattle be ' heavy with ' young: ♦
   may there be no miscarriage or untimely birth,
     no ' cry of dis'tress • in our ' streets.

16 Happy are the people whose ' blessing this ' is. ♦
   Happy are the people who have the ' Lord ' for their ' God.

Psalm 145

Charles V. Stanford

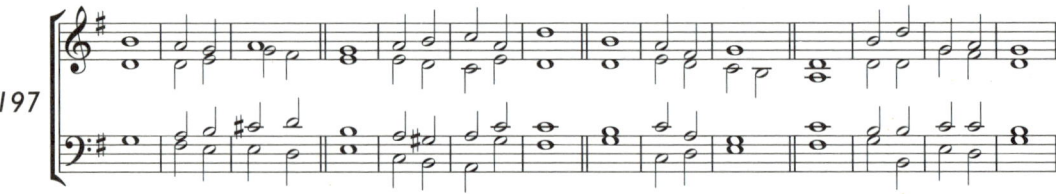

1 I will exalt you, O ' God my ' King, ♦
  and bless your ' name for ' ever and ' ever.

2 Every day ' will I ' bless you ♦
  and praise your ' name for ' ever and ' ever.

3 Great is the Lord and ′ highly • to be ′ praised; ♦
his greatness is be′yond all ′ searching ′ out.

4 One generation shall praise your ′ works • to an′other ♦
and de′clare your ′ mighty ′ acts.

5 They shall speak of the majesty ′ of your ′ glory, ♦
and I will tell of ′ all your ′ wonderful ′ deeds.

6 They shall speak of the might of your ′ marvellous ′ acts, ♦
and I will ′ also ′ tell of your ′ greatness.

7 They shall pour forth the story of your a′bundant ′ kindness ♦
and ′ joyfully ′ sing • of your ′ righteousness.

8 The Lord is ′ gracious and ′ merciful, ♦
long-suffering ′ and of ′ great ′ goodness.

9 The Lord is ′ loving to ′ everyone ♦
and his mercy is ′ over ′ all his ′ creatures.

10 All your works ′ praise you, O ′ Lord, ♦
and your ′ faithful ′ servants ′ bless you.

11 They tell of the ′ glory • of your ′ kingdom ♦
and ′ speak of your ′ mighty ′ power,

12 To make known to all peoples your ′ mighty ′ acts ♦
and the glorious ′ splendour ′ of your ′ kingdom.

13 Your kingdom is an ever′lasting ′ kingdom; ♦
your dominion en′dures through′out all ′ ages.

14 The Lord is sure in ′ all his ′ words ♦
and ′ faithful in ′ all his ′ deeds.

15 The Lord upholds all ′ those who ′ fall ♦
and lifts up all ′ those who are ′ bowed ′ down.

16 The eyes of all wait upon ′ you, O ′ Lord, ♦
and you give them their ′ food in ′ due ′ season.

17 You open ′ wide your ′ hand ♦
and fill ′ all things ′ living with ′ plenty.

18 The Lord is righteous in ′ all his ′ ways ♦
and ′ loving in ′ all his ′ works.

19 The Lord is near to those who ′ call up′on him, ♦
to all who ′ call up′on him ′ faithfully.

20 He fulfils the desire of ′ those who ′ fear him; ♦
he ′ hears their ′ cry and ′ saves them.

21 The Lord watches over ′ those who ′ love him, ♦
but all the ′ wicked shall ′ he des′troy.

22 My mouth shall speak the ′ praise of the ′ Lord, ♦
and let all flesh bless his holy ′ name for ′ ever and ′ ever.

Psalm 146

Charles V. Stanford

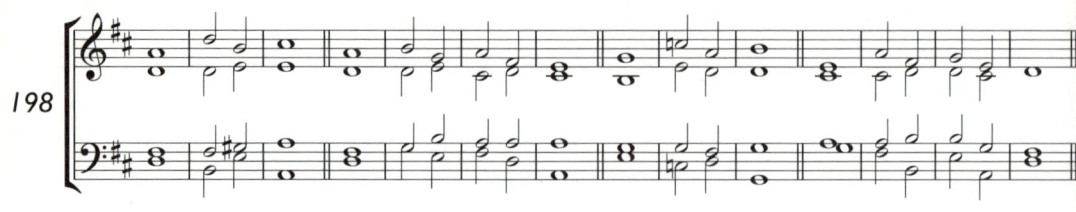

198

1 Alleluia.   [or Praise the Lord.]
    Praise the Lord, ' O my ' soul: ♦
while I ' live • will I ' praise the ' Lord;

1a As long as I ' have any ' being, ♦
I will sing ' praises ' to my ' God.

2 Put not your trust in princes,
    nor in any ' human ' power, ♦
for there ' is no ' help in ' them.

3 When their breath goes forth, they re'turn to the ' earth; ♦
on that day ' all their ' thoughts ' perish.

4 Happy are those who have the God of Jacob ' for their ' help, ♦
whose hope is ' in the ' Lord their ' God;

5 Who made heaven and earth,
    the sea and ' all that is ' in them; ♦
who ' keeps his ' promise for ' ever;

‡ 6 Who gives justice to those that ' suffer ' wrong ♦
and ' bread to ' those who ' hunger.

7 The Lord looses ' those that are ' bound; ♦
the Lord opens the ' eyes ' of the ' blind;

8 The Lord lifts up those who are ' bowed ' down; ♦
the ' Lord ' loves the ' righteous;

9 The Lord watches over the stranger in the land;
    he upholds the ' orphan and ' widow; ♦
but the way of the wicked ' he turns ' upside ' down.

10 The Lord shall ' reign for ' ever, ♦
your God, O Zion, throughout all gene'rations.
    ' Alle'luia.   [or ' Praise the ' Lord.]

Psalm 147

Simon Mold

1 Alleluia. [*or* Praise the Lord.]
 How good it is to make music ' for our ' God, ♦
 how joyful to ' honour ' him with ' praise.

2 The Lord builds ' up Je'rusalem ♦
 and gathers to'gether the ' outcasts of ' Israel.

3 He heals the 'broken'hearted ♦
 and ' binds up ' all their ' wounds.

4 He counts the ' number • of the ' stars ♦
 and ' calls them ' all • by their ' names.

5 Great is our Lord and ' mighty in ' power; ♦
 his wisdom ' is be'yond all ' telling.

6 The Lord lifts ' up the ' poor, ♦
 but casts down the ' wicked ' to the ' ground.

7 Sing to the ' Lord with ' thanksgiving; ♦
 make music to our ' God up'on the ' lyre;

8 Who covers the ' heavens with ' clouds ♦
 and prepares ' rain ' for the ' earth;

9 Who makes grass to ' grow upon the ' mountains ♦
 and green ' plants to ' serve our ' needs.

10 He gives the ' beasts their ' food ♦
 and the young ' ravens ' when they ' cry.

11 He takes no pleasure in the ' power of a ' horse, ♦
 no de'light in ' human ' strength;

12 But the Lord delights in ' those who ' fear him, ♦
 who put their ' trust • in his ' steadfast ' love.

13 Sing praise to the Lord, ' O Je'rusalem; ♦
 praise your ' God, ' O ' Zion;

14 For he has strengthened the ' bars of your ' gates ♦
 and has ' blest your ' children with'in you.

15 He has established ' peace in your ' borders ♦
 and satisfies you ' with the ' finest ' wheat.

16 He sends forth his command ' to the ' earth ♦
 and his ' word runs ' very ' swiftly.

Simon Mold

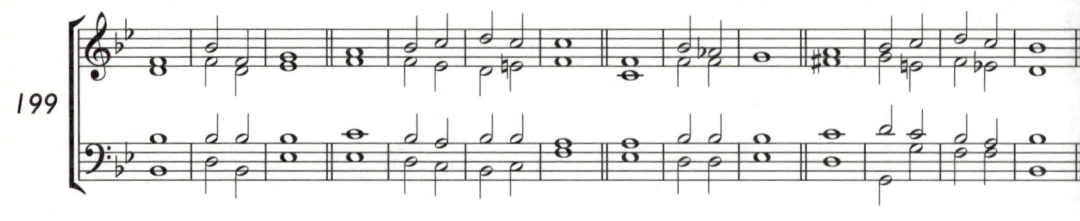

17 He gives ' snow like ' wool ♦
    and ' scatters the ' hoarfrost like ' ashes.

18 He casts down his hailstones like ' morsels of ' bread; ♦
    who ' can en'dure his ' frost?

19 He sends forth his ' word and ' melts them; ♦
    he blows with his wind ' and the ' waters ' flow.

20 He declares his ' word to ' Jacob, ♦
    his ' statutes and ' judgements to ' Israel.

‡ 21 He has not dealt so with any ' other ' nation; ♦
    they do not know his ' laws.
        ' Alle'luia.   [or ' Praise the ' Lord.]

Psalm 148

Walter Parratt

1 Alleluia.   [or Praise the Lord.]
    Praise the Lord ' from the ' heavens; ♦
    praise ' – him ' in the ' heights.

2 Praise him, all ' you his ' angels; ♦
    praise ' – him, ' all his ' host.

3 Praise him, ' sun and ' moon; ♦
    praise him, ' all you ' stars of ' light.

4 Praise him, ' heaven of ' heavens, ♦
    and you ' waters a'bove the ' heavens.

5 Let them praise the ' name of the ' Lord, ♦
    for he commanded ' and they ' were cre'ated.

6 He made them fast for ' ever and ' ever; ♦
    he gave them a law which ' shall not ' pass a'way.

7 Praise the Lord ' from the ' earth, ♦
   you sea ' monsters and ' all ' deeps;

8 Fire and hail, ' snow and ' mist, ♦
   tempestuous ' wind, ful'filling his ' word;

9 Mountains and ' all ' hills, ♦
   fruit ' trees and ' all ' cedars;

10 Wild beasts and ' all ' cattle, ♦
   creeping ' things and ' birds • on the ' wing;

11 Kings of the earth and ' all ' peoples, ♦
   princes and all ' rulers ' of the ' world;

12 Young men and women,
     old and ' young to'gether; ♦
   let them ' praise the ' name of the ' Lord.

13 For his name only ' is ex'alted, ♦
   his splendour a'bove ' earth and ' heaven.

14 He has raised up the horn of his people
     and praise for all his ' faithful ' servants, ♦
   the children of Israel, a people who are ' near him.
     ' Alle'luia.   [or ' Praise the ' Lord.]

Psalm 149

George J. Elvey

1 Alleluia.   [or Praise the Lord.]
     O sing to the Lord a ' new ' song; ♦
   sing his praise in the congre'gation ' of the ' faithful.

2 Let Israel rejoice ' in their ' maker; ♦
   let the children of Zion be ' joyful ' in their ' king.

3 Let them praise his ' name • in the ' dance; ♦
   let them sing praise to ' him with ' timbrel and ' lyre.

4 For the Lord has pleasure ' in his ' people ♦
   and adorns the ' poor ' with sal'vation.

5 Let the faithful be ' joyful in ' glory; ♦
   let them re'joice ' in their ' ranks,

6 With the praises of God ' in their ' mouths ♦
   and a ' two-edged ' sword • in their ' hands;

George J. Elvey

201

7 To execute vengeance ' on the ' nations ♦
 and ' punishment ' on the ' peoples;

8 To bind their ' kings in ' chains ♦
 and their ' nobles with ' fetters of ' iron;

‡ 9 To execute on them the ' judgement de'creed: ♦
 such honour have all his faithful ' servants.
  ' Alle'luia. [or ' Praise the ' Lord.]

Psalm 150

Peter Hurford

Descant v.6

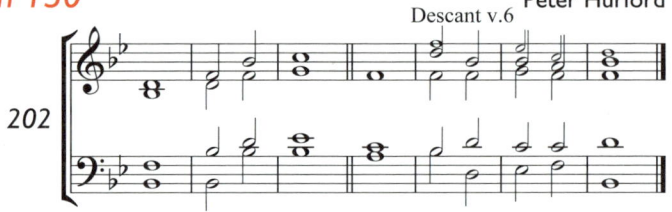

202

1 Alleluia. [or Praise the Lord.]
  O praise God ' in his ' holiness; ♦
  praise him in the ' firmament ' of his ' power.

2 Praise him for his ' mighty ' acts; ♦
  praise him ac'cording • to his ' excellent ' greatness.

3 Praise him with the ' blast of the ' trumpet; ♦
  praise him up'on the ' harp and ' lyre.

4 Praise him with ' timbrel and ' dances; ♦
  praise him up'on the ' strings and ' pipe.

5 Praise him with ' ringing ' cymbals; ♦
  praise him up'on the ' clashing ' cymbals.

6 Let everything ' that has ' breath ♦
  praise the ' Lord.
   ' Alle'luia. [or ' Praise the ' Lord.]

Psalm 150

Charles V. Stanford

1. Alleluia.* O praise God in his ho-li-ness: praise him in the fir-ma-ment of his power.
2. Praise him for his might-y acts: praise him ac-cord-ing to his ex-cel-lent great-ness.
3. (HARMONY) Praise him with the blast of the trum-pet: praise him up-on the harp and lyre.
4. Praise him with tim-brel and dan-ces: praise him up-on the strings and pipe.
5. (TENOR & BASS) Praise him with ring-ing cym-bals: praise him up-on the clash-ing cym-bals.

*In penitential seasons, 'Praise the Lord' may replace 'Alleluia'.

¶ Canticles

Benedicite – a Song of Creation

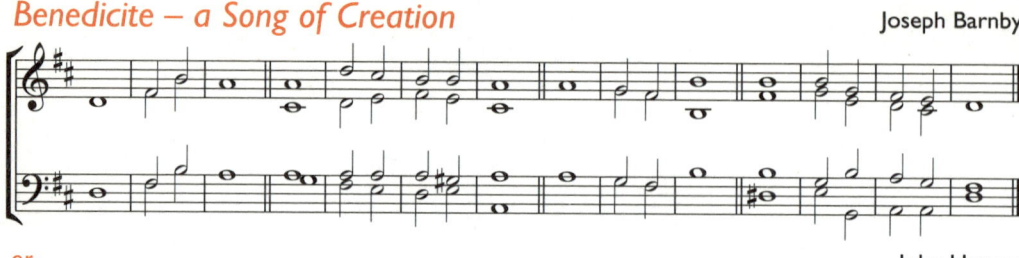

204 Joseph Barnby

205 John Harper

1 Bless the Lord all you ' works of the ' Lord: ♦
  sing his ' praise • and ex'alt him for ' ever.

2 Bless the ' Lord you ' heavens: ♦
  sing his ' praise • and ex'alt him for ' ever.

3 Bless the Lord you ' angels • of the ' Lord: ♦
  bless the ' Lord all ' you his ' hosts;

  bless the Lord you waters a'bove the ' heavens: ♦
  sing his ' praise • and ex'alt him for ' ever.

4 Bless the Lord ' sun and ' moon: ♦
  bless the ' Lord you ' stars of ' heaven;

  bless the Lord all ' rain and ' dew: ♦
  sing his ' praise • and ex'alt him for ' ever.

5 Bless the Lord all ' winds that ' blow: ♦
  bless the ' Lord you ' fire and ' heat;

  bless the Lord scorching wind and ' bitter ' cold: ♦
  sing his ' praise • and ex'alt him for ' ever.

6 Bless the Lord dews and ' falling ' snows: ♦
  bless the ' Lord you ' nights and ' days;

  bless the Lord ' light and ' darkness: ♦
  sing his ' praise • and ex'alt him for ' ever.

7 Bless the Lord ' frost and ' cold: ♦
  bless the ' Lord you ' ice and ' snow;

  bless the Lord ' lightnings and ' clouds: ♦
  sing his ' praise • and ex'alt him for ' ever.

8 O let the earth ' bless the ' Lord: ♦
  bless the ' Lord you ' mountains and ' hills;

  bless the Lord all that ' grows in the ' ground: ♦
  sing his ' praise • and ex'alt him for ' ever.

9 Bless the ' Lord you ' springs: ♦
bless the ' Lord you ' seas and ' rivers;

bless the Lord you whales and all that ' swim in the ' waters: ♦
sing his ' praise • and ex'alt him for ' ever.

10 Bless the Lord all ' birds of the ' air: ♦
bless the ' Lord you ' beasts and ' cattle;

bless the Lord all ' people on ' earth: ♦
sing his ' praise • and ex'alt him for ' ever.

11 O people of God ' bless the ' Lord: ♦
bless the ' Lord you ' priests of the ' Lord;

bless the Lord you ' servants • of the ' Lord: ♦
sing his ' praise • and ex'alt him for ' ever.

12 Bless the Lord all you of ' upright ' spirit: ♦
bless the Lord you that are ' holy and ' humble in ' heart;

The Song of the Three 35-65

bless the Father, the Son and the ' Holy ' Spirit: ♦
sing his ' praise • and ex'alt him for ' ever.

This doxology replaces Glory to the Father…

Benedicite – a Song of Creation
shorter version

1 Bless the Lord all you ' works of the ' Lord: ♦
sing his ' praise • and ex'alt him for ' ever.

2 Bless the ' Lord you ' heavens: ♦
sing his ' praise • and ex'alt him for ' ever.

3 Bless the Lord you ' angels • of the ' Lord: ♦
sing his ' praise • and ex'alt him for ' ever.

4 Bless the Lord all ' people on ' earth: ♦
sing his ' praise • and ex'alt him for ' ever.

5 O people of God ' bless the ' Lord: ♦
sing his ' praise • and ex'alt him for ' ever.

6 Bless the Lord you ' priests of the ' Lord: ♦
sing his ' praise • and ex'alt him for ' ever.

7 Bless the Lord you ' servants • of the ' Lord: ♦
sing his ' praise • and ex'alt him for ' ever.

8 Bless the Lord all you of ' upright ' spirit: ♦
bless the Lord you that are ' holy and ' humble in ' heart;

‡ bless the Father, the Son and the ' Holy ' Spirit: ♦
sing his ' praise • and ex'alt him for ' ever.

This doxology replaces Glory to the Father…

Venite – a Song of Triumph

Thomas Norris

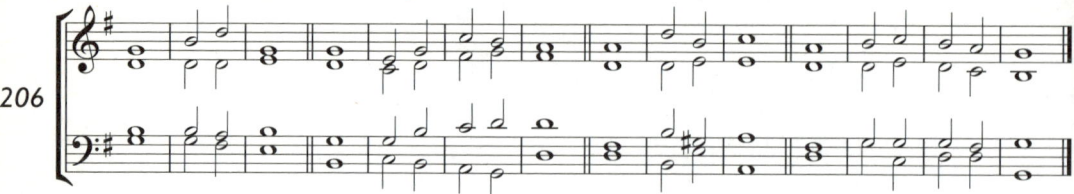

206

1. O come, let us ' sing • to the ' Lord; ♦
   let us heartily rejoice in the ' rock of ' our sal'vation.

2. Let us come into his ' presence with ' thanksgiving ♦
   and be ' glad in ' him with ' psalms.

3. For the Lord is a ' great ' God ♦
   and a great ' king a'bove all ' gods.

4. In his hand are the ' depths • of the ' earth ♦
   and the heights of the ' mountains are ' his ' also.

‡ 5. The sea is his, ' for he ' made it, ♦
   and his hands have ' moulded the ' dry ' land.

6. Come, let us worship and ' bow ' down ♦
   and kneel be'fore the ' Lord our ' Maker.

7. For ' he is our ' God; ♦
   we are the people of his ' pasture • and the ' sheep of his ' hand.

The canticle may end here with Glory to the Father…

8. O that today you would ' listen • to his ' voice: ♦
   'Harden not your hearts as at Meribah,
      on that day at ' Massah ' in the ' wilderness,

9. 'When your forebears tested me, and ' put me • to the ' proof, ♦
   though ' they had ' seen my ' works.

10. 'Forty years long I detested that gene'ration and ' said, ♦
    "This people are wayward in their hearts;
       they ' do not ' know my ' ways."

11. 'So I ' swore • in my ' wrath, ♦
    "They shall not ' enter ' into my ' rest."'

Psalm 95

Glory to the Father and ' to the ' Son ♦
and ' to the ' Holy ' Spirit;

as it was in the be'ginning is ' now ♦
and shall be for ' ever. ' A'men.

Jubilate – a Song of Joy

207 Peter Hurford

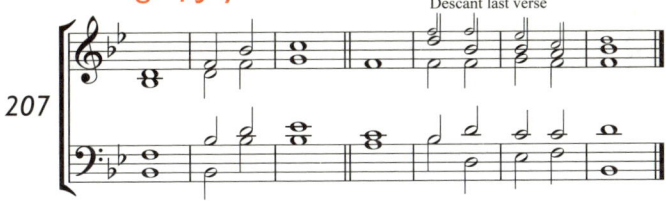

or

208 Frederick A. G. Ouseley

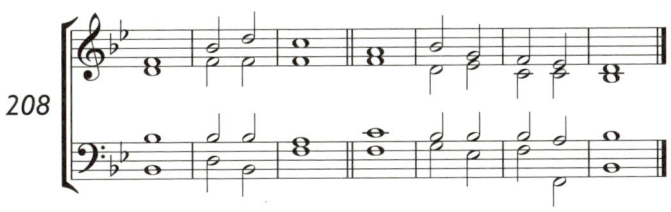

1 O be joyful in the Lord, ' all the ' earth; ♦
serve the Lord with gladness
    and come before his ' presence ' with a ' song.

2 Know that the ' Lord is ' God; ♦
it is he that has made us and we are his;
    we are his ' people • and the ' sheep of his ' pasture.

3 Enter his gates with thanksgiving
    and his ' courts with ' praise; ♦
give thanks to ' him and ' bless his ' name.

4 For the Lord is gracious; his steadfast love is ' ever'lasting, ♦
and his faithfulness endures from gene'ration to ' gene'ration.

Psalm 100

Glory to the Father and ' to the ' Son ♦
and ' to the ' Holy ' Spirit;

as it was in the be'ginning is ' now ♦
and shall be for ' ever. ' A'men.

The Easter Anthems

George M. Garrett

209

1 Christ our passover has been ' sacrificed ' for us: ♦
so let us ' cele'brate the ' feast,

2 not with the old leaven of cor'ruption and ' wickedness: ♦
but with the unleavened ' bread of sin'cerity and ' truth.

1 Corinthians 5.7b, 8

3 Christ once raised from the dead ' dies no ' more: ♦
death has ' no more do'minion ' over him.

4 In dying he died to sin ' once for ' all: ♦
in ' living he ' lives to ' God.

5 See yourselves therefore as ' dead to ' sin: ♦
and alive to God in ' Jesus ' Christ our ' Lord.

Romans 6.9-11

6 Christ has been raised ' from the ' dead: ♦
the ' first fruits of ' those who ' sleep.

7 For as by ' man came ' death: ♦
by man has come also the resur'rection ' of the ' dead;

8 for as in ' Adam all ' die: ♦
even so in Christ shall ' all be ' made a'live.

1 Corinthians 15.20-22

Glory to the Father and ' to the ' Son ♦
and ' to the ' Holy ' Spirit;

as it was in the be'ginning is ' now ♦
and shall be for ' ever. ' A'men.

Phos hilaron – a Song of the Light

George J. Elvey

210

1. O joyful light,
   from the pure glory of the eternal ' heavenly ' Father, ♦
   O holy, ' blessed ' Jesus ' Christ.

2. As we come to the ' setting • of the ' sun ♦
   and ' see the ' evening ' light,

3. we give thanks and praise to the Father and ' to the ' Son ♦
   and to the ' Holy ' Spirit of ' God.

4. Worthy are ' you at ' all times ♦
   to be ' sung with ' holy ' voices,

5. O Son of God, O ' giver of ' life, ♦
   and to be ' glorified through ' all cre'ation.

or

1. Hail, gladdening Light, of his pure ' glory ' poured, ♦
   Who is the immortal Father, heavenly, blest,
   Holiest of holies, ' Jesus ' Christ our ' Lord.

2. Now we are come to the sun's ' hour of ' rest, ♦
   The lights of evening round us shine,
   We hymn the Father, Son and ' Holy ' Spirit div'ine.

3. Worthy are you at ' all times • to be ' sung ♦
   With ' unde'filed ' tongue,

4. Son of our God, giver of ' life, a'lone: ♦
   Therefore in all the world your ' glories, ' Lord, they ' own.

Phos hilaron 209

Verses from Psalm 141 William Croft

211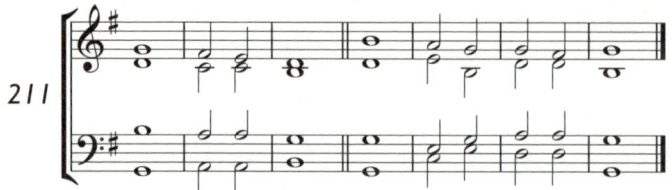

or William Croft

212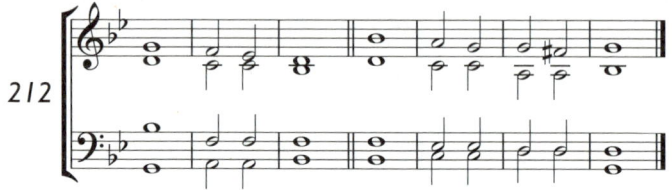

1 Let my prayer rise be'fore you as ' incense, ♦
  the lifting up of my hands ' as the ' evening ' sacrifice.

2 O Lord, I call to you; ' come to me ' quickly; ♦
  hear my voice ' when I ' cry to ' you.

3 Set a watch before my ' mouth, O ' Lord, ♦
  and ' guard the ' door of my ' lips;

4 Let my prayer rise be'fore you as ' incense, ♦
  the lifting up of my hands ' as the ' evening ' sacrifice.

5 Let not my heart incline to any ' evil ' thing; ♦
  let me not be occupied in ' wickedness with ' evil'doers.

6 But my eyes are turned to ' you, Lord ' God; ♦
  in you I take refuge; ' do not ' leave me de'fenceless.

7 Let my prayer rise be'fore you as ' incense, ♦
  the lifting up of my hands ' as the ' evening ' sacrifice.

Verses from Psalm 104

Jonathan Battishill

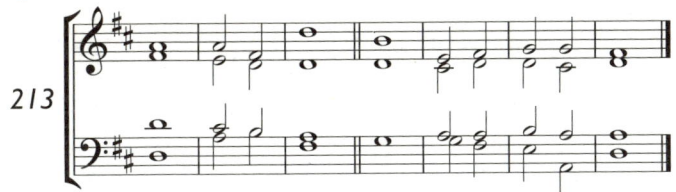

213

1. *Bless the Lord, ' O my ' soul.* ♦
   O Lord my God, how ' excellent ' is your ' greatness!

2. *You are clothed with ' majesty and ' honour,* ♦
   wrapped in ' light as ' in a ' garment.

3. *The sun knows the ' time for its ' setting.* ♦
   You make darkness ' that it ' may be ' night.

4. *Bless the Lord, ' O my ' soul.* ♦
   O Lord my God, how ' excellent ' is your ' greatness!

5. *O Lord, how manifold ' are your ' works!* ♦
   In wisdom you have made them all;
       the ' earth is ' full of your ' creatures.

6. *When you send forth your spirit, they ' are cre'ated,* ♦
   and you re'new the ' face of the ' earth.

7. *Bless the Lord, ' O my ' soul.* ♦
   O Lord my God, how ' excellent ' is your ' greatness!

8. *May the glory of the Lord en'dure for ' ever;* ♦
   may the ' Lord re'joice in his ' works;

9. *I will sing to the Lord as ' long as I ' live;* ♦
   I will make music to my God ' while I ' have my ' being.

10. *Bless the Lord, ' O my ' soul.* ♦
    O Lord my God, how ' excellent ' is your ' greatness!

A Song of the Wilderness (Advent)

Frederick A. G. Ouseley

214

1 The wilderness and the dry land ' shall re'joice, ♦
   the desert shall ' blossom and ' burst ' into ' song.

2 They shall see the ' glory of the ' Lord, ♦
   the ' majesty ' of our ' God.

3 Strengthen the ' weary ' hands, ♦
   and make ' firm the ' feeble ' knees.

4 Say to the anxious, 'Be ' strong, fear ' not, ♦
   your God is coming with judgement,
     ' coming with ' judgement to ' save you.'

5 Then shall the eyes of the ' blind be ' opened, ♦
   and the ' ears of the ' deaf un'stopped;

6 Then shall the lame ' leap • like a ' hart, ♦
   and the tongue of the ' dumb ' sing for ' joy.

7 For waters shall break ' forth in the ' wilderness, ♦
   and ' streams ' in the ' desert;

8 The ransomed of the Lord shall re'turn with ' singing, ♦
   with everlasting ' joy up'on their ' heads.

‡ 9 Joy and gladness ' shall be ' theirs, ♦
   and sorrow and ' sighing shall ' flee a'way.

Isaiah 35.1,2b-4a,4c-6,10

Glory to the Father and ' to the ' Son ♦
and ' to the ' Holy ' Spirit;

as it was in the be'ginning is ' now ♦
and shall be for ' ever. ' A'men.

A Song of the Messiah (Christmas)

James Turle

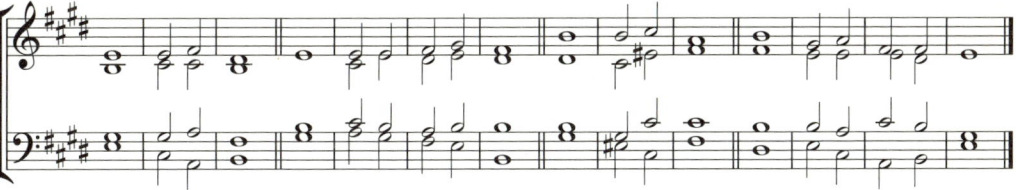

1 The people who walked in darkness have seen a ' great ' light; ♦
  those who dwelt in a land of deep darkness,
    upon ' them the ' light has ' dawned.

2 You have increased their joy and given them ' great ' gladness; ♦
  they rejoiced before you ' as with ' joy • at the ' harvest.

3 For you have shattered the ' yoke that ' burdened them; ♦
  the collar that lay ' heavy ' on their ' shoulders.

4 For to us a child is born and to us a ' son is ' given, ♦
  and the government will ' be up'on his shoulder.

5 And his name will be called: Wonderful Counsellor;
    the ' Mighty ' God; ♦
  the Everlasting ' Father; the ' Prince of ' Peace.

6 Of the increase of his government ' and of ' peace ♦
  there ' will be ' no ' end,

7 Upon the throne of David and ' over his ' kingdom, ♦
  to establish and up'hold it with ' justice and ' righteousness.

8 From this time forth and for ' ever'more; ♦
  the zeal of the ' Lord of ' hosts will ' do this.

Isaiah 9.2, 3b, 4a, 6, 7

Glory to the Father and ' to the ' Son ♦
and ' to the ' Holy ' Spirit;

as it was in the be'ginning is ' now ♦
and shall be for ' ever. ' A'men.

A Song of the New Jerusalem (Epiphany)

George J. Elvey

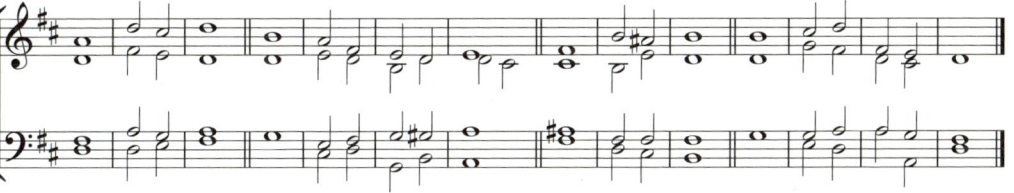

1 Arise, shine out, for your ' light has ' come, ♦
  the glory of the ' Lord is ' rising up'on you.

2 Though night still ' covers the ' earth, ♦
  and ' dark'ness the ' peoples;

A Song of the New Jerusalem

George J. Elvey

216

3 Above you the ' Holy One a'rises, ♦
and above you ' God's ' glory ap'pears.

4 The nations will ' come • to your ' light, ♦
and ' kings • to your ' dawning ' brightness.

5 Your gates will lie ' open con'tinually, ♦
shut neither by ' day ' nor by ' night.

6 The sound of violence shall be heard no longer ' in your ' land, ♦
or ruin and devas'tation with'in your ' borders.

* 7 You will call your ' walls, Sal'vation, ♦
and ' your ' gates, ' Praise.

8 No more will the ' sun • give you ' daylight, ♦
nor ' moonlight ' shine up'on you;

9 But the Lord will be your ever'lasting ' light, ♦
your ' God will ' be your ' splendour.

10 For you shall be called the ' city of ' God, ♦
the dwelling of the ' Holy ' One of ' Israel.

Isaiah 60.1-3,11a,18,19,14b

Glory to the Father and ' to the ' Son ♦
and ' to the ' Holy ' Spirit;

as it was in the be'ginning is ' now ♦
and shall be for ' ever. ' A'men.

A Song of Humility (Lent)

John Goss

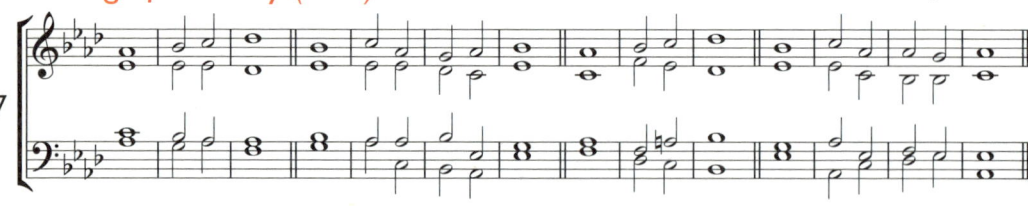

217

1 Come, let us re'turn • to the ' Lord ♦
who has ' torn us ' and will ' heal us.

---

* *or*

7 You will ' call your ' walls, ♦
Salvation, ' and your ' gates, ' Praise.

2 God ' – has ' stricken us ♦
and will ' bind ' up our ' wounds.

3 After two days, he ' will re'vive us, ♦
and on the third day will raise us up,
   that ' we may ' live in his ' presence.

4 Let us strive to ' know the ' Lord; ♦
his appearing ' is as ' sure as the ' sunrise.

5 He will come to us ' like the ' showers, ♦
like the spring ' rains that ' water the ' earth.

6 'O Ephraim, how ' shall I ' deal with you? ♦
How shall I ' deal with ' you, O ' Judah?

7 'Your love for me is like the ' morning ' mist, ♦
like the dew ' that goes ' early a'way.

8 'Therefore, I have hewn them ' by the ' prophets, ♦
and my ' judgement goes ' forth • as the ' light.

‡ 9 'For loyalty is my desire ' and not ' sacrifice, ♦
and the knowledge of God ' rather than ' burnt ' offerings.'

Hosea 6.1-6

Glory to the Father and ' to the ' Son ♦
and ' to the ' Holy ' Spirit;

as it was in the be'ginning is ' now ♦
and shall be for ' ever. ' A'men.

The Song of Moses and Miriam (Easter)

Joseph Barnby

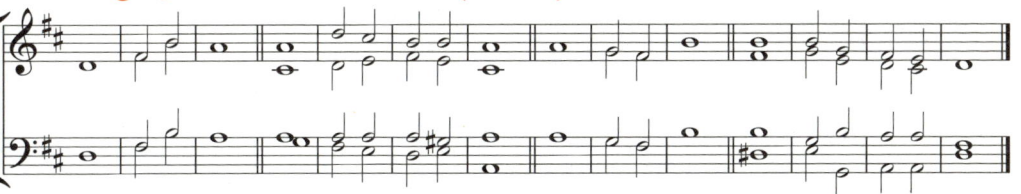

1 I will sing to the Lord, who has ' triumphed ' gloriously, ♦
the horse and his rider he has ' thrown ' into the ' sea.

2 The Lord is my ' strength and my ' song ♦
and ' has be'come • my sal'vation.

3 This is my God whom ' I will ' praise, ♦
the God of my forebears ' whom I ' will ex'alt.

4 The Lord ' is a ' warrior, ♦
the ' Lord ' is his ' name.

Joseph Barnby

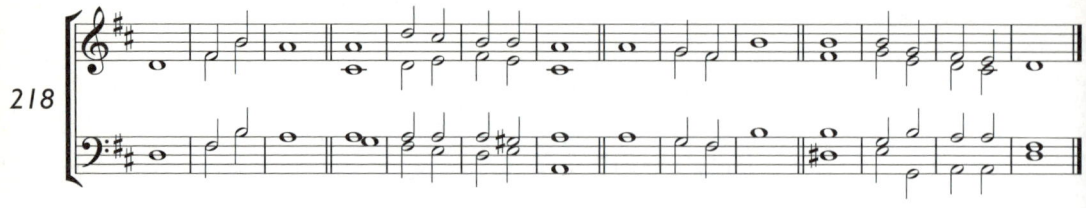

218

5 Your right hand, O Lord, is ' glorious in ' power: ♦
  your right hand, O ' Lord, ' shatters the ' enemy.

6 At the blast of your nostrils, the ' sea ' covered them; ♦
  they sank as ' lead • in the ' mighty ' waters.

7 In your unfailing ' love, O ' Lord, ♦
  you lead the people ' whom you ' have re'deemed.

8 And by your in'vincible ' strength ♦
  you will guide them ' to your ' holy ' dwelling.

‡ 9 You will bring them in and ' plant them, O ' Lord, ♦
  in the sanctuary ' which your ' hands • have es'tablished.

Exodus 15.1b-3,6,10,13,17

Glory to the Father and ' to the ' Son ♦
and ' to the ' Holy ' Spirit;

as it was in the be'ginning is ' now ♦
and shall be for ' ever. ' A'men.

A Song of Ezekiel (Pentecost)

Frederick A. G. Ouseley

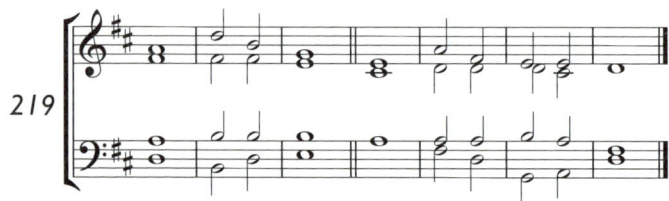

219

1 I will take you ' from the ' nations, ♦
  and ' gather you from ' all the ' countries.

2 I will sprinkle clean ' water up'on you, ♦
  and you shall be clean from ' all ' your un'cleannesses.

3 A new heart ' I will ' give you, ♦
  and put a ' new ' spirit with'in you,

4 And I will remove from your body the ' heart of ' stone ♦
  and ' give you a ' heart of ' flesh.

‡ 5 You shall ' be my ' people, ♦
  and ' I will ' be your ' God.

Ezekiel 36.24-26,28b

216 *A Song of Ezekiel*

Glory to the Father and ' to the ' Son ♦
and ' to the ' Holy ' Spirit;

as it was in the be'ginning is ' now ♦
and shall be for ' ever. ' A'men.

A Song of David (Ordinary Time)

James Turle

1 Blessed are you, God of Israel, for ' ever and ' ever, ♦
   for yours is the greatness, the power,
       the glory, the ' splendour ' and the ' majesty.

2 Everything in heaven and on ' earth is ' yours; ♦
   yours is the kingdom, O Lord,
       and you are exalted as ' head ' over ' all.

3 Riches and honour ' come from ' you ♦
   and you ' rule ' over ' all.

4 In your hand are ' power and ' might; ♦
   yours it is to give ' power and ' strength to ' all.

5 And now we give you ' thanks, our ' God, ♦
   and ' praise your ' glorious ' name.

6 For all things ' come from ' you, ♦
   and of your ' own ' have we ' given you.

1 Chronicles 29.10b-13, 14b

Glory to the Father and ' to the ' Son ♦
and ' to the ' Holy ' Spirit;

as it was in the be'ginning is ' now ♦
and shall be for ' ever. ' A'men.

A Song of the Spirit (Advent)

Thomas Attwood

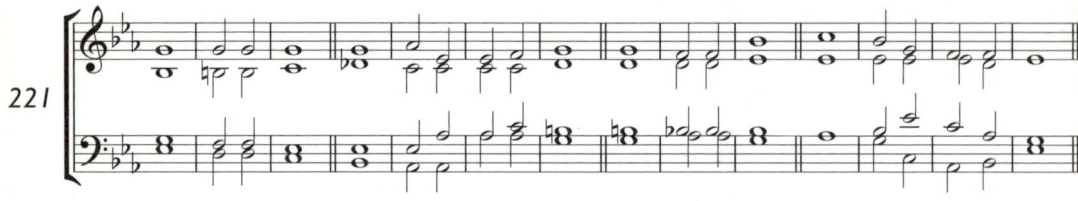

221

1. 'Behold, I am coming soon', says the Lord,
    'and bringing my re'ward ' with me, ♦
   to give to everyone ac'cording ' to their ' deeds.

2. 'I am the Alpha and the Omega, the ' first • and the ' last, ♦
   the be'ginning ' and the ' end.'

3. Blessed are those who do God's commandments,
    that they may have the right to the ' tree of ' life, ♦
   and may enter into the ' city ' through the ' gates.

4. 'I, Jesus, have sent my ' angel ' to you, ♦
   with this ' testimony for ' all the ' churches.

5. 'I am the root and the ' offspring of ' David, ♦
   I am the ' bright ' morning ' star.'

6. 'Come!' say the Spirit ' and the ' Bride; ♦
   'Come!' ' let each ' hearer re'ply!

7. Come forward, ' you who are ' thirsty, ♦
   let those who desire take the ' water of ' life • as a ' gift.

Revelation 22.12-14, 16, 17

Surely I am ' coming ' soon! ♦
A'men! ' Come, Lord ' Jesus!

This verse replaces Glory to the Father...

A Song of Redemption (Christmas)

C. Hubert H. Parry

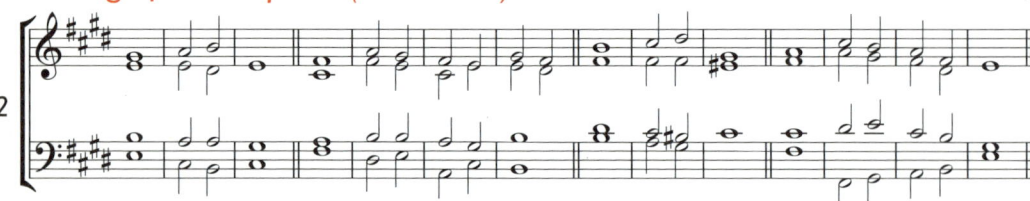

222

1. The Father has delivered us from the do'minion of ' darkness, ♦
   and transferred us to the kingdom of ' his be'loved ' Son;

2. In whom we ' have re'demption, ♦
   the for'giveness ' of our ' sins.

3. He is the image of the in'visible ' God, ♦
   the ' firstborn of ' all cre'ation.

218   *A Song of the Spirit*

4 For in him all things ' were cre'ated, ♦
in heaven and on earth, ' visible ' and in'visible.

5 All things were created ' through him and ' for him, ♦
he is before all things and in him ' all things ' hold to'gether.

6 He is the head of the ' body, the ' Church, ♦
he is the beginning, the ' firstborn ' from the ' dead.

‡ 7 In him all the fullness of God was ' pleased to ' dwell; ♦
and through him God was ' pleased to ' reconcile ' all things.

Colossians 1.13-18a, 19, 20a

Glory to the Father and ' to the ' Son ♦
and ' to the ' Holy ' Spirit;

as it was in the be'ginning is ' now ♦
and shall be for ' ever. ' A'men.

A Song of Praise (Epiphany)

George A. Macfarren

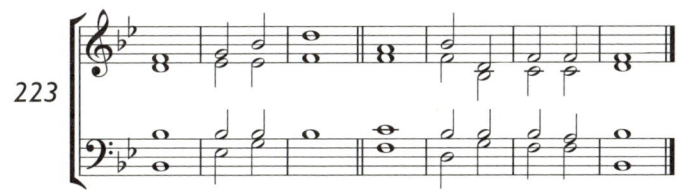

223

This Canticle is also known as Glory and Honour.

1 You are worthy, our ' Lord and ' God, ♦
to receive ' glory and ' honour and ' power.

2 For you have cre'ated ' all things, ♦
and by your ' will they ' have their ' being.

3 You are worthy, O Lamb, for ' you were ' slain, ♦
and by your blood you ransomed for God
saints from every ' tribe and ' language and ' nation.

4 You have made them to be a kingdom and priests
' serving our ' God, ♦
and they will ' reign with ' you on ' earth.

Revelation 4.11; 5.9b, 10

‡ To the One who sits on the throne and ' to the ' Lamb ♦
be blessing and honour, glory and might,
for ever and ' ever. ' A'men.

This verse replaces Glory to the Father...

A Song of Christ the Servant (Lent)

Joseph Barnby

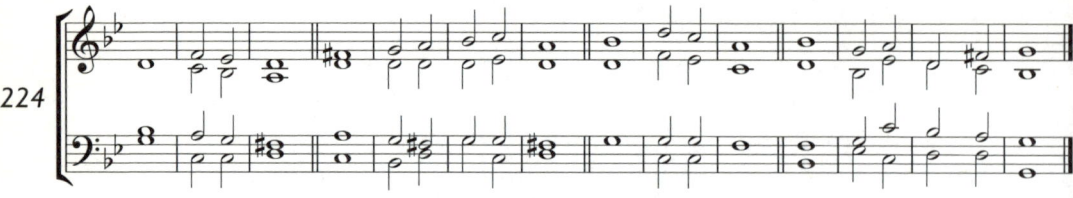

1 Christ suffered for you, leaving you ' an ex'ample, ♦
  that you should ' follow ' in his ' steps.

2 He committed no sin, no guile was ' found on his ' lips, ♦
  when he was reviled, he did ' not re'vile in ' turn.

3 When he suffered, he ' did not ' threaten, ♦
  but he trusted himself to ' God who ' judges ' justly.

4 Christ himself bore our sins in his body ' on the ' tree, ♦
  that we might die to ' sin and ' live to ' righteousness.

5 By his wounds, you ' have been ' healed, ♦
  for ' you were ' straying like ' sheep,

5a but have ' now re'turned ♦
  to the shepherd and ' guardian ' of your ' souls.

1 Peter 2.21b-25

Glory to the Father and ' to the ' Son ♦
and ' to the ' Holy ' Spirit;

as it was in the be'ginning is ' now ♦
and shall be for ' ever. ' A'men.

A Song of Faith (Easter)

George J. Elvey

1 Blessed be the ' God and ' Father ♦
  of our ' Lord ' Jesus ' Christ!

2 By his great mercy we have been born anew to a ' living ' hope ♦
  through the resurrection of Jesus ' Christ ' from the ' dead,

3 Into an inheritance that ' is im'perishable, ♦
  undefiled and unfading,
    ' kept in ' heaven for ' you,

4 Who are being protected by the power of God
    through faith ' for a sal'vation, ♦
  ready to be re'vealed • in the ' last ' time.

5 You were ransomed from the futile ' ways of your ' ancestors ♦
  not with perishable ' things like ' silver or ' gold

6 But with the precious ' blood of ' Christ ♦
  like that of a lamb ' without ' spot or ' stain.

‡ 7 Through him we have confidence in God,
    who raised him from the dead and ' gave him ' glory, ♦
  so that your faith and ' hope are ' set on ' God.

1 Peter 1.3-5,18,19,21

Glory to the Father and ' to the ' Son ♦
and ' to the ' Holy ' Spirit;

as it was in the be'ginning is ' now ♦
and shall be for ' ever. ' A'men.

A Song of God's Children (Pentecost)

John Goss

1 The law of the Spirit of life ' in Christ ' Jesus ♦
  has set us free from the ' law of ' sin and ' death.

2 All who are led by the Spirit of God are ' children of ' God; ♦
  for we have received the Spirit that enables us to ' cry, '
    ' 'Abba, ' Father'.

3 The Spirit himself bears witness that we are ' children of ' God ♦
  and if God's ' children, then ' heirs of ' God;

4 If heirs of God, then fellow'heirs with ' Christ; ♦
  since we suffer with him now, that ' we • may be ' glorified ' with him.

5 These sufferings that we ' now en'dure ♦
  are not worth comparing to the glory ' that shall ' be re'vealed.

6 For the creation waits with ' eager ' longing ♦
  for the re'vealing • of the ' children of ' God.

Romans 8.2,14,15b-19

Glory to the Father and ' to the ' Son ♦
and ' to the ' Holy ' Spirit;

as it was in the be'ginning is ' now ♦
and shall be for ' ever. ' A'men.

A Song of the Lamb (Ordinary Time)
Jonathan Battishill

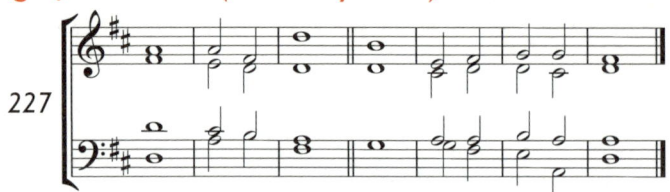

227

1 Salvation and glory and power be'long to our ' God, ♦
   whose ' judgements are ' true and ' just.

2 Praise our God, all ' you his ' servants, ♦
   all who ' fear him, both ' small and ' great.

3 The Lord our God, the Al'mighty, ' reigns: ♦
   let us rejoice and ex'ult and ' give him the ' glory.

4 For the marriage of the ' Lamb has ' come ♦
   and his ' bride has ' made herself ' ready.

5 Blessed are those who ' are in'vited ♦
   to the wedding ' banquet ' of the ' Lamb.

Revelation 19.1b,5b,6b,7,9b

To the One who sits on the throne and ' to the ' Lamb ♦
be blessing and honour and glory and might,
    for ever and ' ever. ' A'men.

This verse replaces Glory to the Father…

Benedictus – the Song of Zechariah

228 — Henry Lawes

or

229 — Edwin Monk

222   *A Song of the Lamb*

or   Noel Rawsthorne

1 Blessed be the Lord the ' God of ' Israel, ♦
   who has come to his ' people and ' set them ' free.

2 He has raised up for us a ' mighty ' Saviour, ♦
   born of the ' house of his ' servant ' David.

3 Through his holy prophets God ' promised of ' old ♦
   to save us from our enemies,
      from the ' hands of ' all that ' hate us,

4 To show mercy ' to our ' ancestors, ♦
   and to re'member his ' holy ' covenant.

5 This was the oath God swore to our ' father ' Abraham: ♦
   to set us ' free • from the ' hands of our ' enemies,

6 Free to worship him ' without ' fear, ♦
   holy and righteous in his sight
      ' all the ' days of our ' life.

7 And you, child, shall be called the prophet of the ' Most ' High, ♦
   for you will go before the ' Lord • to pre'pare his ' way,

8 To give his people knowledge ' of sal'vation ♦
   by the for'giveness of ' all their ' sins.

9 In the tender compassion ' of our ' God ♦
   the dawn from on ' high shall ' break up'on us,

10 To shine on those who dwell in darkness and the ' shadow of ' death, ♦
   and to guide our feet ' into the ' way of ' peace.

                                                 Luke 1.68-79

Glory to the Father and ' to the ' Son ♦
and ' to the ' Holy ' Spirit;

as it was in the be'ginning is ' now ♦
and shall be for ' ever. ' A'men.

Benedictus

Magnificat – the Song of Mary

Edgar Day

George M. Garrett

Walter Parratt

(small notes for organ only)

1 My soul proclaims the greatness of the Lord,
    my spirit rejoices in ' God my ' Saviour; ♦
  he has looked with ' favour • on his ' lowly ' servant.

2 From this day all generations will ' call me ' blessed; ♦
  the Almighty has done great things for me
    and ' holy ' is his ' name.

3 He has mercy on ' those who ' fear him, ♦
  from gene'ration to ' gene'ration.

4 He has shown strength ' with his ' arm ♦
  and has scattered the ' proud in ' their con'ceit,

5 Casting down the mighty ' from their ' thrones ♦
  and ' lifting ' up the ' lowly.

6 He has filled the hungry with ' good ' things ♦
  and sent the ' rich a'way ' empty.

7 He has come to the aid of his ' servant ' Israel, ♦
  to re'member his ' promise of ' mercy,

8 The promise ' made to our ' ancestors, ♦
  to Abraham ' and his ' children for ' ever.

Luke 1.46-55

  Glory to the Father... *as opposite*

Nunc dimittis – the Song of Simeon

Raymond Lewis

234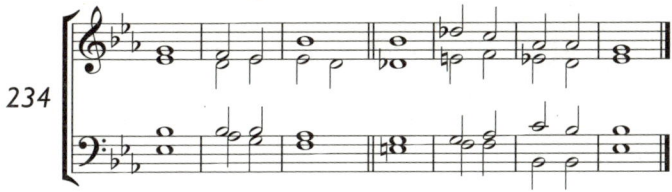

or

Charles H. Lloyd

235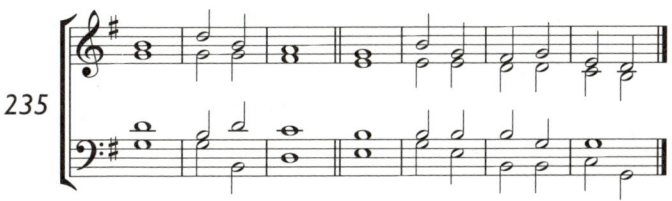

or

Frederick A.G. Ouseley

236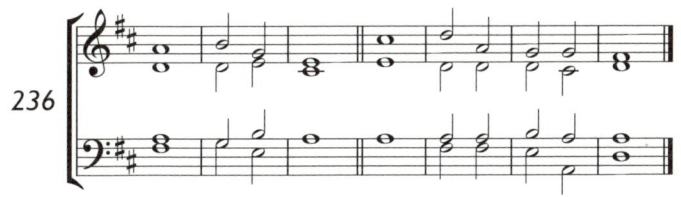

1 Now, Lord, you let your servant ' go in ' peace: ♦
your ' word has ' been ful'filled.

2 My own eyes have ' seen the sal'vation ♦
which you have prepared in the ' sight of ' every ' people;

‡ 3 A light to reveal you ' to the ' nations ♦
and the glory ' of your ' people ' Israel.

Luke 2.29-32

Glory to the Father and ' to the ' Son ♦
and ' to the ' Holy ' Spirit;

as it was in the be'ginning is ' now ♦
and shall be for ' ever. ' A'men.

The Song of Christ's Glory
J. Harrison

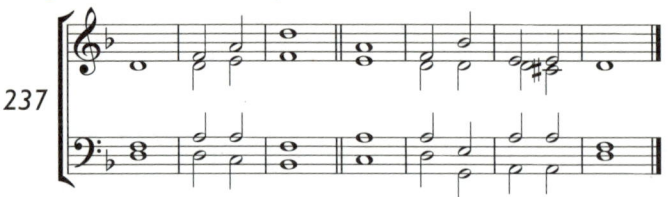

237

1 Christ Jesus was in the ' form of ' God, ♦
    but he did not ' cling to e'quality with ' God.

2 He emptied himself, taking the form ' of a ' servant, ♦
    and was ' born • in our ' human ' likeness.

3 Being found in human form he ' humbled him'self, ♦
    and became obedient unto death, ' even ' death • on a ' cross.

J. Harrison

238

4 Therefore God has ' highly ex'alted him, ♦
    and bestowed on him the ' name above ' every ' name,

5 That at the name of Jesus, every ' knee should ' bow, ♦
    in heaven and on ' earth and ' under the ' earth;

6 And every tongue confess that Jesus ' Christ is ' Lord, ♦
    to the ' glory of ' God the ' Father.

Philippians 2.5-11

Glory to the Father and ' to the ' Son ♦
and ' to the ' Holy ' Spirit;

as it was in the be'ginning is ' now ♦
and shall be for ' ever. ' A'men.

Great and Wonderful
George A Macfarren

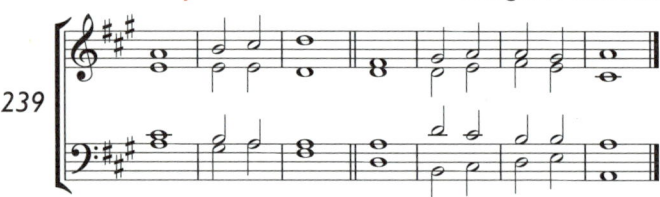

239

1 Great and wonderful ' are your ' deeds, ♦
    Lord ' God ' the Al'mighty.

2 Just and ' true are your ' ways, ♦
  O ' ruler ' of the ' nations.

3 Who shall not revere and praise your ' name, O ' Lord? ♦
  for ' you a'lone are ' holy.

4 All nations shall come and worship ' in your ' presence: ♦
  for your just ' dealings have ' been re'vealed.

Revelation 15.3, 4

‡   To the One who sits on the throne and ' to the ' Lamb ♦
    be blessing and honour and glory and might,
        for ever and ' ever. ' A'men.

This verse replaces Glory to the Father...

Bless the Lord

James Nares

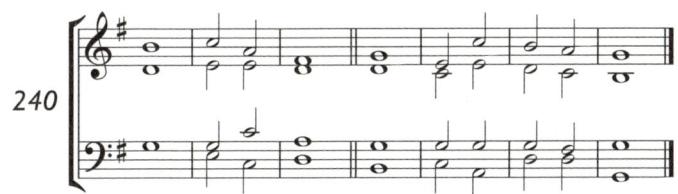

240

1 Blessed are you, the ' God of our ' ancestors, ♦
  worthy to be ' praised • and ex'alted for ' ever.

2 Blessed is your holy and ' glorious ' name, ♦
  worthy to be ' praised • and ex'alted for ' ever.

3 Blessed are you, in your holy and ' glorious ' temple, ♦
  worthy to be ' praised • and ex'alted for ' ever.

4 Blessed are you who look ' into the ' depths, ♦
  worthy to be ' praised • and ex'alted for ' ever.

5 Blessed are you, en'throned on the ' cherubim, ♦
  worthy to be ' praised • and ex'alted for ' ever.

6 Blessed are you on the ' throne of your ' kingdom, ♦
  worthy to be ' praised • and ex'alted for ' ever.

7 Blessed are you in the ' heights of ' heaven, ♦
  worthy to be ' praised • and ex'alted for ' ever.

The Song of the Three 29-34

   Bless the Father, the Son and the ' Holy ' Spirit, ♦
   worthy to be ' praised • and ex'alted for ' ever.

This verse replaces Glory to the Father...

Saviour of the World

Kellow J. Pye

241

1 Jesus, Saviour of the world,
  come to us ' in your ' mercy: ♦
 we look to ' you to ' save and ' help us.

2 By your cross and your life laid down,
  you set your ' people ' free: ♦
 we look to ' you to ' save and ' help us.

3 When they were ready to perish, you ' saved • your dis'ciples: ♦
 we look to ' you to ' come to our ' help.

4 In the greatness of your mercy, loose us ' from our ' chains, ♦
 forgive the ' sins of ' all your ' people.

5 Make yourself known as our Saviour and ' mighty de'liverer; ♦
 save and ' help us that ' we may ' praise you.

6 Come now and dwell with us, ' Lord Christ ' Jesus: ♦
 hear our prayer ' and be ' with us ' always.

‡ 7 And when you ' come in your ' glory: ♦
 make us to be one with you
  and to share the ' life ' of your ' kingdom.

  Glory to the Father and ' to the ' Son ♦
  and ' to the ' Holy ' Spirit;

  as it was in the be'ginning is ' now ♦
  and shall be for ' ever. ' A'men.

228 *Saviour of the World*

Te Deum laudamus

Charles V. Stanford

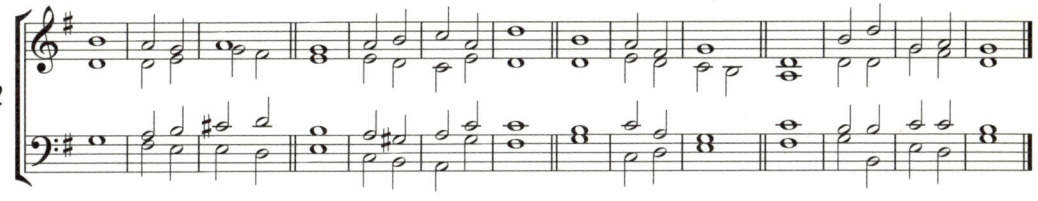

42

or

Thomas A. Walmisley

43

or

Samuel Wesley

44

1 We praise you, O God,
    we acclaim you ' as the ' Lord; ♦
all creation worships you,
    the ' Father ' ever'lasting.

2 To you all angels, all the ' powers of ' heaven, ♦
the cherubim and seraphim, ' sing in ' endless ' praise:

3 Holy, holy, holy Lord, God of ' power and ' might, ♦
heaven and ' earth are ' full of your ' glory.

4 The glorious company of a'postles ' praise you. ♦
The noble ' fellowship of ' prophets ' praise you.

5 The white-robed army of ' martyrs ' praise you. ♦
Throughout the world the ' holy ' Church ac'claims you:

6 Father, of majesty unbounded,
    your true and only Son, worthy ' of all ' praise, ♦
the Holy Spirit, ' advo'cate and ' guide.

Charles V. Stanford

245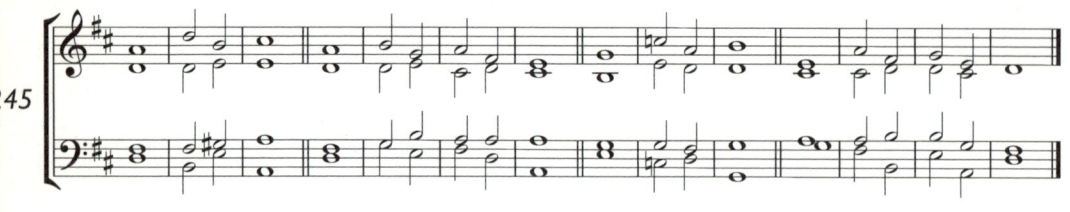

or Thomas A. Walmisley

246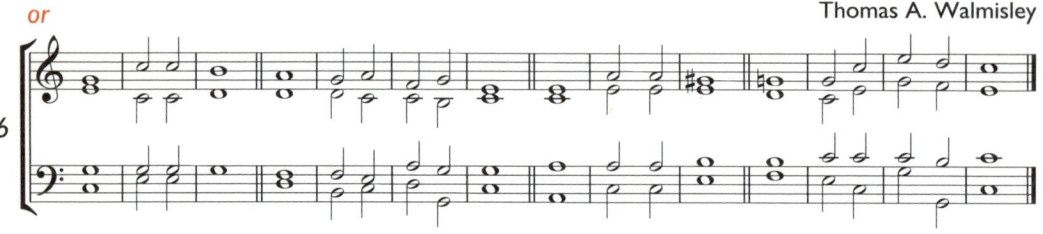

or Samuel Wesley

247

   7 You, Christ, are the ' King of ' glory, ♦
      the e'ternal ' Son of the ' Father.

   8 When you took our flesh to ' set us ' free ♦
      you humbly ' chose the ' Virgin's ' womb.

   9 You overcame the ' sting of ' death ♦
      and opened the kingdom of ' heaven to ' all be'lievers.

 10 You are seated at God's right ' hand in ' glory. ♦
      We believe that you will ' come and ' be our ' judge.

 11 Come then, Lord, and ' help your ' people, ♦
      bought with the ' price of ' your own ' blood,

 12 and bring us ' with your ' saints ♦
      to ' glory ' ever'lasting.

The canticle may end here.

230   *Te Deum laudamus*

Charles V. Stanford

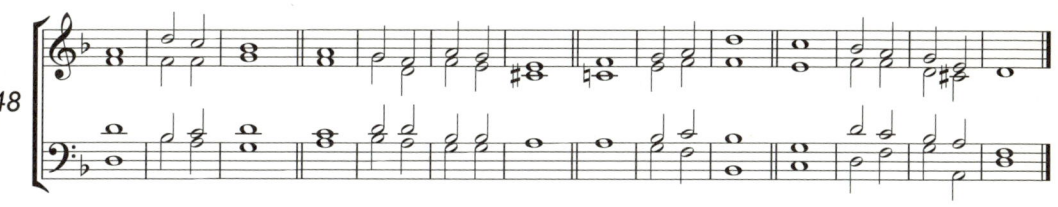

or

Thomas A. Walmisley

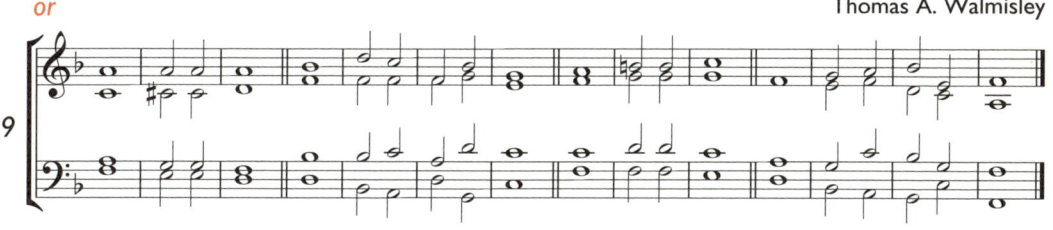

or

Samuel Wesley

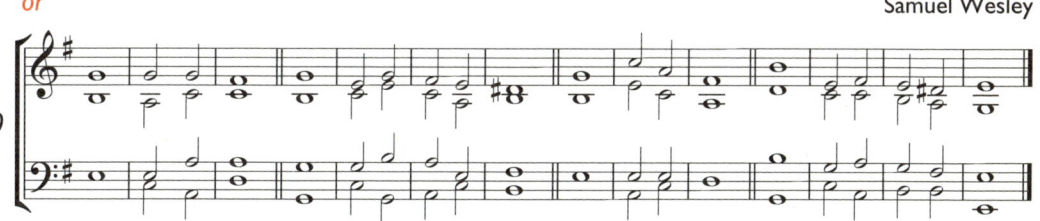

13 Save your people, Lord, and ' bless your in'heritance. ♦
   Govern and up'hold them ' now and ' always.

14 Day by ' day we ' bless you. ♦
   We ' praise your ' name for ' ever.

15 Keep us today, Lord, ' from all ' sin. ♦
   Have mercy ' on us, ' Lord, have ' mercy.

16 Lord, show us your ' love and ' mercy, ♦
   for we have ' put our ' trust in ' you.

‡ 17 In you, Lord, ' is our ' hope: ♦
   let us ' never be ' put to ' shame.

¶ **Canticles from *The Book of Common Prayer***

Venite, exultemus Domino   Edward J. Hopkins

251

1 O come, let us ' sing unto the ' Lord ♦
   let us heartily rejoice in the ' strength of ' our sal'vation.

2 Let us come before his ' presence with ' thanksgiving ♦
   and shew ourselves ' glad in ' him with ' psalms.

3 For the Lord is a ' great ' God ♦
   and a great ' King a'bove all ' gods.

4 In his hand are all the ' corners • of the ' earth ♦
   and the strength of the ' hills is ' his ' also.

5 The sea is ' his, • and he ' made it ♦
   and his ' hands pre'pared the dry ' land.

6 O come let us worship and ' fall ' down ♦
   and kneel be'fore the ' Lord our ' Maker.

‡ 7 For he is the ' Lord our ' God ♦
   and we are the people of his pasture, ' and the ' sheep of his ' hand.

[8 Today if ye will ' hear his ' voice ♦
   harden not your hearts ' as in the ' provo'cation,

8a, 9 And as in the day of temp'tation • in the ' wilderness ♦
   when your fathers tempted me, ' proved me and ' saw my ' works.

10 Forty years long was I grieved with this gene'ration, and ' said ♦
   It is a people that do err in their hearts,
      for they ' have not ' known my ' ways;

11 Unto whom I ' sware • in my ' wrath ♦
   that they should not ' enter ' into my ' rest.]

Psalm 95

Glory be to the Father, and ' to the ' Son ♦
and ' to the ' Holy ' Ghost;
As it was in the beginning, is now and ' ever ' shall be ♦
world without ' end. A'–'men.

The Easter Anthems

George M. Garrett

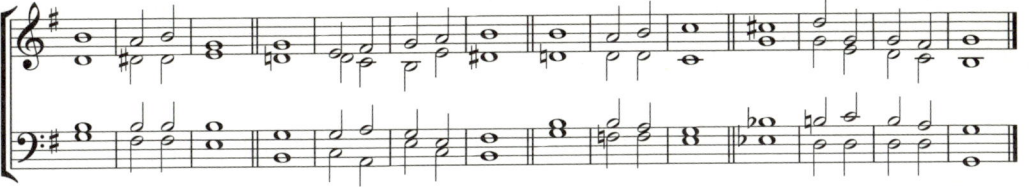

1 Christ our passover is ' sacrificed ' for us ♦
therefore ' let us ' keep the ' feast;

2 Not with the old leaven,
    nor with the leaven of ' malice and ' wickedness ♦
but with the unleavened ' bread • of sin'cerity and ' truth.
1 Corinthians 5.7b,8

3 Christ being raised from the dead ' dieth no ' more ♦
death hath ' no more do'minion ' over him.

4 For in that he died, he died unto ' sin ' once ♦
but in that he liveth, he ' liveth ' unto ' God.

5 Likewise reckon ye also yourselves to be dead in'deed • unto ' sin ♦
but alive unto God, through ' Jesus ' Christ our ' Lord.
Romans 6.9-11

6 Christ is ' risen • from the ' dead ♦
and become the ' first-fruits of ' them that ' slept.

7 For since by ' man came ' death ♦
by man came also the resur'rection ' of the ' dead.

8 For as in ' Adam all ' die ♦
even so in Christ shall ' all be ' made a'live.
1 Corinthians 15.20-22

Glory be to the Father, and ' to the ' Son ♦
and ' to the ' Holy ' Ghost;
As it was in the beginning, is now and ' ever ' shall be ♦
world without ' end. A'–'men.

Te Deum laudamus

Charles V. Stanford

253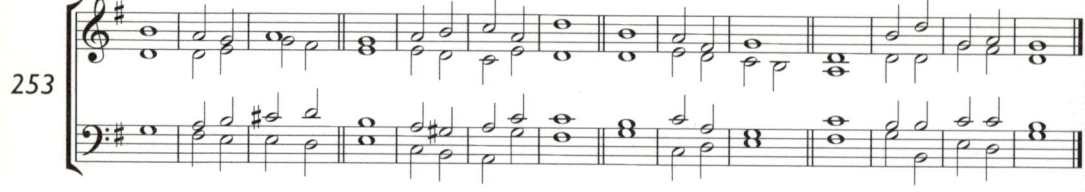

or

Thomas A. Walmisley

254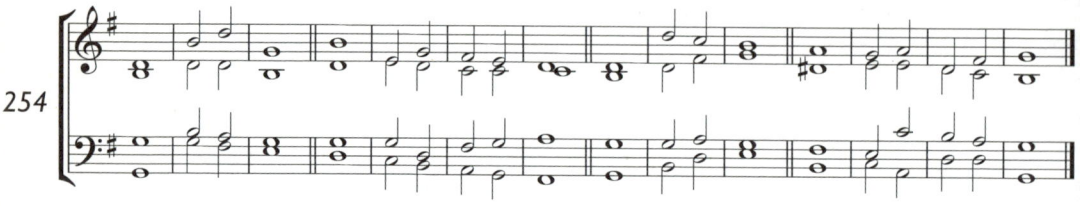

or

Samuel Wesley

255

1 We ′ praise thee, O ′ God; ♦
  we ac′knowledge thee to ′ be the ′ Lord.

2 All the ′ earth doth ′ worship thee, ♦
  the ′ Father ′ ever′lasting.

3 To thee all angels ′ cry a′loud, ♦
  the heavens and ′ all the ′ powers there′in.

4 To thee ′ cherubin and ′ seraphin ♦
  con′tinual′ly do ′ cry,

5,6 Holy, Holy, Holy, Lord ′ God of ′ Sabaoth; ♦
  heaven and earth are full of the ′ majesty ′ of thy ′ glory.

7,8 The glorious company of the Apostles praise thee. ♦
  The goodly fellowship of the ′ Prophets ′ praise thee.
  the noble ′ army of ′ Martyrs ′ praise thee.

9 The holy Church throughout all the ′ world • doth ac′knowledge thee: ♦
  the ′ Father • of an ′ infinite ′ majesty;

10 Thine honourable true and ′ only ′ Son; ♦
  also the ′ Holy ′ Ghost the ′ Comforter.

Te Deum laudamus (BCP)

Charles V. Stanford

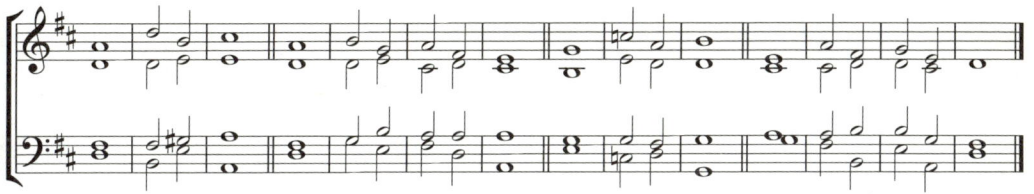

or

Thomas A. Walmisley

or

Samuel Wesley

11 Thou art the King of ' glory, O ' Christ. ♦
   thou art the ever'lasting ' Son of the ' Father.

12 When thou tookest upon thee to de'liver ' man, ♦
   thou didst not ab'hor the ' Virgin's ' womb.

13 When thou hadst overcome the ' sharpness of ' death, ♦
   thou didst open the kingdom of ' heaven to ' all be'lievers.

14 Thou sittest at the ' right hand of ' God, ♦
   in the ' glory ' of the ' Father.

15,16 We believe that thou shalt come to ' be our ' judge. ♦
   We therefore pray thee, help thy servants,
      whom thou hast re'deemed • with thy ' precious ' blood.

17 Make them to be numbered ' with thy ' saints ♦
   in ' glory ' ever'lasting.

Te Deum laudamus (BCP)

Charles V. Stanford

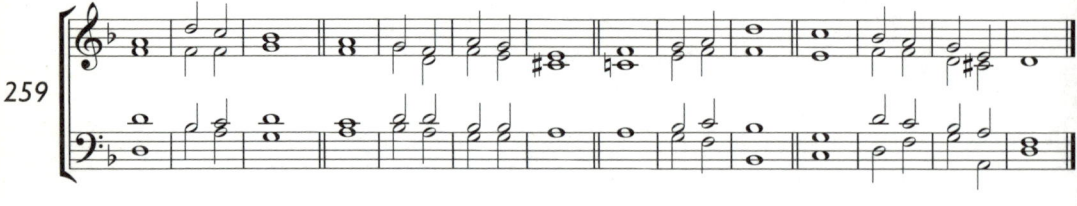

259

or

Thomas A. Walmisley

260

or

Samuel Wesley

261

18 O Lord, save thy people and ' bless thine ' heritage. ♦
Govern them and ' lift them ' up for ' ever.

19 Day by day we ' magnify ' thee; ♦
and we worship thy ' name, • ever ' world without ' end.

20,21 Vouchsafe, O Lord, to keep us this ' day without ' sin. ♦
O Lord, have mercy up'on us, have ' mercy up'on us.

22 O Lord, let thy mercy ' lighten up'on us, ♦
as our ' trust ' is in ' thee.

‡ 23 O Lord, in ' thee • have I ' trusted; ♦
let me ' never ' be con'founded.

236 *Te Deum laudamus (BCP)*

Benedicite, omnia opera

Joseph Barnby

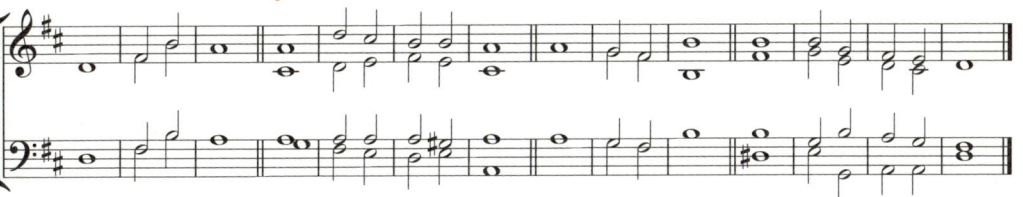

or

John Harper

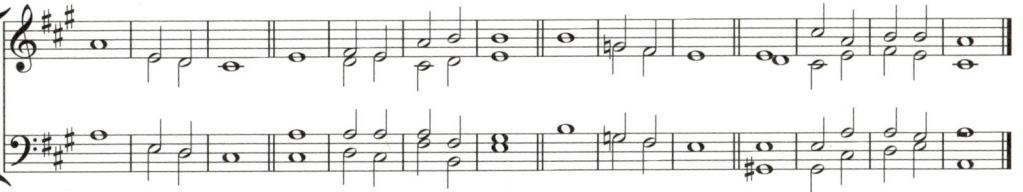

1. O all ye Works of the Lord, ' bless ye the ' Lord ♦
praise him and ' magnify ' him for ' ever.

2. O ye Angels of the Lord, ' bless ye the ' Lord ♦
praise him and ' magnify ' him for ' ever.

3. O ye Heavens, ' bless ye the ' Lord ♦
praise him and ' magnify ' him for ' ever.

4. O ye Waters that be above the Firmament, ' bless ye the ' Lord ♦
praise him and ' magnify ' him for ' ever.

5. O all ye Powers of the Lord, ' bless ye the ' Lord ♦
praise him and ' magnify ' him for ' ever.

6. O ye Sun and Moon, ' bless ye the ' Lord ♦
praise him and ' magnify ' him for ' ever.

7. O ye Stars of Heaven, ' bless ye the ' Lord ♦
praise him and ' magnify ' him for ' ever.

8. O ye Showers and Dew, ' bless ye the ' Lord ♦
praise him and ' magnify ' him for ' ever.

9. O ye Winds of God, ' bless ye the ' Lord ♦
praise him and ' magnify ' him for ' ever.

10. O ye Fire and Heat, ' bless ye the ' Lord ♦
praise him and ' magnify ' him for ' ever.

11. O ye Winter and Summer, ' bless ye the ' Lord ♦
praise him and ' magnify ' him for ' ever.

12. O ye Dews and Frosts, ' bless ye the ' Lord ♦
praise him and ' magnify ' him for ' ever.

13. O ye Frost and Cold, ' bless ye the ' Lord ♦
praise him and ' magnify ' him for ' ever.

14. O ye Ice and Snow, ' bless ye the ' Lord ♦
praise him and ' magnify ' him for ' ever.

Joseph Barnby

262

or

John Harper

263

15 O ye Nights and Days, ' bless ye the ' Lord ♦
   praise him and ' magnify ' him for ' ever.

16 O ye Light and Darkness, ' bless ye the ' Lord ♦
   praise him and ' magnify ' him for ' ever.

17 O ye Lightnings and Clouds, ' bless ye the ' Lord ♦
   praise him and ' magnify ' him for ' ever.

18 O let the Earth ' bless the ' Lord ♦
   yea let it praise him and ' magnify ' him for ' ever.

19 O ye Mountains and Hills, ' bless ye the ' Lord ♦
   praise him and ' magnify ' him for ' ever.

20 O all ye Green Things upon the Earth, ' bless ye the ' Lord ♦
   praise him and ' magnify ' him for ' ever.

21 O ye Wells, ' bless ye the ' Lord ♦
   praise him and ' magnify ' him for ' ever.

22 O ye Seas and Floods, ' bless ye the ' Lord ♦
   praise him and ' magnify ' him for ' ever.

23 O ye Whales, and all that move in the Waters, ' bless ye the ' Lord ♦
   praise him and ' magnify ' him for ' ever.

24 O all ye Fowls of the Air, ' bless ye the ' Lord ♦
   praise him and ' magnify ' him for ' ever.

25 O all ye Beasts and Cattle, ' bless ye the ' Lord ♦
   praise him and ' magnify ' him for ' ever.

26 O ye Children of Men, ' bless ye the ' Lord ♦
   praise him and ' magnify ' him for ' ever.

27 O let Israel ' bless the ' Lord ♦
   praise him and ' magnify ' him for ' ever.

28 O ye Priests of the Lord, ' bless ye the ' Lord ♦
   praise him and ' magnify ' him for ' ever.

Benedicite, omnia opera (BCP)

29 O ye Servants of the Lord, | bless ye the | Lord ♦
praise him and | magnify | him for | ever.

30 O ye Spirits and Souls of the Righteous, | bless ye the | Lord ♦
praise him and | magnify | him for | ever.

31 O ye holy and humble Men of heart, | bless ye the | Lord ♦
praise him and | magnify | him for | ever.

32 O Ananias, Azarias and Misael, | bless ye the | Lord ♦
praise him and | magnify | him for | ever.

The Song of the Three Holy Children 35-66

Glory be to the Father, and | to the | Son ♦
and | to the | Holy | Ghost;
As it was in the beginning, is now and | ever | shall be ♦
world without | end. A|–|men.

Benedictus

Henry Lawes

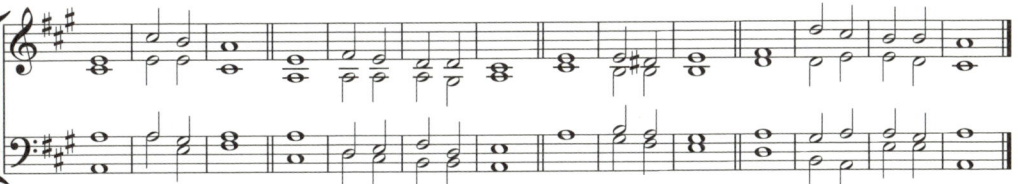

or   Edwin Monk

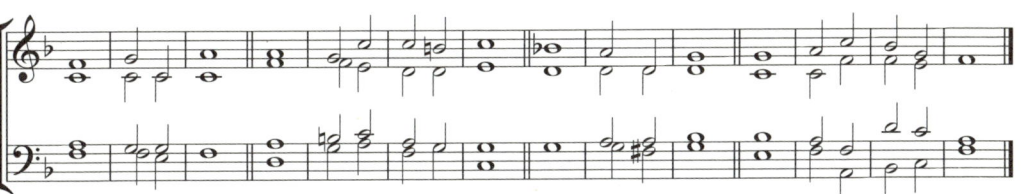

or   Noel Rawsthorne

1 Blessed be the Lord | God of | Israel ♦
for he hath | visited, • and re|deemed his | people;

2 And hath raised up a mighty sal|vation | for us ♦
in the | house • of his | servant | David;

3 As he spake by the mouth of his | holy | Prophets ♦
which have | been • since the | world be|gan;

4 That we should be | saved • from our | enemies ♦
and from the | hands of | all that | hate us;

Benedictus (BCP)   239

Henry Lawes

264

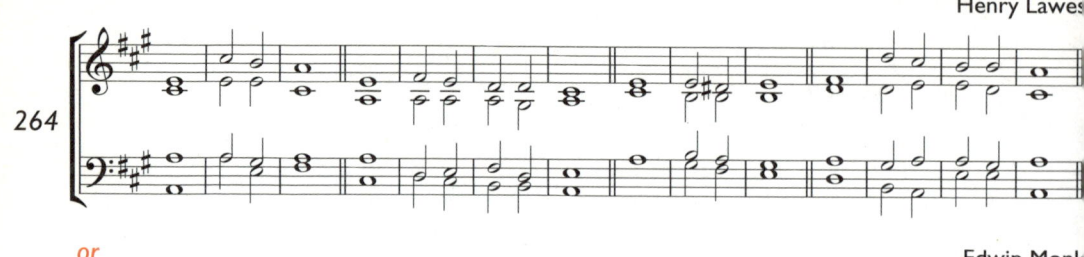

or

Edwin Monk

265

or

Noel Rawsthorne

266

5 To perform the mercy ' promised • to our ' forefathers ♦
and to re'member his ' holy ' covenant;

6 To per'form the ' oath ♦
which he ' sware • to our ' forefather ' Abraham;

7 That ' he would ' give us ♦
that we being delivered out of the hand of our enemies
   might ' serve him ' without ' fear,

8 In holiness and ' righteousness be'fore him ♦
all the ' days ' of our ' life.

9 And thou, child, shalt be called the ' Prophet • of the ' Highest ♦
for thou shalt go before the face of the ' Lord • to pre'pare his ' ways;

10 To give knowledge of salvation ' unto his ' people ♦
for the re'mission ' of their ' sins;

11 Through the tender ' mercy • of our ' God ♦
whereby the ' day-spring • from on ' high hath ' visited us;

12 To give light to them that sit in darkness, and in the ' shadow of ' death ♦
and to guide our ' feet in•to the ' way of ' peace.

Luke 1.68-79

Glory be to the Father, and ' to the ' Son ♦
and ' to the ' Holy ' Ghost;
As it was in the beginning, is now and ' ever ' shall be ♦
world without ' end. A'–'men.

240   *Benedictus (BCP)*

Jubilate

Jonathan Battishill

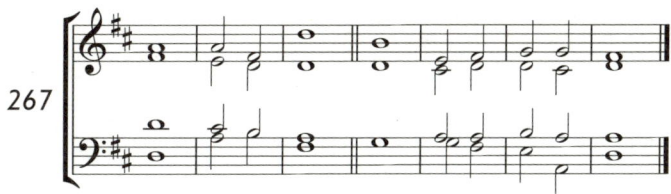

267

1 O be joyful in the Lord, ' all ye ' lands ♦
serve the Lord with gladness,
    and come before his ' presence ' with a ' song.

2 Be ye sure that the Lord ' he is ' God ♦
it is he that hath made us, and not we ourselves,
    we are his ' people, • and the ' sheep of his ' pasture.

3 O go your way into his gates with thanksgiving,
    and into his ' courts with ' praise ♦
be thankful unto ' him • and speak ' good of his ' Name.

4 For the Lord is gracious, his mercy is ' ever'lasting ¨
and his truth endureth from gene'ration to ' gene'ration.

Psalm 100

    Glory be to the Father, and ' to the ' Son ♦
    and ' to the ' Holy ' Ghost;
    As it was in the beginning, is now and ' ever ' shall be ♦
    world without ' end. A' – 'men.

Jubilate (BCP)

Magnificat

268   Edgar Day

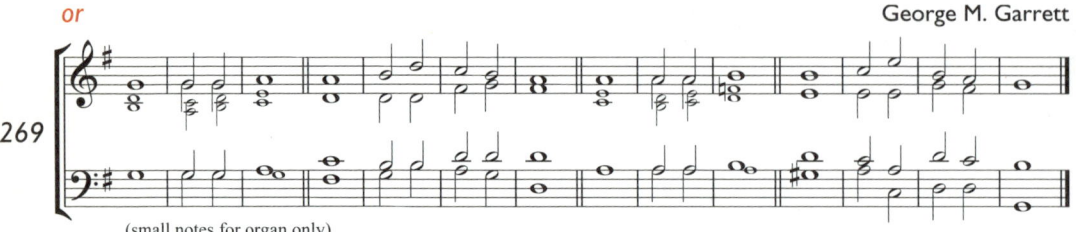

or

269   George M. Garrett

(small notes for organ only)

or

270   Walter Parratt

1. My soul doth ' magnify the ' Lord ♦
   and my spirit hath re'joiced in ' God my ' Saviour.

2. For ' he hath re'garded ♦
   the ' lowliness ' of his ' handmaiden.

3. For be'hold from ' henceforth ♦
   all gene'rations shall ' call me ' blessed.

4. For he that is mighty hath ' magnified ' me ♦
   and ' holy ' is his ' Name.

5. And his mercy is on ' them that ' fear him ♦
   throughout ' all ' gene'rations.

6. He hath shewed ' strength • with his ' arm ♦
   he hath scattered the proud in the imagi'nation ' of their ' hearts.

7. He hath put down the ' mighty • from their ' seat ♦
   and hath ex'alted the ' humble and ' meek.

8. He hath filled the ' hungry with ' good things ♦
   and the ' rich he • hath sent ' empty a'way.

9. He re'membering his ' mercy ♦
   hath ' holpen his ' servant ' Israel

10. As he ' promised • to our ' forefathers, ♦
    Abraham ' and his ' seed for ' ever.

Luke 1.46-55

Glory be to the Father... *as opposite*

242   *Magnificat (BCP)*

Cantate Domino

George J. Elvey

1 O sing unto the ' Lord a new ' song ♦
    for ' he hath done ' marvellous ' things.

2 With his own right hand, and with his ' holy ' arm ♦
    hath he ' gotten him'self the ' victory.

3 The Lord de'clared • his sal'vation ♦
    his righteousness hath he openly ' shewed • in the '
        sight of the ' heathen.

4 He hath remembered his mercy and truth
        toward the ' house of ' Israel ♦
    and all the ends of the world have seen the sal'vation of ' our ' God.

5 Shew yourselves joyful unto the Lord, ' all ye ' lands ♦
    sing, re'joice, and ' give ' thanks.

6 Praise the Lord up'on the ' harp ♦
    sing to the ' harp • with a ' psalm of ' thanksgiving.

7 With trumpets ' also and ' shawms ♦
    O shew yourselves joyful be'fore the ' Lord the ' King.

8 Let the sea make a noise, and all that ' therein ' is ♦
    the round world, and ' they that ' dwell there'in.

9 Let the floods clap their hands,
        and let the hills be joyful together be'fore the ' Lord ♦
    for he is ' come to ' judge the ' earth.

10 With righteousness shall he ' judge the ' world ♦
    and the ' people ' with ' equity.

Psalm 98

Glory be to the Father, and ' to the ' Son ♦
and ' to the ' Holy ' Ghost;
As it was in the beginning, is now and ' ever ' shall be ♦
world without ' end. A'–'men.

Nunc dimittis

272 Raymond Lewis

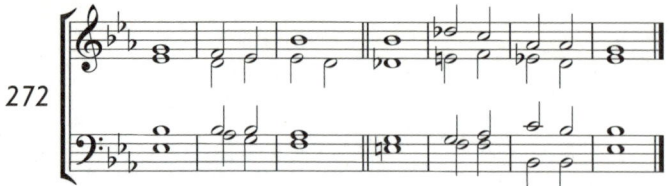

273 Charles H. Lloyd

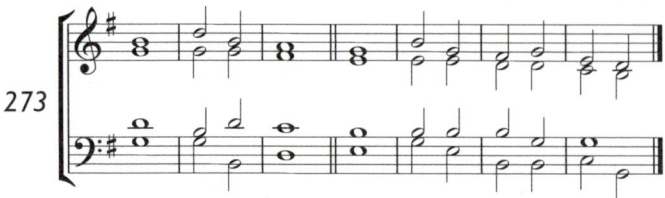

274 Frederick A.G. Ouseley

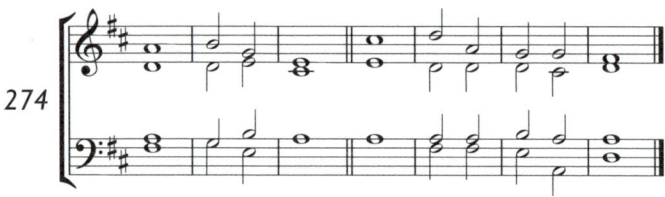

1 Lord now lettest thou thy servant de'part in ' peace ♦
  ac'cording ' to thy ' word.

2 For mine eyes have ' seen thy sal'vation; ♦
  which thou hast prepared before the ' face of ' all ' people;

3 To be a light to ' lighten the ' Gentiles ♦
  and to be the ' glory • of thy ' people ' Israel.

Luke 2.29-32

Glory be to the Father, and ' to the ' Son ♦
and ' to the ' Holy ' Ghost;
As it was in the beginning, is now and ' ever ' shall be ♦
world without ' end. A'–'men.

Deus misereatur

James Nares

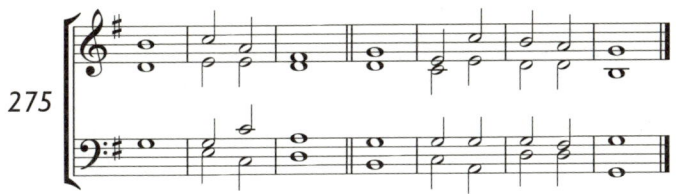

275

1 God be merciful unto ' us, and ' bless us ♦
   and shew us the light of his countenance, ' and be ' merciful ' unto us

2 That thy way may be ' known upon ' earth ♦
   thy saving ' health a'mong all ' nations.

3 Let the people ' praise thee, O ' God ♦
   yea, let ' all the ' people ' praise thee.

4 O let the nations re'joice • and be ' glad ♦
   for thou shalt judge the folk righteously,
      and ' govern the ' nations • upon ' earth.

5 Let the people ' praise thee, O ' God ♦
   yea, let ' all the ' people ' praise thee.

6 Then shall the earth bring ' forth her ' increase ♦
   and God, even our ' own God, shall ' give us his ' blessing.

‡ 7 God ' shall ' bless us ♦
   and all the ' ends • of the ' world shall ' fear him.

Psalm 67

   Glory be to the Father, and ' to the ' Son ♦
   and ' to the ' Holy ' Ghost;
   As it was in the beginning, is now and ' ever ' shall be ♦
   world without ' end. A'–'men.

¶ Index of canticles, hymns and anthems

Opening Hymn and Canticles at Morning and Evening Prayer

Benedicite – a Song of Creation	full text	204
Benedicite – a Song of Creation	shorter version	205
Venite – a Song of Triumph		206
Jubilate – a Song of Joy		207
The Easter Anthems		208
Phos hilaron		209
Verses from Psalm 141		210
Verses from Psalm 104		211

Old and New Testament Canticles at Morning and Evening Prayer

Morning Prayer

A Song of the Wilderness	Advent	212
A Song of the Messiah	Christmas	213
A Song of the New Jerusalem	Epiphany	213
A Song of Humility	Lent	214
The Song of Moses and Miriam	Easter	215
A Song of Ezekiel	Pentecost	216
A Song of David	Ordinary Time	217

Evening Prayer

A Song of the Spirit	Advent	218
A Song of Redemption	Christmas	218
A Song of Praise	Epiphany	219
A Song of Christ the Servant	Lent	220
A Song of Faith	Easter	221
A Song of God's Children	Pentecost	221
A Song of the Lamb	Ordinary Time	222

Gospel Canticles

Benedictus – the Song of Zechariah	222
Magnificat – the Song of Mary	224
Nunc dimittis – the Song of Simeon	225

Other Canticles

The Song of Christ's Glory	226
Great and Wonderful	226
Bless the Lord	227
Saviour of the World	228

Te Deum laudamus   229

Canticles from *The Book of Common Prayer*

Venite, exultemus Domino	232
The Easter Anthems	233
Te Deum laudamus	234
Benedicite, omnia opera	237
Benedictus	239
Jubilate	241
Magnificat	242
Cantate Domino	243
Nunc dimittis	244
Deus misereatur	245

Index of chants

Attwood T	46, 81, 85, 190, 221
Barnby J	6, 9, 22, 31, 65, 66, 74, 75, 79, 116, 148, 168, 170, 173, 194, 204, 218, 224, 262
Battishill J	3, 44, 71, 72, 115, 122, 129, 174, 213, 227, 267
Beethoven L V, see Stainer	
Bramma H	39
Camidge J	29, 101, 105, 157
Camidge M	12, 28, 64, 94, 131, 132
Chipp E	96, 119
Clarke J, see Goss	
Cooke R	162
Croft W	1, 183, 211, 212
Davies H Walford	171
Day E	103, 231, 268
Elvey G J	127, 201, 210, 216, 225, 271
Elvey S	62
Ferguson B	151, 177, 179
Flintoft L	27, 54, 55, 99
Foster J	97, 160
Garrett G M	10, 51, 53, 61, 125, 178, 209, 232, 252, 269
Goodson R	90
Goss J	68, 102, 104, 158, 163, 180, 182, 217, 226
Goss J [Clarke]	49
Harper J	63, 134, 135, 136, 137, 153, 205, 263
Harrison J	14, 15, 175, 176, 237, 238
Havergal W	35, 38, 165
Hawes W	58
Hopkins E J	33, 47, 82, 93, 124, 150, 154, 166, 251
Hopkins J	80
Hurford P	202, 207
Hylton Stewart C	2, 16, 67
Jones J	167
Keeton H	161
Knight G H	117
Langdon R	184
Lawes H	187, 228, 264
Lewis R	112, 120, 130, 234, 272
Lloyd C H	235, 273
Luther M	37, 59
Macfarren G A	17, 110, 185, 186, 223, 239
Martin G C	41
Mold S	199
Monk E	18, 229, 265
Nares J	83, 156, 240, 275
Norris T	206
Ouseley F A G	32, 208, 214, 219, 236, 274
Parratt W	98, 200, 233, 270
Parry C H H	43, 222
Purcell H, see Turle	
Pye K J	73, 164, 193, 241
Rawsthorne N	5, 42, 50, 109, 111, 113, 146, 159, 230, 266
Robinson J	155
Rogers J L	169
Rogers T	84
Russell A	48
Smart H	13, 108, 121, 149, 192
Soaper J	91, 138, 140
South C F	126, 133, 196
Stainer J	4, 52, 95, 114, 118
Stainer J [Beethoven]	78, 195
Stanford C V	20, 21, 23, 69, 144, 145, 197, 198, 203, 242, 245, 248, 253, 256, 259
Stonex H	57, 106
Tonus Peregrinus	152
Trent	92
Turle J	8, 30, 34, 56, 60, 76, 86, 88, 100, 123, 128, 139, 141, 143, 188, 215, 220
Turle J [Purcell]	147, 181
Vann S	45, 107, 172
Walmisley T A	19, 24, 26, 40, 70, 191, 243, 246, 249, 254, 257, 260
Warren N	7, 142
Wesley S	11, 25, 36, 77, 87, 89, 189, 244, 247, 250, 255, 258, 261

¶ Division of Psalms by Morning and Evening according to *The Book of Common Prayer*

Psalm	Day		Psalm	Day	
1-5	1	Morning	82-85	16	Evening
6-8	1	Evening	86-88	17	Morning
9-11	2	Morning	89	17	Evening
12-14	2	Evening	90-92	18	Morning
15-17	3	Morning	93-94	18	Evening
18	3	Evening	95-97	19	Morning
19-21	4	Morning	98-101	19	Evening
22-23	4	Evening	102-103	20	Morning
24-26	5	Morning	104	20	Evening
27-29	5	Evening	105	21	Morning
30-31	6	Morning	106	21	Evening
32-34	6	Evening	107	22	Morning
35-36	7	Morning	108-109	22	Evening
37	7	Evening	110-113	23	Morning
38-40	8	Morning	114-115	23	Evening
41-43	8	Evening	116-118	24	Morning
44-46	9	Morning	119. 1-16	24	Evening
47-49	9	Evening	119. 17-32	24	Evening
50-52	10	Morning	119. 33-72	25	Morning
53-55	10	Evening	119. 72-104	25	Evening
56-58	11	Morning	119. 105-144	26	Morning
59-61	11	Evening	119. 145-176	26	Evening
62-64	12	Morning	120-125	27	Morning
65-67	12	Evening	126-131	27	Evening
68	13	Morning	132-135	28	Morning
69-70	13	Evening	136-138	28	Evening
71-72	14	Morning	139-141	29	Morning
73-74	14	Evening	142-143	29	Evening
75-77	15	Morning	144-146	30	Morning
78	15	Evening	147-150	30	Evening
79-81	16	Morning